All good greetings
WJP

All Good Greetings, gf

Letters of Geraldine Farrar to Ilka Marie Stotler 1946–1958

Edited by

Aida Craig Truxall

Pittsburgh, 1991

Distributed by
University of Pittsburgh Press
Pittsburgh, Pa. 15260

Cover:
Geraldine Farrar in her garden at Fairhaven, 1943.

Frontispiece:
Geraldine Farrar in front of a portrait of herself by the German painter von Kaulbach. She gave the portrait to her devoted friend Mary Cobb Gilmour.

ISBN: 0-8229-7016-3
Library of Congress Catalog Card Number: 90-090433

Printed in the United States

Editorial Services: Fannia Weingartner
Designer: Shelle Lichtenwalter Barron
Typography: D&T Typesetter, Nashville, Tennessee
Printing: BookCrafters, Chelsea, Michigan

For
J.D.S.T.
from
A.C.T.

Contents

List of Illustrations

Credits

Unless otherwise indicated, photographs reproduced in this book are from the collection of the Stotler Family. Any misattribution or omission is entirely inadvertent.

Chicago Historical Society:
Kirsten Flagstad

Geraldine Farrar:
Geraldine Farrar—The Story of an American Singer (Houghton Mifflin, 1916): Sydney D. and Henrietta Barnes Farrar; Farrar as Tosca
Such Sweet Compulsion (Greystone Press, 1938): Crown Prince Wilhelm; Princess Cecilie; Antonio Scotti; Farrar as Joan of Arc

Mrs. Lamar Fearing:
Frontispiece

Louise Johnson:
Mary Cobb Gilmour; Sylvia Blein; Fairhaven

Library of Congress:
Arturo Toscanini

Library of Congress, Music Division:
Lilli Lehmann; Farrar as Carmen; Farrar in *Königskinder*; Farrar as Mimi

Jaqueline Dorothy Porter:
Permission to reproduce photograph of Enrico Caruso from *Enrico Caruso, His Life and Death*, by Dorothy Caruso (Simon & Schuster, 1945)

Mildred Miller Posvar:
Photograph in Foreword

H. R. H. Viktoria Luise, Princess of Prussia:
Kaiser's Daughter, Memoirs (Prentice Hall, 1977): The Kaiser and the Kaiserin.

Acknowledgments

A number of people helped make this book possible. I especially want to thank several individuals and institutions for helping locate illustrations. Mrs. Lamar Fearing, a close friend of Miss Farrar, lent the photograph reproduced in the frontispiece. Louise Johnson, niece of Miss Farrar's companion, Sylvia Blein, contributed several photographs. Others who assisted included William C. Parsons, Music Specialist, Music Division, Library of Congress; Kathryn P. Logan, head of the Music and Art Department, The Carnegie Library of Pittsburgh; and Larry Viskochil, Curator, Photographs and Prints, Chicago Historical Society. Ray Fleming provided photographic skills.

Frederick A. Hetzel, Director of the University of Pittsburgh Press, offered indispensable advice and assistance throughout the project. Margot Barbour was most helpful with advice on production. Kathy McLaughlin typed the manuscript and prepared the index. Meg Moss and Abigail McGuire provided editorial help.

Fannia Weingartner, with whom I passed many a congenial afternoon working on the book, and who became a good friend, served as coordinator of the project and provided chief editorial support. Shelle Lichtenwalter Barron carried out the design of the book with great care and appreciation of my wishes.

I am most grateful to Mildred Miller Posvar for taking the time and thought to add her insightful foreword to Miss Farrar's letters.

To my husband, John, I owe more than I can say.

Aida Craig Truxall

Foreword

No matter how indirectly or how remotely, a legendary person will exert an influence on future generations.

Geraldine Farrar was a legend and I felt her influence.

I never heard her sing, which is not difficult to understand since she retired from her operatic career before I was born. I have heard recordings, of course, but she would agree that no fair judgment can be made from anything less than the live transmission of voice to ear.

Still, she was so legendary that the mere mention of her name could create a quiver of—what? delight? envy? inspiration? For, although never having laid an eye (or ear) on her, I knew that in addition to all of her considerable talents there was something quite special about her, something intangible, something even she with her insights and ability to express herself would be hard put to identify. It was the "something" that no conservatory, no voice teacher, no vocal or drama coach, certainly no make-up artist, wig or costume mistress could impart. For lack of better powers of description we call it personal magnetism, charisma, communication. The great Lilli Lehmann, her teacher, said her greatest asset was her *Geshichtlichkeit,* but even saying she had a sense of the historical or that she brought an "authenticity" to the stage still falls short of the mark.

Her magic often was extolled to me by Marie Sundelius, who had sung with her at the Metropolitan Opera and who was one of my teachers at the New England Conservatory of Music.

From my opera history, I knew that Geraldine Farrar had been one of the first great Carmens, a role I wanted someday to sing and did. I knew also that Geraldine Farrar was an American at a time when very few Americans were on the roster at the Met. I did not know, until preparing this preface, that we also shared the role of Cherubino in *The Marriage of Figaro.* She sang the page in 1909, and brought impetuosity to the role, they say. Cherubino was my debut role at the Met and I sang the role for almost ten years in that house. An impetuous Cherubino? Marvelous, I think Mozart wrote him that way. That Miss Farrar did the right thing by Cherubino goes straight to the heart of it. She did not just sing a role, she became the character. The word we use to describe that ability, of course, is acting. And what an actress she must have been! Primarily billed as a singer, she nonetheless was superb enough as an actress to star as Carmen in a silent movie.

I do not believe any operatic connoisseur would quarrel that she was not among the handful of truly fabled voices of that time. Her vocal endowment was substantial enough for her to sing at the side of the great Caruso and we can leave it at that.

Her great contribution was in being an emphatic affirmation that opera must be more than vocal fireworks. That legacy came to me and to many of my colleagues more implicitly than overtly. What she had been had made a difference. Our lives as performers were being lived in a world that had absorbed and incorporated that difference.

Operatic principals always were expected to do more than just sing, unless, of course, the voice was so stupendous and magnificent that nothing else mattered. It is all very well and good to say this; doing it is another matter. Not all fine singers can manage opera because of the myriad elements that must be juggled. To go beyond that, to add yet another ingredient to that impossible mixture is to become the stuff of legend. Miss Farrar put it all together in a way that has us still talking about it. There is no question in my mind that she would survive today because of the intelligence with which she managed her multiple attributes. She would be able to adapt whereas others of her era might perish in the fierce competition of today.

Some things are different today, of course. Yet, things haven't changed that much. *Plus ça change, plus c'est la même chose.* Opportunities appear slightly more frequently but far from often enough. Europe is still a training ground though not to the extent that it was. We still have young singers ("nit-wits," Miss Farrar called them) who want the end of the rainbow without going out in the rain. They are still with us, those who, as she wrote, "have no idea of the joy of concentration in work." Happily, few if any of them make it to the big houses.

Opera has a way of weeding out the less dedicated. In addition to the radio technicians who drove Miss Farrar to distraction by fiddling with voice levels, we now have a dizzying assortment of television technicians whose tricks boggle the mind and distract from both the visual and auditory effect of the singer. We still have superstars, oversized talents who whisk away astronomical fees while the newer talents starve. And we will have fantastic performances. Miss Farrar was premature in 1947 to "despair that *ever* again we shall have first rate performances." It is possible to get a third rate show in a first rate house, but fortunately not that often.

These issues—the fate of opera, the opportunities for young singers, the relentless and sometimes hurtful march of technology—all were things that meant a great deal to Geraldine Farrar, as these letters attest. Some of these issues remain concerns today. Americans still need to be exposed to opera earlier; opera should be more accessible; the country needs more regional companies hiring more of our excellent and increasingly proficient talent.

In other areas, gradual progress can be noted. Music schools are better than ever, and American training now is recognized as some of the best in the world. I think that would have surprised Miss Farrar.

Perhaps it is not a human weakness, but certainly it is a human trait not to wish to leave accomplishment alone but to seek out the person behind it. What was she "really like," this fiercely private superstar who set her own deadlines and left opera when she was far from played-out or sung-out? Who was behind the magnetism that riveted audiences?

Fans are often shocked, even disappointed, to find that public personages are really simple people with simple desires in life. Often, these personages are uncomplicated and even a bit boring. Happily, this is not true of Geraldine Farrar. Not only was she rather complicated, but she also was able to express herself in writing, so that we can glimpse the complexities of the human being behind the legend.

It was her autobiography *Such Sweet Compulsion* that inspired the first of the letters to her by Ilka Stotler. Miss Farrar's responses fill in many gaps and add to her reflections on life, art, politics, even philosophy and religion. Here is a woman who knew what she wanted and got it and who often stood back and observed herself objectively. Many opera buffs will be fascinated to learn that her almost 30 years of retirement were lived privately, quietly, and, comparatively speaking, uneventfully.

I cannot say that I concur with all she says. I find her criticism of many of my colleagues a bit harsh. Radio with all its faults has done an invaluable service for opera, as has television.

However, I couldn't agree with her more on many other of her well-written observations. Her acerbic and sometimes hilarious evaluations of conductors are on the mark. Her estimation of Flagstad was unerring. I too had the thrill of hearing that great voice. In a way, these opinions seem to have been deliberately solicited with an eye to their preservation. If that is true, we must be additionally grateful to Miss Stotler.

Other than what they contain, the letters seem to me to be important because of their sheer volume and frequency. It becomes evident early on that both correspondents depended heavily on these letters for some kind of sustenance.

In that way alone, the letters fulfilled a worthy function.

Mildred Miller Posvar
February 1990

Mildred Miller Posvar sang for twenty-three years at the Metropolitan Opera as Mildred Miller, and appeared internationally as a recitalist, primarily of German Lieder. In 1978 she founded the Pittsburgh Opera Theater to employ young professionals. She is the company's Artistic Director.

Introduction

The letters included in this volume are but a small part of a much greater number that were written by Geraldine Farrar to my cousin, Ilka Stotler. Their correspondence began in 1939 when Miss Stotler wrote to Miss Farrar in reference to the latter's book, *Such Sweet Compulsion,* which had recently been published. It continued for more than two decades at a lively pace, with letters traveling between Ridgefield, Connecticut, and Wilkinsburg, Pennsylvania, at the rate of two or three a week.

Many have been lost. Only those between the years 1946 and 1958 have survived, and within this span there are gaps of weeks, months, and, with one exception, the entire year of 1952. Even so, it was a great mass of letters, loose and in bundles that Ilka, then a very old lady, turned over to me with the request that I should "do something about them."

Most were typewritten, for which I was thankful, for as Miss Farrar said, her words "rushed on paper like a whirlwind." Since she did not trouble with headings, I have made postmarks serve as dates, and unless otherwise noted all were written in Ridgefield either at Fairhaven or Les Miettes, the cottage to which she moved in 1951. A true New Englander, Miss Farrar was, however, keenly interested in the weather, and many, if not most of the letters begin with some allusion to its state, as though setting the stage for the day.

In reproducing Miss Farrar's letters, I have, as far as possible, kept her spelling and punctuation. This includes her tendency to insert three dots in the middle or at the end of sentences. They appear to indicate that the thought drifted off and was to be left hanging in the air. Similarly, she often underlined words or phrases for emphasis, here reflected by the use of italics. Where references to people or events of some time ago might prove puzzling, explanations have been added in square brackets within the text or in footnotes.

Miss Farrar carried on an enormous correspondence with people of many lands, but it is doubtful if, during the long period of their friendship, there was anyone with whom she had such constant written communication as with my cousin, a source of real pleasure to both. Always they retained the formal use of the surname. Miss Farrar called me "Miss Aida," or sometimes just "Aida," probably because I was much younger.

Ilka was the daughter of my mother's cousin, Dr. Fulton R. Stotler, and a Munich lady, Elise Johanna Cecelia Boxhammer. The Stotlers (the name originally "Stadtler," meaning "city dweller") came to this country from the Bavarian Palatinate about the middle of the eighteenth century and were among the early settlers of Western Pennsylvania, taking up tracts of land in what are now Penn and Plum townships, Allegheny County.

In the year 1869, young Dr. Stotler graduated cum laude from the Jefferson Medical School in Philadelphia. After several years of practice in the village of Wilkinsburg, a suburb of Pittsburgh, he left for Germany to continue his surgical training at the Nussbaum Clinic in Munich. With him in Munich was a Pittsburgh friend, John W. Beatty, later a distinguished artist and the first Director of Fine Arts at the Carnegie Institute of Pittsburgh.

Both men naturally took up the study of the German language, and after some time Dr. Stotler wrote home that he had had three teachers but that Fräulein Elise Boxhammer was the best. The romance that began over German grammar continued in a pen courtship after his return home. In 1878 the couple were married in New York. Ilka recounted that her mother had qualms during the long transatlantic crossing, her mind teased by the thought that it could still be changed. "But no," she told herself, "I have given F.R. my word!"

After a brief wedding trip, the couple set up housekeeping in Wilkinsburg where Dr. Stotler practiced all of his long life, being indeed the beloved physician to the residents of the two homes for the aged and the School for the Deaf, where he was visiting doctor.

Our family was quite won by the pretty, intelligent bride. She had been educated at Nymphenburg at a school for daughters of government officials and in London, and must have found her new surroundings different, to say the least. However, she adapted gracefully to life in the village, which at that time was not without considerable character of its own. Formerly called McNairstown, it had been laid out in 1790 by Colonel Dunning McNair, an officer in the

Revolution. In the year 1884, when Ilka Stotler was born, many of the resident families still bore the names of early settlers.

An only child, and probably a lonely as well as a precocious one, little Ilka spent more time with her much-loved dogs and in the company of her mother's friends than with children of her own age. Mrs. Franklin Gordon, born Eliza McNair Horner, was a great favorite. A beauty and a belle, her popularity extended far beyond the bounds of the village. Widowed after only one year of marriage, she indulged her taste for travel and turned up in some very interesting places.

Ilka has passed on to me two souvenirs given her by Mrs. Gordon. The first is a pretty enameled cup made for the coronation of Czar Nicholas of Russia in 1896. These cups had been the cause of a dreadful disaster. Filled with sweets, they were placed on stands at one end of the Khodynka Meadow, a field used for military maneuvers and criss-crossed with shallow ditches, as part of the celebration. The excited crowd rushed forward to seize the czar's gift, lost control, fell, and piled up in heaps. Three thousand lives were lost that day, and the tragedy darkened the reign of the last czar at its very inception.

The other memento, of happy memory, is from a court ball celebrating the sixtieth anniversary of the reign of Emperor Franz Josef of the Austrian-Hungarian Empire. Mrs. Gordon attended the ball in Vienna in 1908. Each guest received a handsome medallion with a raised portrait bust of the Emperor in silver and the imperial coat of arms in gold. The case is of white leather decorated with ribbons in the Austrian colors.

Another intimate friend of the Stotlers was that distinguished woman and excellent piano teacher, Miss Elizabeth Davison. She had studied at the Leschetizsky School in Vienna and returned to take an active part in the musical life of Pittsburgh. She was a charter member and for several terms president of the Tuesday Musical Club, which still flourishes.

Ilka took piano lessons from her, but became more interested in the art classes that she attended at the School of Design, founded by Mr. Beatty and another prominent artist, George Hetzel. Later she became a member of the Associated Artists of Pittsburgh.

In spite of—or perhaps because of—being reared in a conservative and rather formal atmosphere, Ilka in her teens became much interested in the life of an earlier resident of the district, the famous Jane Grey Swisshelm, journalist, abolitionist, and feminist. I have always felt that certain spirited and exuberant elements of my cousin's personality may have been stimulated by her youthful admiration for this colorful figure.

From an early age Ilka had been taught to write pretty letters in several languages to connections abroad. In 1908 she accompanied her mother to Europe and spent four and a half months there, miserably homesick, although she did enjoy meeting friends and relatives from whom she had heard for so long.

For a number of years she assisted her mother in translating correspondence pertaining to the Carnegie International Exhibition of Painting, which began under the directorship of John Beatty.

In 1935, her parents having died, Ilka built her house, Dogwood, high on a hill in a wooded area eight miles from Wilkinsburg. Later she moved to a second Dogwood on the edge of her property next to the road. In 1978 she entered a nursing home near Pittsburgh where she died in September 1982, aged ninety-eight. Having tried for most of her life to conceal her age, she claimed, on her last birthday, to be a hundred. When challenged she said simply, "It makes it more interesting."

Naturally the Stotler family followed with interest the career of the fair New England girl who, at the age of nineteen, became the darling of the Royal Opera of Berlin. Miss Farrar's letters will tell of her life and activities; here a brief outline will suffice.

Her triumphant career in grand opera began in 1901 and ended, as she had planned, when she was forty. She appeared for the last time on the stage of the Metropolitan on April 22, 1922, singing the title role in Leoncavallo's *Zaza*. Although she was glad to be relieved of opera duties, this period was a difficult one for her. The sudden death of her adored mother and the breakup of her marriage to Lou Tellegen, an actor of Dutch-Greek descent whom she had married in 1916, left her nervously depleted.

Tellegen had been leading man to French actress Sarah Bernhardt and was the model for Rodin's famous statue *Eternal Springtime*. He and Miss Farrar met in Hollywood when both were starring in motion pictures. Handsome, with a John Barrymore-like profile and a superb physique, he was also stupid and amoral. As Miss Farrar said, it was her own lack of wisdom to have been misled by his charm, as were her usually clear-eyed parents.

Her panacea was hard work, to which she had been accustomed all her life. Accompanied by her devoted father, she crossed and recrossed the country in her private railway coach, singing programs of exquisite Lieder varied with a condensed version of *Carmen*, with scenery, costumes, and orchestra. Concluding a concert at Carnegie Hall in 1931, she surprised her audience with a simply worded speech of farewell, thus definitely ending her singing career.

Lecture tours followed, in which Miss Farrar spoke of the future of American music and careers for young artists. She is credited with having done more than any other person to stimulate interest in these subjects so close to her heart. There was time now for leisurely travel; trips to Mexico, and, after World War II, two journeys to Europe to see such friends as had survived that tragic time.

After her retirement from the Metropolitan, Miss Farrar bought, in the delightful village of Ridgefield, Connecticut, a large property which she called Fairhaven, and such it proved to be. She spent many happy years there during which she involved herself in organizational work both civil and military.

Mr. Farrar lived on his thirty-acre farm, which he greatly enjoyed, at the other end of the village. A kindly man, he had many friends, and his daughter was much touched when, at his death in 1935, the Town Hall flag was lowered to half-mast.

Although Miss Farrar and Miss Stotler had been corresponding for some months, they met for the first time when Miss Farrar came to Pittsburgh in November 1940 to lecture on "A Golden Age of Song" at the Twentieth Century Club. Ilka called on her at the Hotel Schenley and they had a long conversation during which Miss Farrar suggested that since Ilka and I were planning a week in New York to see some plays, we should drive up to Ridgefield one day and spend the afternoon with her. This we did, and so began the series of pleasant spring and autumn visits that were to continue, almost without a break, into the 1960s.

I well recall that first afternoon when Ilka and I pored over the elaborate written instructions that directed us to Fairhaven. Once we had located the little red Peter Parley School, it was only a moment until we arrived at Miss Farrar's twenty-two-room "Early McKinley" house where she was devotedly looked after by Miss Sylvia Blein, who was French, and Mrs. Margaret Gellatly, a native of Aberdeen.

Miss Farrar welcomed us at the door, a handsome figure indeed, dressed in a powder blue teagown, a velvet bow in her silver hair. On our later visits she always wore either her American Women's Voluntary Services uniform or a simply cut pastel-colored suit or frock.

That afternoon we sat most of the time in the pretty upstairs studio where Miss Farrar spent most of her leisure hours. I recall that we looked at her precious collection of Meissen and Dresden pieces, mostly gifts from friends of long ago, which were assembled in various vitrines.

Miss Farrar spoke much of Lilli Lehmann, her revered teacher, whose photograph inscribed "To my dearest child, with all my love" stood on her dresser with those of her parents.

When Ilka and I departed after tea, we were so stimulated that I believe we took more than one wrong turn on our way back to the city.

On subsequent visits we usually arrived in time for luncheon. Afterward, if the weather permitted, Miss Farrar liked to take us for a leisurely drive on the pleasant back roads of Fairfield County in one of the series of blue Fords that she favored. Back for tea and more talk, which was always very animated; lively discussions of affairs of the day, musical, literary, political, or just human. We were most pleased when the conversation turned—and Ilka was adept at turning it—to events and personalities of the earlier Golden Age of Opera days.

I count it a high privilege to have known Geraldine Farrar. Surely one of the greatest musical figures of her time, she was still, long after the singing years were past, a woman of rare charm and outstanding intelligence and integrity. She had a happy nature and a keen sense of fun. She could and did become highly incensed on occasion, especially if something occurred to offend her idea of fair play, but her usual attitude toward those with whom she came in contact was one of kindly interest.

I never heard the living voice in song. Ilka, who did, spoke of its rich beauty and varied tone color. Critics of her era wrote of its appealing personal quality, a vibrant intensity, a joie de vivre that was hers alone.

In her letter of January 22, 1948, commenting on what she called "chemical magnetism" between individuals, Miss Farrar wrote, "It is a special flow of good-will and communication that takes place spontaneously. . . . I think of it as a stream of kindliness, gushing forth without undue thought, and directed toward the other person with unconscious gesture of sympathy." I would say that she herself possessed this fine quality to a high degree.

Pittsburgh columnist Florence Fisher Parry called Geraldine Farrar "a complete human being. . . . Through living she has absorbed into her ample heart the very stuff of greatness. Abundantly endowed, touched with a great talent and crowned with a great success, she still has managed to become a greater woman even than an artist. She has found the secret of life: Grace. She has accepted her portion of life with grace . . . and in her heart burns the unquenchable torch of *interest, interest.*"

Geraldine Farrar died March 12, 1967. Thinking of her when the news came I was reminded of an afternoon at Les Miettes, when, over the tea table, someone brought up the subject of life after death. And I remember that she said, "I shall not be afraid. I shall be very curious."

Aida Craig Truxall
Pittsburgh, Pennsylvania
December 1990

THE ENTERTAINMENT HALL OF FAME FOUNDATION

Honoring Creators and Performers of the Twentieth Century
not for what they last did, but for what they did that will last

hereby certifies that

Geraldine Farrar

WAS A NOMINEE IN 1974

President

1946

June 16, 1946

Dear Miss Stotler:

I hope that your trip has not been too fatiguing and that you are comfortably settled at the Savoy Plaza.[1] Do not fear, we shall have enough food for you and Miss Aida. Advise you that lamb will be served you on Sunday, so govern your Manhattan fare accordingly.

I am trying to do some garden work, but in such hot weather it is backbreaking. I am just too lame for words.

We shall expect you at 12:30 on Sunday. I fear we shall have a wet weekend from all reports. Too bad. We anticipate your coming, and meanwhile, our best welcome.

In a tearing hurry, GF

June 22, 1946

Dear Miss Stotler:

A hot, humid day for our Fashion Show. It is for charity and all the village attends. I act only as spectator, thanks be, and pity my young friends who model. My shades are drawn and the house is cool.

More peeps into the Wagner volume[2] which you brought me. Concise writing, vivid pictures of the moment. What an upheaval going on at all times in the Wagner household! They lived their theater daily.

Our warm greetings, GF

June 24, 1946

Dear Miss Stotler:

We have again a day of heavy fog and humidity, trying to all. It reminds me of Munich, where it always seemed to be so moist when there was not an actual downpour. One had an umbrella always at hand.

---

[1] On our semi-annual trips to New York City, Ilka and I always stayed at the Savoy Plaza.

[2] *The Truth about Wagner,* letters selected by Philip Dutton Hearn and Waverly L. Root, published by Frederick A. Stokes (1930).

You asked me about the dates of my "Kur"[3] in the lovely sanitorium just outside Salzburg. From 1908 to 1914, war time, I spent a part of the two Summer months there. The nuns, since the institution was Catholic, wore the familiar black dress and long veil, with the white coif framing the face. They were educated in the same degree as our secular hospitals. All very fine young women, and we became good friends.

The Bavarian Alps were not far distant. I remember many charming holidays when Olga Samaroff[4] was a fellow guest of friends there. We wore the costume of the country and walked and climbed to our hearts' content. Sometimes we found a piano in some sequestered inn and Olga and I would give an impromptu concert—always incognito.

I have read the Wagner volume. I find that in my own case one needed the ebullience of youth to lend glamor to this most detestable of humans—as a person. I cannot conceive of the submergence of so independent a woman as Cosima,[5] admitting the glory of the musical intoxication, but then it was an era of forced passions and obvious flouting of convention, and I suppose the more extreme it became the greater the satisfaction to the ego.

However my first days of Wagner, in Munich, at 18, were certainly thrilling and the environment lent its particular charm. It was wonderful to be young, untried, and with the world before one.

At this later date I think the more classical grandeur of Brahms and Beethoven give more appreciation and inspiration. So often in listening to the Wagner I am torn between the thrill of yielding

[3] Each year Farrar was in Europe she took a course at a spa as a means of toning up the system after an arduous season.

[4] Born Lucy Mary Olga Agnes Hickenlooper in San Antonio, Texas, in 1882, the same year as Farrar, Olga became a distinguished pianist and teacher. She was married to and divorced from Leopold Stokowski, for many years renowned conductor of the Philadelphia Orchestra. Her friendship with Geraldine Farrar dated from their student days in Paris. After returning to America they toured together under the management of Charles A. Ellis, manager of the Boston Symphony. The young ladies, bored by long train journeys, amused themselves by treating William Brennan, at that time Mr. Ellis's assistant and later his successor with the orchestra, to displays of artistic temperament. They would demand all sorts of delicacies difficult or impossible to obtain. A favorite prank was to quietly turn their publicity photographs upside down in shop windows and come to him with loud reproaches for allowing such a thing to occur. Antonio Scotti, Metropolitan colleague of Miss Farrar, who met them for a concert in Chicago, was not spared either. Upon their return to Boston, Mr. Ellis met them and presented each of his naughty stars with a huge Teddy bear.

[5] Richard Wagner's second wife, the illegitimate daughter of Franz Liszt.

wholeheartedly to the rich spell of picture and music, and then, at the interminable lengthy narratives, wondering why I allow myself to be humbugged by such arrogant demand on nerves and time, in a ridiculous exposition of song negation and ham-strutting, as per old Wotan, for instance. Well, we all change.

With best greetings, GF

June 29, 1946

Dear Miss Stotler:

I was up betimes for a little church service in Stamford, the edifice having been purchased by Mrs. G.[6] and put in order for worship of the small community. It is a tiny church but pretty in its simple New England fashion. The silver altar service has just been delivered, otherwise I would not have been bowling over the hills at such an early hour—9 A.M.

I have friends in for tea to say addio to one of our nice Red Cross workers who is leaving for the Summer in Maine, so Miss Sylvia [Blein][7] and Margaret [Gellatly] have been busy getting dainties in order.

Yes, I loved horse racing—never won a cent on them, but the animals in stride are to make one gasp at their rhythm and beauty. I did not care for whippet racing for the dogs looked so pitifully lean

[6] Born in Lexington, Virginia, in 1882, the same year as Geraldine Farrar, Mary [Mrs. Howard G.] Gilmour met the young singer when they were neighbors on New York City's West Side. Miss Farrar was devoted to the Gilmours' only child, Nancy, and shared their grief when she died at the age of eighteen. After the death of Miss Farrar's father and her own divorce, Mrs. Gilmour accompanied the singer and Miss Sylvia as they criss-crossed the country en route to various singing engagements. On several occasions Mrs. Gilmour offered support to Miss Farrar's young protégés.

[7] Sylvia Blein was born in the French town of L'Argentiere in 1890, the youngest of a large family of children. In 1901, after both parents died within the same week, Sylvia went to live with an uncle. She remained with him until 1916, when she took service as lady's maid in the home of the Surgeon General of French Hospitals. She also did marketing for a Red Cross contingent which occupied a nearby castle loaned by the French government. In 1917 she came to the United States and, recommended by a friend, joined Miss Farrar just as the latter was leaving for Hollywood to make a motion picture. She remained with Miss Farrar for fifty years. A close friend wrote, "Sylvia was an angel. She treated Miss Farrar like a queen and was happy to do her every bidding." After Miss Farrar's death she lived on at Les Miettes for two years, then went to live with her niece, Mrs. Lea Stempel, in Stamford. Here she was happy and content until her death in 1980. She lived surrounded by mementos of the person she had dedicated her life to and loved.

and nervous. I have been thrilled at bullfights—they really are something for grace and agility; but the sight of two men battering each other I can not endure to watch.

My little Hansi[8] is supposed to come home next week as the vet says he will need only simple nursing. Miss Sylvia will be in her element for she loves to "baby" anything, human or animal. The poor little tyke is isolated and pining for company. We shall give him a warm welcome.

Our best greetings, GF

June 30, 1946

Dear Miss Stotler:

A day of intense heat so we shall do no gardening, but keep the house cool and darkened. I went to the garden early for roses. They fill every niche and are just too lovely with the dew still trembling upon them.

I am not given to "arrangements"; in fact know very little about such disputed form of flower exhibition, but I do love my flowers to have space and water. Thus, two iris poised in half an inch of water give me the feeling that they languish. Mine are plunged into deep, refreshing water up to their pretty blooms after I have smashed their stem ends.

I am hoping to get a little space in the cellar for my personal tools. I would love to have the tiny preserve closet there, near the door, but it would disturb Miss Sylvia's beautifully arranged jars . . . so I say nothing.

We had our Garden Club meeting in a fine old house overlooking the hills. I carried an interesting little volume on soil erosion. How we have abused and wasted our precious blessings . . . like careless, greedy children.

Are you not pleased to be once more alone, with no guest, however dear, to hinder your routine? As time goes on I am more and more inclined to short hours, lunch or tea, rather than a visit of several days. I know I am unwilling to devote time to chat and energy expenditure, which does not make for a good hostess. I resent too, subconsciously, the eternal cigarette ashes and the leaning to cocktails. Trays seem always to need replacement and the aroma of unfamiliar beverages and smoke permeates my house. I suppose I

[8] Miss Farrar's dachshund.

am a bit too particular. This has always been a bone of contention with friends who do not mind this constant catering. I find the women abuse more than the men.

Mr. Kreisler[9] improves, a letter from his wife tells me.

Yes, I knew the late Mr. Hart[10] on the studio lot years ago in Hollywood. God's most homely man, but he had a tremendous following even in Europe. We all wondered how he ever persuaded a woman to marry him. The divorce followed soon after the birth of the son.

I keep relaxed in the middle of this hot day with a pitcher of lemonade and a book. I did like the Wagner and thank you for bringing it. It revives many memories of the young conductors who later became well known and, in some instances, famous, Nikisch, Muck, Strauss, Seidl, Humperdinck, for instance.

The Red Cross book is a gift to you from our chairman, Mrs. Louis Twyefort, to whom you have written. The record is an exceptional one for such a small village.

We have our last O.P.A.[11] meeting. I consider my duty over by the end of the month which means the finale for me.

In the absence of your factotum do not kill yourself with overwork. Learn to do only the important things, and then one at a time!

I view with a certain equanimity now the tangled masses of the garden in the absence of my little Scot. He is not able to come and I am well pleased, as the heat would finish him. The handy-man mows the lawn—otherwise the riot is on!

All good wishes from us here. GF

July 5, 1946

Dear Miss Stotler:

We brought our dear little Hansi home yesterday. He seems all right. His joy to see us was hysterical. He now needs only feeding and home sympathy. I had hoped to get someone to rake the hay that now lies in an untidy mess. The little Scot is out of the picture, as he

---

9 The Austrian violinist, Fritz Kreisler, and his American wife, Harriet, were dear friends of Miss Farrar's. Kreisler was recovering from an appendectomy.

10 William S. Hart, star of early Westerns, died June 23, 1946, at the age of seventy-three.

11 The Office of Price Administration, a government agency, regulated and monitored rents and prices during World War II. Many civilian volunteers, like Miss Farrar, served at the local level.

should be in this awful weather. But these Scots are hardy and obstinate so I must find some excuse to keep him at home without wounding his pride.

A sad contretemps this early morn. Cows from a neighbor broke into our place and, where the gardener's widow had a wonderful field of early corn, the seven Holsteins ate their fill. We got the neighbor and her man. She is so unhappy and is putting up an electric fence. She is alone on a big place and her lot is a hard one with this labor shortage.

No, I never won much at gambling although the excitement was amusing. Monte Carlo was a rare experience for a teen-ager, what with its fine opera and large fees that were much appreciated. Then too, the notables came from Paris and Milan, and if the impression was good, engagements in these cities would follow.

It was there that I first met Caruso.[12] I shall never forget my first sight of him, in the loudest of checked suits, but with the blackest eyes and such a friendly expression. A warm and generous human being.

I am very glad to have the nice notice from the critic[13] of the *Sun-Telegraph*. It gives me an idea.

Last week I had a letter from Munich, from the artist who made fine portraits of Lilli Lehmann[14] for the Mozarteum[15] in Salzburg. He relates that they have disappeared from that lovely edifice and wants me to bring it to the attention of the present authorities with the object of replacing them if recovered. As she was the soul of the Mozart Festivals at the very inception, I felt this to be quite right. I shall write to Mr. Lissfelt, who has always been a great admirer of hers, to see if he can bring it to some attention.

All good wishes to you, GF

---

12 The great tenor Enrico Caruso and Geraldine Farrar made their Monte Carlo debuts together in Puccini's *La Bohème*. It was the first time she had sung with him, and she all but missed her cue, so enthralled was she by his glorious voice.

13 Fred Lissfelt, Pittsburgh music critic.

14 The greatest dramatic soprano of her day and Farrar's beloved teacher. Lilli Lehmann (1848–1929) left the Royal Opera of Berlin to perform at the Metropolitan Opera in New York on various occasions during the years from 1885 to 1889. Describing her performance as Isolde in Wagner's *Tristan and Isolde*, critic Henry Krehbiel wrote, in 1886, "She has grasped its passionate intensity . . . and disclosed the wealth of musical, vocal, and histrionic gifts which qualify her to interpret the passionate heroines of Wagner. It is seldom given to the public to observe so complete a devotion of an artist to her task."

15 Built in 1910–14, the Mozarteum included concert halls and a school of music, as well as the Mozart archives.

July 6, 1946

Dear Miss Stotler:

Thanks in advance for the delicious raspberry juice, but what work you make for yourself in this hot weather! We are very fond of the iced fruit juices. I drank light beer in Mexico, since the water there is dubious. I wish I could get the same brand here, but it is not to be had.

The insects are abundant in this humid air. They penetrate my smock and babushka . . . I am covered with welts.

I appreciate how you felt in the primitive retreat with your friend. I loathe all such woodsy places, I am too juicy a prey to the biting insects. Camp life was not for me at any age, and made me very homesick the few times I tried it. My father had a fishing place in the Adirondacks with motorboats and all that such places offer. Not for me, although he tried hard to interest me.

I spent a good part of the Sabbath burning the old O.P.A. records. It was a huge pile, and I tremble to think of the accumulation in the official files. No more of this nonsense for me, thank goodness.

As to O.P.A. rentals, it seems to me that the landlord is entitled to some recompense for deterioration. The O.P.A. strikes me as unworkable in this and other avenues.

For instance, Miss Sylvia could not put out a wretched, dishonest tenant, who defaulted on checks and left the place in shocking condition, until he was ready to move on—and was really driven out of town, and none too soon. Now she has a fine tenant who could easily pay more, but having had the former rental, she cannot change.

I spent the 4th with Mrs. G. [Gilmour] in her country home in Stamford [Connecticut], just the two of us, to discuss the state of her sister. Neither of us had any interest in other invitations.

I do not share your feelings about putting out the flag. It is our glory at all times and nothing in the nature of changing administrations can change its symbol and its challenge. The flag does not falter even if we should, in our confusion and distress. I find all the more need to solidify my belief in our land, though disagreeing heartily with many who profane it. In the end, nothing can impair it; we only disgrace ourselves.

Cheerio, and may the sick tooth have improved. They can be brutes indeed.

GF

July 14, 1946

Dear Miss Stotler:

The invalid still lingers, but with lowered pulse. Close friends have prepared all the last details that must proceed when the time comes; and so we wait to offer our services.

After the ordeal is over and the inevitable let-down occurs, we shall very likely go to the Saranac Inn [Lake Saranac, New York]. I want to be at my friend's command in this sad emergency. We have gone through many sorrows together, and she knows she may rely on me.

How could I have a cousin, since my parents had no brothers or sisters? Let the lady go her way. I am used to all kinds of publicity stunts, that is part of the professional froth that one accepts as such.

I am credited with progeny, numerous, too. I place this in the category of the same careless gossip. You would be surprised to know that people who spread such reports do *not want* to be corrected, or to have the actual truth told.[16]

Hansi is less well today. He adores Miss Sylvia above all, then hangs on me; but I do not feed him, so when mealtime comes he goes to the full hands.

I am weary with tussling with weeds in the garden. The little Scot came today and managed a good deal of work. He is wonderful for his 81 years, but I am a total flop after an hour and have to come in and attack another occupation, best known as sedentary.

The whole atom bomb affair is horrible to my mind. I wish we had never invented it; and the second launching on Nagasaki had no excuse.

I do not see that we hold out one Christian gesture toward matters at home, either. If our Constitution declares that all men are created free and equal (though I do quarrel with this for God has not ordained such equality, as anyone with eyes can see) then we should find a way to abide by it and not pay lip service and continue to do the opposite.

The position of the Negro is no different from that of the uneducated immigrant. Both are unhappily susceptible to pressure and exploitation while awaiting the generations to come. I do

[16] Miss Farrar told of having been approached by a German couple who wished to adopt the semiroyal children she was supposed to have mothered.

not think segregation is the answer either, but I can give none myself.

Now to chores in the village.

Our best greetings to you. GF

July 15, 1946

Dear Miss Stotler:

The little sister of my friend lies at the point of death. We are fortunate that with the heavy drugs she will fall asleep quietly and not have to meet the change face on, which would send her into a fright. Nature itself is often kind at the last and induces a stupor to allow the departure of the spirit.

No, I have no bleak mood, as you would put it, even though this is a serious time. I can lay this to my dear mother whose early communications along this line were a wonderful source of strength to me. If you believe your Bible you will know that there is no dissolution, though a change. If we regard nature with a perceptive eye we realize that *nothing* dies, only is transformed, and life renews itself constantly . . . we must progress, even if not allowed in this life to understand the wonder of it all.

If I do not write for a few days you will know that I am engaged in trying to be of some help to this family, who will take things very hard.

My best to you with greetings, GF

Saranac Inn
August, 1946

Dear Miss Stotler:

The rain is upon us so the fire is cheerful and we hug its cozy vicinity. No, I do not turn my back on the water sports, for the adventuresome young on their aqua planes are a pleasure to watch, and the easy rhythm admirable to the eye—but I do not care to be *on* the water. Silly, too, for why then was I born in the water month, signified by fish?

I hope you will not be offended if I do not share your enthusiasm for the nautical volume [Richard Dana's *Two Years Before the Mast*]—I much prefer other kinds of reading.

On large ships I have been the victim of the annoying persuasion of the officers, and have visited every corner from the captain's bridge to the boilers below in their company. To my credit I did not become actually ill, but the knowledge obtained in no way contributed to the enjoyment of the voyage which always distressed me. And in those days I had to make four crossings a year. It was an agony.

Yes, I do have the Cobb[17] book, *Speaking of Operations.* He was a good friend of my father. Indeed, I own the pen sketch of Cobb, in bed, as he wrote the book. I liked him very much, easy and good humored. He and Bob Davis[18] were forever scolding each other, in play, and it was great fun to hear them. Cobb's spontaneous wit did not lend itself to much polishing, or so it seemed to me.

He had a delightful spouse, but one who was socially inclined, toward which desire Cobb did his best to contribute. Financially, it went, but he was more at home in other scenes, and given to menfolks' sports and companionship. A very real man and a delightful one.

Speaking of ships, I was taken by Bob Davis to see the celebrated *Convict Ship* as she lay in the Hudson River many years ago. It was viewed as a curiosity, and the small fee collected went to the seamen's benefit. It was replete with awful torture instruments. There were printed labels of the poor devils who had sailed on it to prison life in New Caledonia. One man was put in the solitary dark hole below the water line for stealing a loaf of bread. Numerous labels attested to the many who had been imprisoned for debt. It was pretty gruesome. Perhaps we have improved in some ways after all.

Mrs. G. is not well and must go through this nervous tension. She is doing her best and is a sweet hostess, always, but I know her so well and what weighs on her that I fear it will be some time before she is quite calm.

All good wishes to you. GF

Saranac Inn
August, 1946

Dear Miss Stotler:

A pale sun is trying to warm us, but not to much avail, as the lowering clouds presage more and constant rain. A friend on Cape Cod says it is too dismal there for words; only a scattered group of

17 Irvin S. Cobb, writer of humorous works.

18 Prominent sports writer.

people to carry on till Labor Day. Those dunes in a fog or rain to my mind would spell dreariness beyond description.

Yes. I love to write as a means of communication, and when time does not press with irksome business matters; then one is harassed and out of humor for pleasant chat. So long a traveller, and forced to conserve energy of voice and body, it was always a delight to write and find response. I have correspondents all over the world, or did have till this and the last war, when so many were killed. I was happy to know them at their best in this wise, and no strain to adjust in a personal contact. Then there is apt to be an unease, as though striving for the more facile expressions that come with the pen confidences.

Miss Sylvia will be here for me on the 4th with my car and the handy-man to drive. More and more I would find it a hardship not to have my own roof and to live with those intimate things that mean precious memories. I know the care is great, and my two willing girls have more than I would put on their shoulders, could we find others to aid us. But it seems domestics are inclined to places where the harvest is rich and the perquisites enormous. I have seen some of my friends hand out tips at the door of a hotel, or to a waiter, that made me blush for shame for them all. Out of all proportion to the grudging service. It did not engender any respect, if they themselves failed to inspire it.

We drive every day, rain or shine. It affords the only time when Mrs. G. can relax and sleep, probably due to the steady hum of the wheels and the lovely quiet of these pine avenues we traverse. It is truly fairyland. So long as I need not go on foot, I am content.

Now to lunch, and the afternoon drive. All good wishes, and fireside tranquility, if you have this down-pour in your vicinity.

GF

September 2, 1946

Dear Miss Stotler:

Your pen sketch[19] of my welcome home is to the life. The dogs clamored for a caress and notice, howling for joy. I was so glad to see them.

My desk is piled high. The printed matter that goes to waste is enormous.

---

[19] Ilka Stotler sent frequent "pen fancies" to illustrate incidents in Miss Farrar's life.

Did you hear the Stuttgart speech of Byrnes?[20] He sees that a unified Germany is necessary, otherwise we shall have a return to barbarism in the action of Russian ideology.

If Churchill is quoted correctly as advising a combine of England, Germany and France for the balance of Western Europe, I would say he has come awake very late, and may live to ponder how the Allies ever allowed their mistaken pity to take in the Russians as loyal and competent companions. I never thought it other than the gravest error, and now we shall have a problem made all the more complex by reason of the radical elements here, and in high places, too.

I found the receipt of CARE,[21] acknowledgment of the six orders not specified, but it would seem to be all right, and I do not quarrel. The agency is probably swamped with orders.

Yes, I do know the young singer, Miss Williams.[22] She is having quite a season here with the New York City Opera, where she made her debut last Fall with *Butterfly*. She now adds the role of Nedda, and most attractive photographs are being used.

Indeed I would like the Finletter book.[23] The family has been active so long in affairs of music. The father, Leopold Damrosch, was the real musical talent. Both sons have done well for themselves, however, though Walter Damrosch[24] has been a thorn in the side of many. His wife comes of good old New England stock, and the family is amusing enough. The Frank Damrosch school has been in existence for years; at the head is son-in-law David Mannes.

Dolls. I love them to this day and can well understand the obsti-

---

20 As U.S. Secretary of State (1945–47), James F. Byrnes first tried to negotiate with the Soviet Union after the end of World War II, but finally concluded that this was impossible and took a firm anti-Soviet stand.

21 The acronym for Cooperative for American Remittances for Europe, a private, non-profit organization founded in 1945 to send $10.00 food packages to victims of the European war. Miss Farrar was able in this manner to care for many of her European friends, although not for those in the Russian Zone.

22 Camilla Williams, winner of the Marian Anderson prize, scored a great success as Bess in Gershwin's *Porgy and Bess*. She was the first black woman to sing in the Vienna Opera. She gave many concerts in Europe and was noted for her sensitive interpretations.

23 *From the Top of the Stairs*, by Gretchen Damrosch Finletter, daughter of Walter Damrosch.

24 Walter Johannes Damrosch, born in Germany, was one of the best-known American symphony and opera conductors of his era. He composed several operas but is remembered especially for his early use of radio as a means of developing music appreciation in American children.

nate Frances in her determination to hold on to the one she had purchased. I would have sustained her, I think, despite mama's and your objections. Why hope to bribe her away from Lana—as good a name as any, in a child's opinion, and without the frivolous air the adult might deplore?

I recall well the tussle I had with a young teen-ager when I myself was only about sixteen. This girl was enamored of a photo of the lovely, soft-eyed Cleo de Merode.[25] She vowed she was going to waylay the dancer, who was then performing in New York, and talk with her. The mother was stupid and confused, trying to explain why this was not to be thought of. I was the referee and managed to show the child that, owing to the many who would have the same idea, the lady would be exhausted trying to be gracious, and could not possibly see everyone. I suggested that she write to the dancer and request her autograph. This was done, the autograph was forthcoming, the child was happy, no harm was done.

The photograph of the little Frances is very attractive to my mind. A gay face and sturdy frame. I like the little girls to have dolls for loving. Wait till you see mine, my big girl from Berlin of some forty years ago. She is in her high chair here, having done her bit at the Red Cross these latter years, and now can rest on her laurels.

Perhaps my own family life gave me a high opinion of the usual function of women. There are too many who deny it, and those who have the talent to point a career out of this circle know best if their urge has been completely fulfilled.

All good wishes, GF

September 4, 1946

Dear Miss Stotler:

Rain, rain, rain, unceasing, and a bore indeed. One cannot go out on the slippery roads and it is just as well. Much too chill.

There is a collection of photographs (in which I figure) in the Mozart Haus[26] in Salzburg to commemorate the casts when we sang under Lilli Lehmann. In the Mozarteum, the large bronze plaque in the foyer was the insignia of our Mitwirkung [collaboration].

The artist who inquired about Lilli's portraits has had a mean

[25] Cleo de Merode was a Parisian dancer of great beauty and dubious reputation, at that time the toast of three continents.

[26] Mozart's birthplace at No. 9 Getreidegasse, now a museum.

time among the Russians, but is now in the American sector in Freising, and can write freely. I would not know why Lilli's portraits have been removed, it could have been a protective measure; but as both she and the artist were stout monarchists, perhaps there was a political reason of petty spite. One never knows.

I do know that Leo Blech,[27] the Czech conductor, a Jew, and a good comrade of mine, was kept at the opera, despite fierce opposition, by Goering,[28] who appreciated him. What came about later, I do not know. There were all kinds of party machinations, as in every political machine no matter what the avowed purpose.

Yes, the Prince Auwi[29] who was very much inclined to the Nazis, is the youngest brother of the K.P. [German Crown Prince]. His unexplainable joining up with this organization was looked on very unfavorably by the rest of the family. His testimony at the jewel loot (and more shame to the Americans who did this) would be for purposes of identification only.

The K.P.[30] was never a Nazi, and had plenty of trouble to keep his head at the time of their power. I hardly think the French officials will stoop so low as to betray their trust in his captivity. It would give them a very black eye and serve no useful purpose as he is quite harmless as a political figure now.

He had plenty of sense, but of course as a younger member of the circle around his father, his voice was the least heard and understood. When there were differences of opinion, he was quietly sent off on maneuvers till the hour passed. There has always been a desperate rivalry in the Hohenzollerns between fathers and sons. This was no different than in previous eras. The father was *not* democratic, but the son was very well aware of the growing influence of the laborites, socialists and left wingers. He was a good comrade, easy of access among the people, and far too popular to suit the cabinet of his father, and later, the evil men around Hitler.

---

27 Leo Blech (1871–1958) conducted at the Berlin State Opera from 1926 to 1937. He returned from exile in 1949.

28 A World War I flying ace, Hermann Wilhelm Goering (1893–1946) became an early member of the Nazi Party and rose to be one of Hitler's chief supporters. Once Hitler came to power Goering held many important posts, helping rearm Germany and building the air force. He was also an art lover and prided himself on his cultivation.

29 Kaiser Wilhelm's fourth son, August Wilhelm, later changed his views and was placed under house arrest by Goering. The "testimony" was probably identification of his mother's jewelry which had apparently been "liberated" by American soldiers.

30 Crown Prince Wilhelm was living in a small villa in Hechingen, Swabia, under French custody.

I believe the only thing that kept Hitler from finishing him off was the fact that the army would have had something very opposite to offer. After all, even Hitler and his youthful fanatics could not have hoped to do the widespread damage outside Germany unless the army supported them. Even so, there were many officers purged who resented the tactics employed. We shall never know the cost paid by such patriots . . . it is all so terrible a tragedy . . . who will be the truly honest historian to set down all the facts?

Now to lunch by our cozy fire. Perhaps a nap later, and more letters.

Good wishes from all here. GF

October 2, 1946

Dear Miss Stotler:

A most beautiful Indian Summer day . . . too warm for much activity. I shall try to get a letter off before I go to chores in the attic.

Last night I attended a concert to hear the young protégé of several ladies interested in her musical education (voice). We had a delightful hour or two until it was time to go to the concert, well attended and with a public disposed to be more than friendly and responsive.

But . . . it was my disagreeable experience to find the nineteen year old hardly worthy of so much concentration. She is the daughter of illiterate Italians, the father, a good-for-nothing, and the numerous family, grasping, and ignorant of the finer things that I can well believe this girl yearns to attain. Happily, she is placed out of their immediate reach, lives in a Catholic home, is very studious and well behaved.

Unlike many of such peasant types, who have a vocal endowment of promise, I did not find enough talent to warrant the oversight of so much else that will be required if she is to have a real career.

She is definitely *not* ready for any public appearance and should be put back on scales and allowed to mature. There is, in my opinion, little to merit undue interest, save as to lift a human being out of unhappy surroundings to a betterment, and even this is problematical. I was troubled, but spoke freely to my hostess, as I assumed it was intended.

Mrs. G. and I have had so much to do with such incidents, that I am beginning to feel that it is hardly worthwhile to try to pound into limited heads any idea of what is truly needed. Though the idea also comes to mind that since glorified mediocrity seems so generally accepted today, perhaps one is out of tune in expecting higher standards. I came home vowing I would *never* again get into such a situation. I may be quite wrong in view of present acceptance of performers.

The Philharmonic of New York gave a fine program at the Norwalk Community Concert Series. It was good to see many young people as patrons, and attentive to the classical music.

It is an excellent band, though I prefer not to watch the present day leaders who dramatize themselves after the manner of the flamboyant [Leopold] Stokowski. He started the vogue for prima donna podium stars; it does not add to one's enjoyment. The posterior of any leader is not an engaging sight—so much swishing of tails.

Now to the attic, before the cold becomes too unpleasant there. Three stories are really too much for our furnace to supply adequately.

All good wishes, GF

October 7, 1946

Dear Miss Stotler:

A pouring rain that is very conducive to desk work, if not of much inspirational value. The garden which I had seeded for lawn, thus cutting down on the flower beds, is doing nicely; green, with a fresh new fuzz that bodes well for the coming Spring. Is it not odd, that all of us in nature, plant, animal or human life, have to prepare for the coming events? I think this should be stressed in the teaching of children.

How reduced we are now to elementary thinking . . . just the technic to keep going to our best ability, to survive. Last week at the various events in which I participated, no one mentioned fashions, new decors, etc.; our principal topic of conversation was food, and the distress its shortage now causes.

Mme. Fremstad[31] is now in the Roosevelt Hospital, greatly improved and out of danger, per news yesterday from her sister. But the broken hip, with its new theory of the pin, and constant exercise in walking, is painful still. I fancy the patient is none too certain that this

[31] Olive Fremstad sang at the Metropolitan from 1903 to 1914, principally in Wagnerian roles.

forced walking is her preference . . . Myself, I would be inclined to its benefits, for attrition comes so easily, when a limb is immobilized.

Yes, I have always liked to write, and it saved my voice much, and yet kept me in touch with friends. My mother wrote an excellent and humorous letter, in a neat, graceful hand; mine was always sprawling, and [my words] rushed on paper like a whirlwind.

My mother had a talent for painting and needlework, always dainty and fine; I have none for either, though I can manage at intervals to trace a few simple stitches. Too active at all times, I think, to have the required patience.

I have greatly enjoyed the Oscar Wilde [book][32] which you sent. A sympathetic narrative, yet not prurient, dwelling upon the complex nature of the man. This type of human does not alarm me; our musical world is full of these gifted prisms of expression . . . not to mention some of the greatest geniuses in other forms of art. Just how much the divergences contribute to the interpretation is debatable, but I do not enjoy the Russian Peter[33] the less for his aberrations from the usual pattern.

I agree that Fulton Lewis [Jr.][34] is wonderful in his search for truthfulness, but why does he seem so breathless, and at times make such stammering and hesitant effects? He is almost my favorite commentator, for I believe him to be authoritative; only the manner of speech is at times annoying. I wonder if he does not use notes.

I like [H. V.] Kaltenborn best of all. [Lowell] Thomas is a good reporter. [Drew] Pearson breathes scandal. Rupert Hughes has been very deaf these last years so I suppose this is a handicap.[35]

May your trip to Erie be a happy one, and *Brava* for the sale of the property.

All good wishes and greetings, GF

October 11, 1946

Dear Miss Stotler:

Yes, I heard [President] Truman's back-slide speech. All he needed to have said in one sentence would have been "Ladies and

[32] *Oscar Wilde and the Yellow Nineties,* by Frances Winwar (1940).

[33] Composer Peter Ilyich Tchaikovsky.

[34] and [35] Radio commentators and journalists prominent during the war years and after and known for their strong views on political issues.

gentlemen of the listening radio audience, I realize I have been a d–d fool as leader of the nation and declare prices abolished."

Is it not ridiculous to have to beg for such commonplace commodities as paper for personal use of all kinds, with pulp trees being cut down freely and *not* replaced? Today I asked for an article not obtainable, and ten minutes later had the shop-keeper murmur, "Will you give me 27 cents for a parcel sight unseen?" Of course I did. Now that the country is being led by the villains and the gamblers, I can gamble too . . . and to hell with the whole sheebang!

We have tried to do the best for each other in the emergency, with much forbearance in all ways, but it was too easy for the rotters to keep on the pressure. Now it will be every one for himself, since there is no decency from the leaders.

The visit here Sunday with my medical friends was delightful, though we spoke of serious things and the professional needs in general. So much misery in the world.

Pitiful letters from overseas friends, one in particular is [from] an English girl married to a Russian. Since they were in Germany before the war declaration, they are, under present regulations, stateless persons, and as such have not received one jot from UNRRA[36] or even from the Quakers. This is heartless indeed; they are humans caught in a horrible web. Though I have sent parcels[37] before, our post here advises waiting till the strikes are over, as millions of packages are in the storehouses, not only immobile but likely to be misplaced. I am going to try to post cigarettes, as the lady tells me they are a means of barter more to be desired than food or clothing.

Is it not terrible that anyone should go hungry, cold and helpless while so little is accomplished to bring order to these ruined countries and despairing people? It makes one heavy hearted, indeed.

Greetings from us all. GF

October 20, 1946

Dear Miss Stotler:

The weather is fine and mild, and the glorious flaming trees are a delight to the eye. I do hope that on your trip, you and Miss Aida

36 United Nations Relief and Rehabilitation Administration, founded in 1943 to provide emergency aid to countries liberated from Axis occupation. It functioned in Europe until 1947 when its work was assumed by various United Nations agencies.

37 Miss Farrar helped many European friends this way.

may have this beauty in abundance. I think I had best send this to the Savoy Plaza as of yore, as it would not arrive in time at Dogwood to greet you before departure.

Until we meet, as ever, GF

October 28, 1946

Dear Miss Stotler:

Thank you again for your continued thought of us, and for the dainty gifts left behind. I am happy that you had an entertaining time in Babylon. After the long drive you needed the relaxation . . . if any can be found in the excitement of the city.

You cannot imagine what pleasure it afforded me to be able to find for you the spare tire. I should have been very sorry to see you depart and have to rely on a chance finding on the road. I have little faith to believe that in New York you could have found it. It seems one must know "ropes" for everything.

Your letter has just arrived saying that you found your little Toto very uncomfortable. Why not give him a merciful whiff of chloroform? I have done this, even with police dogs, tying their muzzle with a handkerchief. Sleep at once—no struggle.

A disturbing letter from my young Russian friend. There is no opportunity as yet for them to get to England, her home. The young man carefully avoids present Russian circles. His father belonged to the old aristocracy and he knew the Bolshevik misery as a child, first hand. They live now in a small room, his piano, for he is a professional, at the foot of the bed . . . "a miserable affair, out of tune, and of small size"—I suppose she means upright. She is very frail, heart and lungs failing. All in all a sad outlook, multiplied no doubt by similar thousands. Our soldiers have been helpful and generous in sharing, this has kept them alive, but usually there has been shifting of forces, and they have to begin all over again, making acquaintances . . . a dreadful uncertainty.

Now I shall post this letter with our heartiest greetings. GF

November 2, 1946

Dear Miss Stotler:

The *Lost Treasures*[38] came, a beautiful book of poignant memories, indeed. Many thanks for this mark of enjoyment.

How pretty are the Austrian stamps that will swell Miss Sylvia's collection. I wonder why ours have to be of such depressing similarity in the profiles of various politicians. The European examples are of real beauty.

I shall be glad to have the election campaigning over. Such a flood of twiddle-twaddle over the radio makes one weary.

The Republicans would seem to be on the upward trend, with [New York Governor Thomas E.] Dewey quite certainly in the lead for president [for the 1948 election]. Almost anyone would be better than Harry Truman, who has to cope with such inferior material in his entourage. Not being a giant himself, he is snowed under by the more radical elements while the conservatives of his party seem very much disturbed.

No, I am not chairman of the Garden Club, but serve only as a member of the committee. We belong to the Federation of Garden Clubs of America, and our aims are anything from village improvement and tree conservation to soil erosion and pest controls. In the realm of horticulture, we are interested in flowers and vegetables for show and use.

This village, as well as many others, owes to the efforts of such clubs the preservation of its loveliness. Where the town or state cannot grant monies for certain projects, the garden clubs take upon themselves such as are worthwhile; for instance, there was such decimation of the superb California redwoods, that the clubs banded together for subscriptions, in the form of naming each specimen saved for a soldier killed in the last war, in memory. This was a project that was widely approved by the entire country.

Here at home, I have six dozen more daffies to plant, then my labors are over in this line. I worked yesterday till I could hardly stand up straight. A lovely day of blue sky and errant breezes.

We keep well, and certainly there is something to challenge us every day.

Our best wishes, GF

38 *Lost Treasures of Europe*—a collection of photographs edited by Henry La Farge.

Later. I have here what I can loan you from my costume notes. I hope they will help you in making up the series.

Costume Hints

Lenora [*Il Trovatore,* Verdi]: Black chiffon and satin, as in my book [*Such Sweet Compulsion* (1938)].

Angela [*Le Domino Noir,* Auber]: Powder blue silk skirt, black velvet bodice. Orange velvet bolero, gold trim. Coral necklace and earrings. Own dark hair with red flowers. Two colored ribbon on skirt, blue and orange.

Gilda [*Rigoletto,* Verdi]: Dress of white cloth embroidered with seed pearls and silver. Own dark hair. White veil, diamond band on forehead.

Marguerite [*La Damnation de Faust,* Berlioz]: Mauve cloth laced with deeper shade. Deep purple on cape and hood. Beige guimpe. Own hair.

Maddelena [*Andrea Chénier,* Giordano]: Costumes provided by Opera of Warsaw, style of Manon. One performance only.[39] I do not recall the colors.

Amica [*Amica,* Mascagni]: Black velvet bodice, beige guimpe, silver ornaments. Dark green skirt, beige pleated apron, multi-colored shawl. A very unusual Italian peasant dress. Gold earrings. Own hair.

Sita [*Le Roi de Lahore,* Massenet]: Light blue dress hung with gold and turquoise chains. Bodice of darker blue velvet, with seed pearls and silver embroidery. Necklace and head dress of same motif as chains. White aigrette. Sheer gold veil held aloft. Dark skin make-up, Indian color. Black hair.

Zephyrine [*Le Clown,* Camondo]: Vari-colored orange-yellow chiffons. Sequins and same on head. Blond wig. Red shoes.

Margarita [*Mefistofele,* Boito]: Pearl grey pleated skirt, under petticoat of blue. Repeat motif in head dress, dark blue with gold trim. Pocket and belt of gilt leather.

Cherubino [*Le Nozze di Figaro,* Mozart]: Louis XIV brocade, predominant color greenish blue. Laces at throat and wrist. Stiffly

[39] The patriotic theme of *Andrea Chénier* was considered too provocative at this time, in 1904, when Poland was seething with resentment against Russian rule.

starched. Green slippers, red heels. Stockings of grey silk with clocks of silver sequins. Large grey felt hat with blue plume.

Ariane [*Ariane et Barbe-Bleue,* Dukas]: Very ornate head dress over brown hair. Colors of diamonds and rubies. Same motif on chains and arms. Dress, princess style, with same colors applied.

Rosaura [*Le Donne Curiose,* Wolf-Ferrari]: Very like first act of *Manon.* Blue taffeta dress, green velvet bows down the front, with gay flowers of the period. Own hair, blue ribbon band.

Susanna [*Il Segreto di Susanna,* Wolf-Ferrari]: The period was as of *Bohème,* save that I wore a long dress. Own hair, dressed high, of the period. Dress of pink brocade with ruffles at throat and wrist. Pink rose in hair.

Lodoletta [*Lodoletta,* Mascagni]: Dark brown dress, buttoned tight, a "Little Women" style. Blond wig. Dutch lace cap. Wooden sabots. Dress to floor, skirt turned up like an apron, lined with red.

Thaïs [*Thaïs,* Massenet]: Nun's costume. Grey chiffon with blue cross at forehead. The yoke and sleeves had a slight thread of scarlet beads to indicate the folds and outline the shoulders.

Orlanda [*La Reine Fiamette,* Leroux]: Very ornate Renaissance dress of white satin. Mantle of gold. Ermine cape and sides to the floor, very regal. Fire red hair in the Botticelli style. Crown of sparkling stones.

Anita [*La Navarraise,* Massenet]: Simple black peasant dress with basque. Black kerchief-like fichu around shoulders. Black hair, very long.

Queen Elizabeth [*Don Carlos,* Verdi]: Velvet dress of aqua heavily embroidered with gold and silver. Cape of deeper green satin, traced with silver and gold threads. Ruff of starched white linen with edge of silver. Purple velvet hat with grey plumes. My own dark hair.

1947

Columbus Day, 1947

Dear Miss Stotler:

I was not sure we would have letters today but our cheery old postman arrived in good time so I have your amusing pen fancy. It is quite remarkable how these little bulbs resemble faces—especially the crocus ones, their protective fuzz like hair and beards.

The Sans-Gêne sketch of me arrived yesterday. An unusual pose that may very well have been executed by that very free and easy woman. I saw Rêjane[40] as the protagonist of the original play; she was superb in her easy comedy and effrontery; a little woman of my size, so that I did not feel the lack of heroic stature of the earlier Italian ladies who portrayed the role. Several were quite large, and I fancied some of the inoffensive pertness was lost in too sweeping a series of dramatic gestures.

Amato[41] was the spitting image of Napoleon even to the folded cross-arm, which history says was a pose necessary for the scratching of an intolerable skin irritation.

Yes, Olive Fremstad was one of the great artists of my period. She has become a recluse almost—a strange nature that does not become more extrovert with time.

I have been immensely interested in *200 Years of Musical Criticism,* by Dr. Max Graf, apparently a Viennese. Delightfully written and not pedantic.

We shall look forward to welcoming you and Miss Aida on November 2nd. I shall keep the entire day free, and pray for fine weather for your journey.

Our best greetings, GF

October 15, 1947

Dear Miss Stotler:

More bulbs in the ground this charming Summer day. I have been out in my blue apron, scarf and heavy gloves. The leaves are falling in sheets of vivid colors.

---

[40] Gabrielle Rêjane, star of the French classical theater.

[41] Pasquale Amato (1878–1942), Italian baritone, sang at the Metropolitan at intervals between 1908 and 1933. He and Farrar sang principal roles in the world premiere of Giordano's *Madame Sans-Gêne,* based on a play by Victorien Sardou, at the Metropolitan on January 25, 1915, with Toscanini conducting.

The Fall cleaning season is on, the curtains down and screens out of windows. I think it too early because of the heat, but say nothing. The insects drift in and I give battle royal—mostly to the wasps.

No, I have no feeling for jewels anymore. They belonged to an era when one dressed superbly and did not run the gauntlet of bandits who now infest all places of entertainment—and are even ready to kill for the baubles. How can one expect to go about the streets of New York, or any large city, with the riff-raff who lie in wait for such foolish creatures?

Jewels should be worn on fine occasions, and in their setting; not under loose hair and ready for the most opportune robber. . . . Mine are locked up, and give me no concern—a favorite ring or two, all I care to don at present. Country dress suits my taste and causes no uneasiness.

Remember when I once wrote, "Blessed is he who has nothing?" Not to be taken in too drastic a sense; but the lessening of responsibility allows more freedom of thought . . . do you not think?

How amusing that you failed to recognize your own pastel of me!

Our best greetings till we meet. GF

October 19, 1947

Dear Miss Stotler:

Thank you for the items re Miss Truman.[42] The program photo is the nicest that I have seen to date. A pleasant face, probably a very nice young girl, though to my mind there is nothing to indicate an allure for the general public. Perhaps she varies in expression with her song?

Mr. Lissfelt has been kind and gentlemanly, with sound advice as to the choice of a professional teacher. For her sake I hope she heeds this well intentioned hint.

I recall the sad singing adventures of President Wilson's daughter, Margaret. Poor woman, I fancy she had a difficult life. She died lately in India, a member of some esoteric sect there. Nature did not favor her too much—her father's features did little for a feminine

[42] Mary Margaret, daughter of President Harry S Truman, had a relatively brief singing career during which she was treated unfavorably by the critics and boldly defended by her father. She later became a successful mystery writer.

face, whereas the little Truman looks like a nice, pleasant lass . . . and one hopes she has some measure of content with the results of her determination to warble.

I can sympathize with you in your concern to keep off the hunters, but certainly the state is to blame. Here, for instance, hunting licenses are issued, but *there is no place to hunt,* save over the protesting owner's grounds. My father used to go out to meet the trespassers with his gun, but only while he watched did it do any good.

I have been driving my guests about. The foliage is beautiful and the days have been warm and sunny. This prelude to Winter is all the more poignant because it is so fleeting. The valley over the hills to the Hudson is a canvas of glowing colors; something lovely to see from my study window.

Now to the post, and a concert this evening; an all Negro chorus, that functioned in this manner during the war. It should be good to hear.

Our best greetings, GF

October 20, 1947

Dear Miss Stotler:

A light shower that will no doubt clear, but has not cooled the humid air. I am beginning to wish to be into the wools and out of the cotton frocks at this late date. The earth is like powder, the reservoirs very low, the trees shrivelled; the leaves fall, but not with frost invitation.

Miss Sylvia's tenants leave and new ones come in; the house has to be cleaned and made ready; she must supervise all with an eagle eye. My Ford has to go to the service station for a week so we must make do with the temperamental Crosley.

Branchville has already raised $2,000 by private donations for their recreation area, and more power to them to have refused town help . . . an independent gesture I applaud.

I do not observe any special plea for sympathy from my friends abroad. They state their circumstances, the good fortune to have a roof over their heads. They reply as to what articles they most need, at my inquiry, and make no issue of their plight. Many of the husbands and fathers are gone; the presence of the children and grandchildren seems the one important concern—for their daily living. . . .

Your report of the various observations re Farrar-Garden,[43] is typical. I have been a listener—in a group—to the same heated reflections and many amusing tales that are related with authority. There was much publicity for the stars of yesterday, which stemmed mostly from the active press agent, rather than from the singers themselves . . . a not very laudable avenue of exploitation.

In my day there was no necessity to participate in any outside function, unless one desired a more intimate connection with the public. For me, it was a very wearing ordeal, after one's performance to be besieged in the dressing room; but it was part of the show, and considered wise to allow.

Now to the post, and chores in the village.

Our best greetings, GF

October 22, 1947

Dear Miss Stotler:

No, I know nothing about Holland's reigning family. The Queen[44] is indeed entitled to some rest, after a long and arduous service to her country. No doubt there is much to worry her in the loss of her richest crown land. She will be a poor power indeed, without those colonies [in the East Indies].

I am re-reading the bloody yet fascinating history of Rome from Dr. Durant's book, *Caesar and Christ.* It is the same pattern we now see.

He speaks of the change in the ethnic character of the Roman citizenry due to the overcrowding by freed slaves attracted by the dole. The birthrate of the native stock was low, that of aliens, high. Augustus began too late to try to check the imbalance, fearing that an overwhelming population of former subject peoples could not be relied upon for loyalty. Durant suggests that had more time been

[43] As Geraldine Farrar did in Berlin, so Scottish-American soprano Mary Garden (1874–1967) achieved an immediate success in Paris. She sang for seven years at the Opêra-Comique before being brought by Oscar Hammerstein to his Manhattan Opera House in 1907 where she starred in modern French operas. The press of the day tried its best to pit the two singers against each other, which worried neither and did no harm at the box office.

[44] Because of ill health and exhaustion, Queen Wilhelmina had been temporarily relieved of her official duties on October 10, 1947, and her daughter Juliana had been appointed regent. On September 4, 1948, the much-loved Wilhelmina, queen since her eighteenth birthday in 1898, abdicated in favor of her daughter. She died in 1962.

allowed for the assimilation of aliens, the story of Rome might have been different.

The same pattern today unrolls before our very eyes, unless we have a stern and speedy volte face—almost too much to hope for.

I have just attended a funeral and a birthday, some few minutes apart; a wedding is scheduled for tomorrow; so goes the design of this old world in its repetitious routine . . . only the players are different.

All good wishes, GF

November 10, 1947

Dear Miss Stotler:

We are glad for the good news that you arrived home safely without too much unpleasantness. The weather here has been growling this past week, and the down-pour Saturday a real flood.

I had a visit from a friend just back from Germany, and his narrative is of the most pitiful kind; conditions there must be horrible. His dismay at the change in the people, reduced like animals to forage the best they can for food, was acute. He found his parents in a pretty bad way (French occupation), while the terror is general of the Russian. All who can, escape from them and fall on their knees in prayer once they get over the border. The looting of those in command beggars description.

It is a horrid post-war picture. When, if ever, it betters, is questionable.

I found the Seltsam volume[45] which you brought me very well compiled; and certainly an addition to one's library. The author is a true music lover. He had hoped to make dancing his career, but was stricken with deafness. With a hearing aid he now manages to discern the different values of recordings, and is responsible for the IRCC [International Record Collectors' Club].

He has an enormous correspondence, and a good insight into the values of such mementoes of the past.

The Opera Guild has pushed the publicity and he is to be [the] honored guest at a special luncheon in December. I have "regretted" much to his disappointment. A seat at a long table to be stared at like some strange animal does not amuse me. I do not like ballyhoo.

---

[45] *Metropolitan Opera Annals. A Chronicle of Artists and Performances,* compiled by William H. Seltsam (1947), covers sixty years of opera history. It is dedicated to Geraldine Farrar, American soprano, and Martial Singher, French baritone.

I have not seen the Schumann film [*Song of Love*, 1945] but the choice of Hepburn for Clara would seem to me most unfortunate. Ingrid Bergman would have been the person, in my opinion.

Hollywood does such odd things. Little Margaret O'Brien is dreadful in the *Unfinished Dance*. This quaint little child, who can be so touching, is in this picture a lanky ballerina in the children's class and attached to an inane story. Some of the choreography is pretty, but not outstanding. Great expense—nothing of value.

Our housecleaning lingers on a bit, but the main struggle is over, and I am spared the siren call of the vacuum.

All's well for today, best greetings, GF

November 13, 1947

Dear Miss Stotler:

Beautiful red roses greeted me when I came home from shopping. I do thank you for the thought, and the lovely glow they afford my study; doubly so in the bitter cold.

I'm taking the household to the movies to vary the day's routine. *Forever Amber* [a somewhat sensational film starring Linda Darnell], no doubt the usual trash, but at least no jazz! Perhaps I may ignore for a time my very sore jaws from yesterday's bout with the drill. Again, thank you for the lovely roses.

As ever, GF

November 20, 1947

Dear Miss Stotler:

The last of the bulbs went into the ground this morning. I very much feared we should have to contend with frost, in which case I could not have spaded the earth, but the rain had softened it, all to the good, and now the beds are covered with leaves and can drowse till Spring.

Yes, the radio *Tosca*[46] was very bad. I listened carefully to all three acts; there was not merit in it. Oh yes, I often had poor criticisms, and can give you no reason, save that the critics found me not acceptable to their ideas at the time. I was always mindful of a very

[46] Miss Farrar usually listened to the Saturday afternoon radio broadcasts of the Metropolitan Opera.

tender throat, and had frequent bronchial difficulties, so that my rest time was passed indoors, and much of the time in bed to conserve all the energy possible. I daresay there were many times when I was not as effective as I would have wished.

Those days are so far away now, that I confess they interest me very little. I am grateful to have had good fortune crown my hard work, but enough is enough . . . there is no nostalgia connected with my memories, and when I think of the infernal insomnia that plagued me, well, I want no more of such worries.

The MET had no understudy, but at times, when several artists shared the same role, the management would call upon one to help out in an emergency. There were many singers who, by reason of a sudden indisposition have "held" over the curtain, with an apology from the management, but I can recall no time when the house had to close, once a performance had begun.

I have no pleasure in the pompous interludes now.

The idea to snatch artists from their contemplation to speak into the mike before a performance smacks of a cheap bid for praise. It gets no one anywhere. When the curtain goes up, there is the real battleground!

I do not know how the piano sequences were made in the Hepburn-Schumann opus. I should imagine Hepburn would be trained in the correct position of the hands in the close-ups.

In re *Tosca,* the drop from St. Angelos, with mattress protection, was about as deep as I am tall. It is not without danger; one must be well poised to jump straight.

Please accept the auto gadget, which I hope you will never need to use; but it is a comforting thought that it is at hand. This business of jacking up heavy wheels is nothing for a woman.

All good wishes, GF

November 22, 1947

Dear Miss Stotler:

The two books are here. A hasty glance into the Seibel volume [George Seibel's *Stories He Told* (1947)] would suggest stories along the lines of [Kahlil] Gibran. The Duse[47] will be the usual Harding frame for some colorful phrases.

---

[47] *Age Cannot Wither,* by Bertita Harding (1947) is the story of the renowned Italian actress Eleonora Duse (1859–1924) and her lover Gabriele D'Annunzio (1863–1938), novelist, poet, soldier, and fiery nationalist.

Duse would not have been cremated in any case, being a Catholic, even if not a steady attendant, due, perhaps, to professional activity. She was greatly in need of money, thanks to that rotten D'Annunzio, and the last tour was for the living needs, so I have been told.

I was not an ardent admirer of this strange lady, though I am willing to credit a zealous press agent in the matter of her soulful misery and constant suffering. I think she was a neurotic, a hardworking artist, and certainly not in robust health; but to play roles of glamor and youthful passion, it gave me no pleasure to see a woman of years, without make-up, artifices or illusion, gray hair in untidy profusion and awful dresses. . . . She did nothing to help herself at the age when I last saw her, whereas Sarah Bernhardt was an element of any illusion she chose; and what a voice! Duse's was a wail most of the time. To my way of thinking, the theater *is* the theater, and should create illusion especially in the realm of poetry and legend.

To die in smokey Pittsburgh was certainly a sad suffocation for Duse. She was a very ill lady and drove herself on, as so many do.

I found the soot in Pittsburgh very hard to cope with, though the public was one of the warmest ever, and a concert in the Carnegie Museum [Carnegie Music Hall] near the Schenley was a perfect setting for communication with the audience . . . but remembering how the dirt settled over the most carefully arranged frock, I can well appreciate how poor Duse agonized, in the dead of Winter, with the black outpour on her tortured lungs . . . a far cry from her beloved Italy.

To speak of a happier event, I listened with great sympathy to the wedding of [Princess] Elizabeth and [Prince] Philip.[48] My own thoughts swept back to the time when I read with avid delight as one does a fairy tale, of the nuptials of the young Czar and Princess Alexandra. I could not help breathing a silent prayer that this young couple might never meet with the anger and disorders that brought about the horrible fate of the Russian bridal pair. I was in High School at that time, and the reading material of the occasion was also very romantic and glamorous.

I was amused to hear the commentator speak of the heartiness of Winnie [Winston Churchill], while the face of Atlee [British Labor Prime Minister Clement Atlee] was without expression. I opine that aside from the bridal couple, the most commanding figure would have been the stately Queen Mother, Mary.

[48] The wedding of Her Royal Highness Princess Elizabeth of England to Philip Mountbatten, the Duke of Edinburgh, November 20, 1947.

Well, it is now time for the young people to be off on their honeymoon, and may it continue to be such for many years to come! They have so much on their young shoulders.

Our best greetings as I fly to a dinner in the neighborhood. GF

November 23, 1947

Dear Miss Stotler:

A windy, blustery day, but enough sun to be cheery. I was able to send you a letter yesterday on my way to the city; before that could not hold a pencil in my languid hands. These bugs simply make one helpless for a short time; three days in bed seemed to drive away the intruders.

Thank you for the *Manon* sketch at hand. I know of no more poignant scene, as to song and action, than the lovely St. Suplice moment. The seduction is so elegant, so much of the period of laces and brocades, but with real emotional appeal.

I have never cared for *Ballo in Maschera* [*The Masked Ball,* Verdi, 1859]; there is a confused plot, and the various phrases that recall other operas, more to one's liking, do not continue into haunting melodies. The radio cast was adequate, though one feels, in justice to them, they should also be seen; the action is so important to the whole effect.

I think I dismissed the *Tosca* with brief lack of enthusiasm. It was while leaping to the finale, in the stage version, that Bernhardt did herself the irreparable knee injury, causing the later removal of her leg. The mattress of protection had not been properly placed.

In such matters I always surveyed the scene myself, not trusting to stage hands to know my own plan of action.

In the second act, with candles and crucifix, I never looked at the position of the knife, but kept my eyes on the Scarpia at his desk, the while, feeling for the weapon. This was an effective gesture I learned from Bernhardt,[49] always to have the face express the fleeting emotions. . . . It was not hard to arrange the necessary steps, and follow the carpet line, giving a wonderful play of watchfulness; the idea being to convey the uncertainty of the Scarpia's action by cat and mouse concentration.

I got nothing out of the Seibel book, for I do not respond to these fairy tales and parables. I have never been unduly warm about [Rabindranath] Tagore, when the whole world was swooning over his

[49] Miss Farrar had studied the stage business of *Tosca* with Sarah Bernhardt in Paris.

neat little volumes. One must have a predilection for such phraseology, perhaps.

The Duse-D'Annunzio book was a trite attempt to revive an old story, but in their poor little pecuniary affair (on his part, the rascal), she was nothing like the Bernhardt, who was at all times mistress of the situation.

Bernhardt had her trials and misfortunes and had to labor at being the star she later became. Her type was unusual, her ultra-slender figure[50] a perfect one on which to hang the caricatures, but she turned all to account, and defeated her detractors. She was proud of her son, her life and her adventures; like an empress, believing in herself, she made all accept her own estimate. The Duse, retiring, and with far less ability to defend herself, made of the usual theater routine and its incidents, a tragedy.

Sarah had extraordinary clouds of red-gold hair, worn in a long bang over a broad forehead, and the most marvelous eyes. The upper part of her face was like a tigress—the nose heavy but with palpitating nostrils. The mouth, never pretty, for she did unutterably silly things with her teeth. They were not good, and when I knew her, she was her own dentist. She managed some kind of plaster over the entire denture. It was all right en scène, but pretty strange at near view . . . she did not care.

She was not as tall as I, but had such grace of gesture, in caress or command, that she seemed to tower over men much taller, and swamped them. Her hands were small and most eloquent. Her back was charmingly modelled, but her breast was null. There was no fleshy volupté in her body, as such, but it conveyed the most violent of passions, seconded by a voice, truly molten gold.

I believe she never lost control of herself at any time, though she had moments of great generosity. She was a slave to her husband, a good for nothing Greek animal of no talent, though she hoped to make him great. For many years she nursed him through the most repulsive orgies (narcotic) and finally had to divorce him to prevent his complete grasping of her rich finances . . . so was the husband-wife law in those days. From then on she never harnessed herself to a domestic routine.

I call her an element . . . she had no time or era; a remarkable brand. I was in Paris at the time she gave her theater to Duse, and saw

[50] A familiar quip of the time was "An empty carriage drew up, and Sarah Bernhardt got out."

them both frequently. I seem to recall but one dolorous expression of Duse, Sarah had a thousand faces . . .

Best greetings from us all, GF

November 25, 1947

Dear Miss Stotler:

I am glad that you, too, heard the two hour radio report of the royal wedding. I thought it a very beautiful impression conveyed over the ether. The form of High Church was solemn and devout, and both Bishops had such tenderness and fatherly feeling. I thought the cheering crowds and the music, the thud of those superb horses, all gave a fine impression of a vanishing era; a proud echo of an older England that is now fighting for her life and her traditions.

I agree that it was slightly out of manner not to include the bridegroom's family, since he himself had for some time replaced the Germanic name with Mountbatten; but no doubt there had to be concessions, re protocol. As to the non-inclusion of the Windsors,[51] since he had renounced everything that pertained to his former estate, there was no reason why this couple should be included. Listening carefully to the marriage service, one could realize there would be no place in it save for those who have empire interests at heart; for there is not only the holy state of matrimony, but, as well, the reiterated insistence on family life and progeny, to carry on the succession.

I do not take it as a slap to an American, as you feel; this particular American, like all the other expatriates, has no call on our feelings, and seems pleased to consort with the less agreeable humans who make up some of this world's saddest society. A pitiful couple at best.

After Thanksgiving I shall begin to think of Christmas greens. The time will be upon us before we know it.

All good things to you. GF

December 4, 1947

Dear Miss Stotler:

I shall settle to the opera music—nothing can dim the enchant-

[51] Edward VIII had abdicated from the British throne in 1936 when refused permission to marry Wallis Warfield Simpson, an American divorcée. He was given the title of Duke of Windsor and married Mrs. Simpson in 1937.

ment of Mozart. And then the radio *Otello*[52] of Toscanini. A joy that I do not have to contend with the elements; the cold is intense and the streets are a sheet of ice. The sandman has not yet made his rounds; our hills are dangerous till he does.

Perhaps Burton Holmes[53] is grooming the young man to replace him. I should think the present day travel would be a great hardship and more than discourage him, though he has a public that has been loyal these many years. A good friend and a delightful gentleman.

There used to be a man named Fitzpatrick, who showed superlatively lovely scenes illustrating delightful tales. I recall one in particular, a Swiss romance, where the guide had an accident and was lost for some time. Later a party discovered the body, still preserved in life-like pose, at the bottom of a gully; the features and color of the Tracht [clothing] were very distinct. It made quite an impression. The inference was that the sorrowing family left him where he lay, with some fine references to the immutability of the eternal snows and their protection.

I wrote about *Forever Amber* a few letters ago. It was a bit dull, on the order of a similar huzzy movie, *Kitty* [1946], with Paulette Goddard. The costumes were pretty, and the technicolor covered many sins; the actors were constrained and the various scenes only repeated themselves in other color combinations. Most appealing were the adorable King Charles spaniels who frisked in and out at the call of their master.

I do listen frequently to the Detroit Orchestra. That body of men is sustained by the wealthy Reichold,[54] who is considering a large musical project. If it goes through, it would supply a field of small houses for the employment of opera companies. As you know, this idea has always been close to my heart, and I have spoken of it in many

---

[52] Sunday evening program with his NBC Orchestra.

[53] E. Burton Holmes, noted travel lecturer, was indeed introducing to his audiences Thayer Soule, who was to carry on his work. Holmes was enchanted by Farrar's Butterfly and brought her from Japan the pretty toys used in the first act and the exquisite dagger for the hari-kari scene.

[54] A German immigrant who made a fortune from a chemical company he established in Ferndale, Michigan, Henry H. Reichold was a fervent patron of music. On several occasions during the 1940s he rescued the Detroit Symphony from extinction by covering the orchestra's deficits. The beneficial effect of his patronage was undermined by his strong views on personnel and artistic matters, and clashes with various sections of the orchestral community eventually led to his withdrawal from active participation in the symphony's affairs.

lectures in the past. I heard of the Reichold project from the man who came to see me about Lilli Lehmann's 100th birthday material.

The difficulty seems to be, as expected, with the labor unions . . . quite especially, one Petrillo.[55]

I shall be home for Christmas Eve, then off to spend Christmas Day with Mrs. Gilmour and a group of friends.[56]

I hope the fair weather delights your area.

Best greetings, GF

December 9, 1947

Dear Miss Stotler:

Yes, I saw the article, "Met Singer Sings Under Guard" re the threats to the life of Regina Resnik,[57] if she appeared on the stage at the Saturday performance of *Don Giovanni*. The affair must have been very disagreeable for the young singer; having had this form of nuisance I can appreciate the situation. One man had to be restrained by law—he was definitely unbalanced. One never knows what harm these people may do, no pleasant outlook. This young lady is a pupil of a friend of mine, an excellent teacher. For both their sakes, I hope it is only a temporary annoyance.

Manon[58] has always been a great favorite of mine, superb en scène, with the lovely attire of that era, and ravishing melody . . . fascinating little tramp she was, and most endearing despite her amoral activities.

You asked about the diligence of *Manon*. We always had, in

[55] James C. Petrillo was the highly influential and long-time president of the American Federation of Musicians. Among his most effective means for securing the conditions requested by union members was the calling of general strikes.

[56] Geraldine Farrar, Marion Telva, Lily Pons, and Rosa Ponselle were the friends who often gathered on holidays at the home of Mary Gilmour, the only member of the group who was not a professional performer.

[57] Born in New York in 1923, Regina Resnik studied at Harvard and won a Metropolitan Opera prize. Her debut at the Metropolitan Opera as Leonora in *Il Trovatore* on December 6, 1944, was highly acclaimed but impromptu, with only one brief rehearsal. She remained a popular singer there for many years, her voice changing from dramatic soprano to mezzo. She is perhaps best remembered for her role as Fricka in Wagner's *Ring* cycle.

[58] Manon was a favorite role of Berlin audiences and, with Butterfly, was said to have been the exclusive property of Farrar until the First World War. "Manon" was Miss Sylvia's special name for Miss Farrar.

Berlin, a very fine coach and pair loaned from the royal stables; a dim recollection of a model viewed in museums, of another era.

Talking with the Maestro's [Toscanini's] secretary this morning, preparing for the second half of *Otello* [on radio] he tells me the rehearsals are twice daily with cast and orchestra. No wonder the results are perfection. Yet one of the smaller singers ventured to remonstrate, saying that she could not come back for the last rehearsal, but that she would, even so, be letter perfect. This is indicative of the young people today—no idea of any concentration or joy in work. Imagine the *glory* any of us older singers would have felt to be chosen for such an occasion. The hours we rehearsed, without food or rest, all intent on the lovely results, and these little nit-wits—truly it is to despair that *ever* again we shall have first rate performances.

Miss Garden has, as yet, brought forth no book, but she should. It would be good reading of a fascinating era. She comes from Aberdeen, but has lived here from her early youth. Her father was in the automobile business, Packard, I seem to recall, while her mother and a second daughter were present.

Miss Garden was a protégé of a wealthy lady (as we have all had the good fortune to be, or we would have had retarded achievements indeed) but in making her career she had need of no such assistance. She owed her first Paris engagement to the goodwill of a charming American singer, Sybil Sanderson,[59] and from then on her career soared, and quite rightly.

There was much in her like Fremstad; they seemed always restless and dissatisfied; both women of difficult tempers.

I dash to the post before we have either snow or sleet; best be in the warm house when the wind rises, as I now hear it.

Again, our good wishes, GF

December 11, 1947

Dear Miss Stotler:

A brilliant snowy morning of blue sky and dazzling ermine. The air is like wine and the birds are swooping down from all sides,

[59] American prima donna Sybil Sanderson (1865–1903) was a dear friend of Massenet, several of whose roles she created. When Farrar visited the composer in Paris to discuss the Manon that she was to sing at the Royal Opera in Berlin, she found him overcome by grief, having just come from Sybil's funeral. A painting by Albert Aublet of Massenet rehearsing Sybil in *Manon* appeared in the Paris Salon in the 1880s.

eager for the contents of their feeding box. Oh, it is wonderful to be in the country and partake of this wholesome freshness. Phone calls from the city speak of mud and slush; what a pity that anyone must inhabit such a mart for his livelihood. I am happy to be out of it; to see only a patch of azure through the towers of Manhattan would be to me a suffocation.

I do love all the dear sentiments of Christmas, and my home recollections of this season are always of tenderness. My mother made all that I received—dresses and costumes and stuffed dolls. Music books I had to earn by good marks; save for arithmetic, this was not too difficult. We trimmed our own tree and others for our neighbors. There were the usual Christmas carols, both at home and in church, our family always in place. To this day I try to choose gifts that are pleasing, either by phone or wire, well in advance. I will not make shopping the finale.

The *Otello* with Toscanini was rarely beautiful. It just goes to show what careful preparation and a certain amount of talent will do. Singers blossomed out under the Maestro's baton. He told me he had rehearsed them two hours, morning and afternoon, for four weeks. Well, the results indeed repaid his care.

I took a chance, from a stray bit of gossip, that Mary Garden was in her native Aberdeen (my Margaret's home, by the way) so I sent Miss Garden a Christmas card with greetings to her and her mother. This morning came an airmail reciprocation, with a pencilled addition to the printed phrase. The design of the card amused me; no Madonna or Christ Child, but a myriad-colored peacock on a delicately drawn tree branch, Japanese in style, I would say, quite in the manner one would associate with her.

My thought of Grace Moore[60] was always of a Broadway singer; a pretty voice and face, but no proper opera foundation, and too pleasure loving to accept the stern discipline that would have made her a better singer.

But the whole picture is so changed now that one is at a loss to judge, save by the fine standards of earlier days, and those I shall not lightly cast aside. Their memory is precious and suffices for my content.

Now I shall hop into my cozy bed, turn on the radio and be

[60] Grace Moore (1901–1946) was an American soprano who sang for three seasons with the Metropolitan Opera. Best remembered as a singing actress in motion pictures, she was killed in a plane crash near Copenhagen.

grateful for the warm comfort and tranquility I am privileged to enjoy.

Our best wishes, GF

December 19, 1947

Dear Miss Stotler:

Our porch at last is in its Christmas dress with green, fragrant sprays and the spruces on either side of the door decked with silver tinsel and gaily colored globes. No matter the weather, we shall have them quite perfect in this enclosed setting.

Another brilliant sunny day it is a joy to welcome. I would not mind a sled and a spill on the nearby Country Club incline!

Letters from England are amazing in the courage and spirit of my friends there. That a great empire should fall afoul of such times is scarcely believable; all speak with pride and affection of the royal wedding party, and of their gladness in a brief glimpse of something beside the austerities that are their portion now.

I hope the crank who bothers Miss Resnik will be disposed of. Most professional people have had to struggle with this unpleasant thing, and one tries to give it no publicity, as this incites others to similar annoyance. I had several experiences, and resorted to law. Cranks but not guttersnipes, just, I think, a bit off balance. I have a letter writer these many years who has hallucinations. Though he has never presented himself, I am very careful about strangers. He is given to poetry and such illusive matters, and as I know the writing I drop his communications into the wastebasket. An anonymous case, and so far, harmless.

You mentioned Westbrook Pegler.[61] He is a very conscientious man, but I think he and his wife are killing themselves over the job. They have a most lovely farm here, up for sale, since he has to travel much for certain information, while their ranch in Arizona hardly ever sees them. He is fighting a nervous breakdown and his wife goes from one heart attack into another. The pace is killing, and the role of crusader, for the morons who never learn, and the politicians who never falter in their evil ways, seems to me to be losing very valuable energy that could be better applied. This, of course, is only my

61 An ultra-conservative, Pegler had won the 1941 Pulitzer Prize for his exposé of labor unions. His most virulent columns, written for King Features Syndicate (1944–1962), were directed against Communists in the unions and the government.

personal view. Perhaps if one has the ink on his desk and the fervor to use it, one cannot be denied.

I hope your holidays will continue merry. This morning from 6 to 7 there was a very pretty program of carols, and some records particularly seasonable, one of which was Schumann-Heink[62] in her traditional "Stille Nacht" ["Silent Night"]. It gave me quite a thrill, in memory.

Our best wishes and greetings, and a very joyous Christmastide.

GF

December 24, 1947

Dear Miss Stotler:

A perfect winter day, after a whirling snow storm. It is truly Christmas weather in the familiar and traditional scene that now gladdens the eye.

I did not listen to *Manon*. I like Bidú Sayão,[63] but I was busy with other matters. Sometimes a voice does not properly warm up, which may induce off-key strain. The caliber, also, has to do with steady pitch. Some delicate voices, like [Lily] Pons, often overshoot the mark; there is no support, only the most tenuous of head voice, which means an unreliable pitch if there is the slightest thing wrong with the general condition. Deep breath control is the great essential.

The higher voices often suffer from this, while large volumed instruments, sometimes forced beyond normal control, are so strained that they, too, adhere badly to the given note.

Vibrations play such an eerie part. Woodwinds have a different vibration from the strings, while the brasses often seem off pitch, due to the air pressure of the players that must be handled with great skill . . . a fine ear plays the guiding part.

Back to *Manon*—I had so many costumes I could not tell you off hand the color combinations. The first, second and last acts, I

[62] Ernestine Schumann-Heink (1861–1936) was a Czech-born contralto who became an American citizen in 1908. She sang throughout Europe and at the Metropolitan, before retiring to give concerts. It became a tradition for her to sing "Silent Night" on the radio every Christmas.

[63] Bidú Sayão (b. 1902), Brazilian soprano, sang leading roles at the Metropolitan from 1936 to 1947. She was especially admired as Manon.

played in my own dark hair. The white wigs were combined with the luxury costumes befitting the lady's climb to notoriety.

The Massenet *Manon* is the true Gallic expression. The virile music of the Puccini opera, while most effective, has not the style or elegance for this fragile story; it is the more emotional outpouring of free Italian throats.

Put the majority of Italian singers into a French style, and you will readily see how deficient they are in the elegance of the diction. French is a very difficult tongue to sing, but it *is* beautiful.

The doorbell is ringing and the parcels keep arriving, all very exciting on this sunny Winter's day. As I wrote before, the wonderful cheeses have come and I have had them in several delicious ways, one of which is gnocchi, with beer for supper, very pleasant.

Several little handmade gifts from overseas, a pitiful attempt to return for the food reminders of friendship. I hate to think of conditions there, in this grim Winter.

I agree that the last years have been far from happy ones for the world in general, but I do feel we have to fashion the Christmastide according to our means and spirit. It would be a sad universe indeed were there not some hope, and some return, even for a few days, to the faith of our fathers. My own reactions are perhaps a bit juvenile but I am not ashamed of them. My household joins in reiterated good wishes and greeting.

GF

December 29, 1947

Dear Miss Stotler:

Hurrah—the bulldozer has freed a part of the drive, enough to allow me to get out the car and drive to town; but Oh, the costly new cover of last Summer is a wreck from the cleats of the machine. It will cost me a pretty penny to put it in order again. As Miss Sylvia says, "Nothing *ever* stays put!"

However we must be grateful to be rid of the snow. I had the Matterhorn on one side and the peak of Mt. McKinley on the other. We are counting on a party tonight; the husband of a friend is driving, which spares me the nervous strain; one is a bit apprehensive in negotiating our hills.

Crank mail? Oh, yes, to this day. It does not concern me. But there is someone who always sends me the most lovely roses—just a card saying "With admiration." The florist says the person phones and sends a money order. This is silly, for I should like to thank the donor. It *is* frustrating.

You speak of investments; I do not know that I approve of autos as a backlog. Every one has a particular idea. Some of my friends, having interests in Mexico, invest in silver bars, others in diamonds, since the need for these in precision instruments is great. My money is in savings, if one goes, all will go, and there is little use to try to fathom the whirlpool.

There is so much hysteria, and one wonders if for a purpose. The radio has been banging away about fuel shortages, but our dealer this week said he certainly would look after his customers as usual.

With the immense oil reserves in Arabia, and the disputes there, Palestine versus Arabia, anything can happen, and probably will end in a holy war, with the usual carnage.

If oil fails, scientists will evolve something else, at our generation's expense.

As for a business venture, well, that is indeed a headache for honest people. We have a new silver factory here that should have success, in a trade and repair work, with the laudable idea of giving home youth the opportunity to learn a paying trade. I went to see the proprietor, a silversmith who had been with Gorham and Jensen. He said frankly that he could no longer work under New York conditions. I grasped at once the reason, for the fine old firm of Jensen has sold out; they now deal in anything, like a department store. Not the elegant porcelain figurines that used to be, with silver, their specialty. The world has low grade tastes and habits.

The Detroit concern has, according to report, a barrel of money to further many musical ventures. One almost started, with several companies of youthful aspirants, but some hitch occurred; one hears of Petrillo bans. Now we shall see what happens to the recording business. I see no difference between this particular czar and Capone.

We have seen nothing of Wallace[64] in church. He seems too busy with his public speaking. The rector of our Episcopal church here is a staunch Democrat and a great admirer, so perhaps he

[64] Henry A. Wallace had a varied political career. From 1941 to 1945 he served as Vice President of the United States under Democratic Presidents Roosevelt and Truman. Although starting out as a Republican, he had become an ardent New Dealer, serving as Secretary of Agriculture under Roosevelt and Secretary of Commerce under Truman. In 1948 he helped form and ran as presidential candidate for the Progressive Party.

may get some friendly circle; not with me, however. Few of the townspeople, outside of the stores where perhaps he may trade, would be inclined to mingle. We are a very stubborn Republican crowd. I admit we should better our ways also. I am not enthusiastic about our present candidates.

Meanwhile, may the year 1948 bring us all health, confidence and humor for the daily routine of living, and may we find some honest and competent men who *will* bring to some order the chaos and misery of those we have to sustain.

Best greetings, and again thanks from us here.

Happy New Year! GF

1948

January 2, 1948

Dear Miss Stotler:

The salami came as a very pleasant surprise this forenoon. Our aged postman has been heroic and delivered mail in drifts almost up to his waist. He gets his hot coffee and sandwich, little enough for his valiant devotion. No thought of getting food from the stores, as they have no delivery in such weather. Miss Sylvia has some yeast and is baking rolls; a delicious delicacy.

The last act of *Tristan* is in progress but I do not heed the gross [Lauritz] Melchior. At the advent of Isolde [Helen Traubel] I shall turn the dial to normal. It is a gorgeous tapestry of sound, but, what pompous entr'actes, culminating in Deems Taylor's plea to have his *Peter Ibbetson* grace the boards again.

My castagnettes may very well have been used by the lovely Rita Hayworth. I had many pairs from Spain and Mexico, all sold at my auction of long ago. I keep very few of such souvenirs; do not believe in having mountains of stage property in storage to rot and pay for. I see such folly in the case of Fremstad, who still clings to these things. Better to have them in use by others when time comes for the owner to exit. Also, take the ready cash for them; in my case it was a sizable sum indeed.

We were most fortunate to get to Mrs. G. for the New Year's gathering. The roads were passable and the sky without rain or snow, another story now.

I wore an aqua dress, plain with green palliates on the sleeves, sprinkled more to sparkle than to decorate. As we were all bundled to shapeless monstrosity, there was no question of wearing a lovely evening wrap.

We were rather quiet; the circle of other days has diminished considerably, and while we were happy and content to be gathered, it was not a noisy hilarity.

Music and conversation were enjoyed, and we had a remarkable magician who did such fascinating sleight-of-hand things, all very dainty and all to bewilder the less quick eye . . .

I came home at 4:30 A.M. dead tired, and devoted all of yesterday to resting.

Thank you for the picture of Miss Aida. I like the hair-do she wears, it becomes her style and manner. She has the somewhat illusive air of an earlier century lady . . . a bit studied, but with a hint of purpose behind it all.

The sleet is wicked. The trees bend beneath encrusted ice, cracking now and then; a heart-breaking sight and sound.

We send our best greetings, and do not worry about us, we are in good order.

GF

January 5, 1948

Dear Miss Stotler:

I have no considered opinion about my own records. It is a sort of anguish for me to hear them, not for the technical effects, these I do not consider, but the vocal renditions that I always could have done better, for I can view the past with a very objective eye. One record that I do think is an excellent one in style and color is one very few people ever care to hear. It is from that delightful *Donne Curiose*[65] and is called "Tutto per te, mio bene." It has the elements of Mozart, and for tone, does please me. Also a Mozart, "Dove sono" [from *Figaro*], a half finished record done in the studio to prove a point to myself. Mr. Seltsam begged permission to re-record it, with proper notation as to its inclusion.

Yes, I find Rita Hayworth a most glamorous girl and a beautiful dancer—if a point too thin, that is required by Hollywood. Her family is a famous dance group, Spanish, the Cansinos; her name, Marguerite Cansino. I believe there was an English connection somewhere that accounts for the Hayworth.

I like Irene Dunne very much, a refined type and a sweet person. Likewise, Ingrid Bergman. Both of them carry sincerity. I cannot bear to look at the present [Marlene] Dietrich. Nothing can cover the sad attempt to keep on being glamorous. When she first came here she was a wonderful creature, but her many odd directors have imposed their whims, and now she is just mechanical, to my mind.

I think beauty has much to do with the style of an era. Certainly a gracious manner and feminine apparel gave to women of no outstanding beauty an impression of loveliness that is lacking today.

I knew Ada Rehan, an Irish beauty and a good actress; Lillian Russell—skin like a peach and wonderful blue eyes; Nordica too. Julia Marlowe had a fascinating face and expression, not to mention

[65] Opera by Ermanno Wolf-Ferrari (1876–1948), German-Italian composer.

the rich voice. I could name many whose graces were rightly the talk of the town.

You are disposed in my favor, but we will leave *me* out of it. I am grateful for health and humor . . . I have no vanity; the mirror has always been a truthful confidante . . . and not unduly consulted.[66]

I listened to Harry Truman for ten minutes and then gave up. Fulton Lewis summed it up beautifully—that Truman had no need to reiterate the Wallace theories. It was certainly a play for all kinds of votes.

Well, at least the sun shines and it is good not to peer too far into an uncertain future.

A happy weekend. GF

January 14, 1948

Dear Miss Stotler:

You ask what qualities I most prize in people? I think first of that honesty that inspires trust. Even as a young person to find that a friend would hedge and dodge issues was to me very unsettling and disturbed my association. I like to know where I stand with none of the deviations that some find so fascinating. If one has close ties there must be some rock ribbed foundation that allows complete confidence.

I did not listen to [Charpentier's] *Louise*. It is not a favorite opera and I had more interesting guests to entertain. The role of course now is out of style. When I accepted to sing I made a stipulation that I would *not* wear the conventional shirt-waist affair. This caused much criticism and I was reproved, but went my own sweet way all the same. My dresses were simple but had good line. Nor did I wear the ridiculous sailor hat and stiff hair-do.

---

[66] Geraldine Farrar was considered a great beauty. Years later, Arturo Toscanini, recalling her appearance in *Königskinder*, mused, "Yes, she was beautiful; she was very beautiful." After the premiere of Humperdinck's opera at the Met, on December 28, 1910, critic Henry Krehbiel wrote, "With what exquisite charm an artist like Miss Farrar might invest a character like the Goose Girl her admirers could easily fancy before they entered the theatre. But it is doubtful if anyone's imagination quite reached the figure which she bodied forth. It was a vision of tender loveliness which she presented, and as perfect in conception as in execution."

At the close of the opera her audience was much amused when the star appeared with a live goose under her arm.

Dorothy Kirstan[67] was a protégé of Grace Moore, so I am told, who was very kind to her. Miss Kirstan came here with her manager. I found her a very agreeable young lady, very pretty, a worker and with a fine voice. Not really a theater talent, I would say; she is, however, not at all Broadway, as Moore. I found her sincere and unaffected.

[Kirsten] Flagstad leaves soon for London and has 22 Wagnerian operas there. My London friends are keen on her, and report glorious success in former appearances there. She will be back in the Spring.

As I listened to *Tristan* at the MET I could not help wondering at the stupidity of the officials there. I am fond of Traubel and admire her fine potentialities, but she is doing too much running hither and yon, and it is telling on the voice. She is too fine to jeopardize her best self; as for Melchior we will not speak of this person, now relegated to the category of radio comic.

I listened with bewilderment to the Philharmonic *Jeanne d'Arc at the Stake* [Paul Claudel's poem set to music by Arthur Honegger]. The poem was highly interesting, but I could find nothing in the musical setting. A pity . . . the subject matter affords such opportunity for beautiful music.

Our best wishes to you, GF

January 22, 1948

Dear Miss Stotler:

The heavens have opened again as was foretold, and the flakes are pouring down to add to the general covering of ice and snow. We have been shovelling a path here and there to allow ingress for milkman and postman, but the ice underneath is immovable; one must proceed with caution. I carried the birds their food but never have seen it disappear in such quantities; they must be without provender of any kind in the woods.

The garage cat and dog come daily for their food also, and Mutzi casts a sour eye on it all. She is very jealous.

I did not hear the Detroit Orchestra, but I do thrill to *Death and Transfiguration,* a noble and beautiful composition. The Strauss mu-

67 Born in 1917 of a musical family in New Jersey, Dorothy Kirstan was sent by Grace Moore to Rome for vocal study prior to World War II. Back in the states she sang with several companies, including the Chicago and San Francisco operas, before making her debut at the Metropolitan in 1945. Here her clear lyric soprano voice and acting ability made her the glamorous heroine of French and Italian roles for thirty years, the longest span for any prima donna at the Met.

sic is so at variance with his personality; it seems incredible that the gift so transcends the man, but it seems to be so in many instances. Perhaps another soul working through . . . who knows?

I am concluding Emil Ludwig's *Beethoven,* a gift from the translator. It is so very somber, as to the character, that I find it unpleasant, almost. I would rather authors did not "suppose" or draw conclusions about a genius . . . who wants to think of the commonplace when soaring to the heavens? Not I.

No, I am not beguiled by physical beauty, having seen much of it and its frailty. It is a very temporary endowment, and often leads astray its possessor. Even as a younger woman I was not misled by the transient loveliness that I could admire without envy.

I recall my dear grandmother, full of her New England proverbs at hand when needed, "Beauty comes from within. Never forget." She was most anxious that inner worth be established and recognized . . . well, this was not poor advice for one to have in early years.

Refinement is so elusive an attribute; some peasants have it to an exquisite degree, while those who should, by birth and education, be saturated in its rare charm, are often boors, piggish and quite distressing. Education does not always refine, nor intelligence induce kindness of feeling.

I do think that chemical magnetism is one fine gift that has little to do with sex appeal. It is a special flow of good-will and communication that takes place spontaneously, and is of great value to anyone in public life . . . also to those who nurse, preach or comfort. I think of it as a stream of kindliness, gushing forth without undue thought, and directed toward the other person with unconscious gesture of sympathy.

One of the nicest things ever said about me, I think, was the remark of a relative when asked if he did not find the superficial qualities a little overwhelming. He replied very simply, "Oh, Geraldine is quite normal."

I am so happy to know that two of my friends, the young English girl and her White Russian husband, have finally made their way to their home outside London, after years of dreadful suffering. I fear she will have come home only to die . . . but happiness may lend such strength as will help recovery . . . we shall hope it.

No, my god-children are not named for me, but bear the names of their relatives. If there are Geraldines elsewhere, they have nothing to do with my particular youngsters.

We're still busy as bees—all good wishes. GF

January 24, 1948

Dear Miss Stotler:

The snows are falling in a heavy veil; the cold is intense. Before the thunders of the *Walküre* begin I will send off a few lines in answer to yours of yesterday.

Re the re-recording of older records, I doubt if it is successful. I have heard some, notably Caruso's, and the voice is sacrificed to whatever "arrangement" the master-mind of the studio desires. In the early days of recording the voice was the primary consideration, and insofar as mechanics can give some idea of the individual gift, they are far more the true caliber than the manipulated sounds now obtained by the technical geniuses . . . I still feel too, that to understand the whole talent of a performer, one must hear him without broadcast or record manipulation . . . the voice is so tangible a part of the human being, it cannot be impressed on a surface with the same effect as coming to the ear, all fresh and vibrating with the actual—not, for want of a better word, "canned" sound.

I do not know what are the fees of the present-day performers. I understand in the last years of Mr. Gatti,[68] when finances were at low ebb, all the artists were asked to take considerable cuts, and all did, save Gigli,[69] for which, to my mind, he was unjustly excoriated. The number of performances is limited, so concerts, radio and screen have to supplement what should be 50 or 60 opera appearances.

The fees in my era were large and permanent, first, because the box-office warranted it, and then because there were only a few singers in the stellar class.

The European salaries were much less, because the number of opera houses made up the difference, in money and réclame, at the season's end.

Lilli [Lehmann] earned much, for she was busy all her life, but she was like most of the stars of her period. Their fortunes were swallowed up by the wars and their aftermath; they were left with property they could not hold, or investments that were frozen, as is the case now with many foreign artists.

Lilli spoke much of her mother, with only a passing observation for a father who seemed to be too often an habitué of the Wirtshaus

[68] Guilio Gatti-Casazza was manager of the Metropolitan Opera, 1908–1935.

[69] Beniamino Gigli, popular Italian tenor, sang at the Metropolitan between 1920 and 1932, and again between 1938 and 1939.

[inn]. I have heard the rumor often of her possible parentage, re Wagner; also noted was the name of Karl Muck, as being his son, a wonderful director, whom you have heard with the Boston Symphony. He, at least, looked enough like Wagner to give the story credit. The blond [sister] Marie was the image of the mother, but Lilli bore no family mark that I could see. Marie died shortly after Lilli.

Lilli's manner to me was very affectionate after she realized my complete devotion to learn. She could be jolly and very human; she was at her best when we were in the Scharfling Summer Resort; there she could relax and enjoy her mountain climbing and outdoor existence.

A great woman, indefatigable; she wanted *only* to sing. We did not therein share the same idea. I could not see an entire life with only one such outlet, because the advance of years would have to exercise a natural change. The voice is so delicate and responsive an instrument; in some it is of longer duration than in others, but the sum in essence is the same, whether a few or many years, and here plays the role of the individual and the mentality of the person in question. Each to his own time.

I did hear parts of *Rosenkavalier* and agree that it is highly desirable to see as well as hear it; a lovely picture with much of emotional appeal. The present cast needed to be seen also for the voices were not happily balanced on the radio. No, I should say you are quite right in preferring *Carmen* for auditory joy. It is sustained music at every page; could be given in concert form, which is the test.

Flagstad's manager has sent me her opera schedule in London, a wonderful one that keeps her busy, and very successful . . . bless her.

Now to the opera. We shall see what goes on in this mythical Wagnerian world.

Our best greetings, GF

January 28, 1948

Dear Miss Stotler:

The dull grey skies hint at more snow, and the zero chill approaches. The birds have been fed, such little greedy things, I can scarcely keep them supplied.

I look like a bear ready for hibernation when I go out on my shopping excursions. In fact yesterday out in the heavy snow swirls, a gentleman in passing laughed at my get-up and said, "Your New York friends should see you now!"

Your poor doctor friend—it were a blessing if she could sink to oblivion with no operation to tax her. If only there were some kind and wise way that persons need not suffer these last agonies; that when their hour came they might be permitted to close their eyes, freed from the body.

I lost my mother in January 1923. It seems incredible that she has been gone so long; but in a sense I have not felt her absence, for she seems so near, and so gay, as was her nature.

Mother was such a self-reliant person that I never worried about her eventual destination; whereas I did in the first months of my father's passing. He was not sure of himself in this transition. His only thought was to find my mother again, and I believe that he did.

I do not feel sad about either of them, for I am confident that we shall rejoin our loved ones—how and where and when does not concern me. It was my mother's teaching and I have never lost it.

My best greeting to you, GF

February 2, 1948

Dear Miss Stotler:

Speaking again of Lilli, well, perhaps in her later years she could have been more mellow, but certainly she was kind to me. I have known her to be very harsh with a few pupils whose lessons preceded mine; but then, fundamentally, it was her fault to have accepted them. Lilli liked to be asked and to explain her manner of teaching. Some were overwhelmed by her personality and used no individual thought of their own, or made an inquiry as to the whys and wherefores.

I remember one girl, an American, crying her eyes out, and when I asked the reason for her distress, said that she was hopelessly enamored of Lilli, and could summon no courage to ask anything. In fact she moaned, "If she should ask me to jump off the roof, I would do it." She never made any career, and should not have begun one. She had no idea of the real goal.

As to my first audition with Lilli, I was not overcome by her person, though I was ever so respectful and most eager to have her accept me as a pupil. As she was then on tour a good part of the time, and also had her own ideas about early debuts and thought I was too young for the one I had made, it might well have been that she would not have cared to enroll me.

But fate ruled otherwise and we became good and trusted friends.[70] She had a throat of iron, no nerves, and a willpower that was formidable, so I had to adjust the values she presented to my own case. As time went on she saw that my greatest asset was, as she wrote it more than once, my *Geschichtlichkeit* [authenticity] and this is more valuable in all fields than the stubborn forcing of all aspirants into one mold.

Her mouth was small, her teeth like perfect pearls. Those arched brows over dark eyes could be raised in anger or delight. She had the grace of the statuesque; a pliant body that was economical of gesture and movement, a handsome Germania. On the stage she was regal. The only other with this superlative line of distinction was Fremstad, but she marred her facial expression by one of disdain, and was not clever with cosmetics, so that she was not her most handsome back of the foot-lights.

I think the Crown Prince would not now be the man to take up the very difficult task of welding Germany together. He is my age, and has been too long a solitaire, and would never enjoy the confidence of the present Allies—memories of 1914 are still strong in the matter of any Hohenzollern. One wonders if the German people are not doomed to scattering and servitude, a mournful picture.

I sleep very well in this cold; have warm covers and the house is never without heat. We keep it at 68° and turn it down to 60° at night. I am in bed early; it seems the nicest way to enjoy the radio and keep warm.

All good wishes to you, GF

February 7, 1948

Dear Miss Stotler:

A dull, grey morning, but the odor of mimosa lends a tropical air to my study. Yesterday a friend sent me a sheaf of pink gladioli that are breathtaking. My African violets are blooming also, one has a

[70] Miss Farrar told of an embarrassing incident which occurred when Frau Lilli was coaching her own husband, the tenor Paul Kalisch and Farrar for a proposed production of *Otello*. Lilli became so caustic in criticizing her husband that that gentleman, an excellent singer and the favorite of the Royal Opera of Wiesbaden, finally picked up his hat and went back to Wiesbaden—bringing to an end that particular *Otello*.

Spring garden in the room. I have a superb fern that is sending forth lovely luxurious fronds like silken draperies.

Yes, I was often classed as a prodigy, which my mother discouraged at every turn. She had her mind set on development, and was in no haste to have the light of publicity shine on the immature stage. She believed implicitly in the eventual success, but was too wise to push before the proper hour. She wanted the best, always; at least we worked to this end.

I gravitated to all things connected with music; my mother had the same urge. Though her voice was sweet and pretty, it held no professional appeal. This she very well knew, but it did not prevent her from establishing a musical club and quartette. She played the piano well, and often accompanied my father, who had a fine baritone voice and was soloist with his Amphion Club and me, a little unabashed tot in the childrens' Sunday School class.

I was often on the "outs" with grown-ups, because it was difficult to express myself in the class-room way. School irked me, it took me away from music and books. There were days when I simply raised my hand, was excused for the usual purpose of temporary retirement, and failed to return at all—I had gone home to sing. I had that sweet teacher who now lives in the South to understand the situation; she and my mother came to a compromise, that if I did not do this anymore, I would be granted the privilege of playing on the piano for the (stupid) calisthenics every Friday. It was an honor arrangement—and I went no more a-roaming.

I had German and French in school, loved the English literature course and history, and was very poor at anything relating to figures—I am to this day; it is very difficult for me to keep such things in order.

Great doings here in the laundry. The expert is cutting up the Angus, and what a juicy beast he is! He just fills our two freezers.

All good wishes to you, GF

February 14, 1948

Dear Miss Stotler:

Rain and sleet; I am glad to be home from shopping, as cars are crawling along with little security on the glazed surface.

When I returned for lunch, there was the most beautiful bouquet in the world—a breathtaking Valentine. The violets and roses are arranged as they used to be, in those heavenly bouquets of another era, and their perfume is delectable. Coming on this wretched dull day, they are doubly welcome. You are ever so thoughtful and good to have this lovely tribute sent. It smiles in fragrance before a large picture of my father in my study. . . Last evening a friend called to tell me of Fremstad's 80th anniversary on the 16th. I was glad to know of it and sent her an armful of those wonderfully cheerful Picardy gladiolas, that look like a cloud of orchids.

Poor woman, always seeking perfection, but making her art more of an agony than a joyous release.[71] Her nature has no doubt much of the reputed introvert quality of the Scandinavians. She is highly intelligent, but will think only of the past. . . As I recall, she was always difficult.

I have just had news of Flagstad who is carrying all London before her in a tremendous repertoire of Wagner, singing practically every third night. It is good to know that she does not have, as here, the miserable line of pickets; only the normal demonstrations of the admiring throngs.

Thank you for the pretty picture of the Boito Gretchen.[72] Do you know this lovely music? It is singable, and the stage scenes are highly pictorial. The chief role is the Mephisto and [Feodor Ivanovich] Chaliapin was superb as the evil one.

Then came the operatic version of the Berlioz *Damnation of Faust,* a much more restrained work in its original oratorio form, but still adaptable to the theater. The role of Gretchen is only incidental, the men play the prominent parts. It was interesting to sing all three Gretchens, variations on the theme in keeping with the character of the composer: the girl, however, always a lovely, pathetic creature.

Many thanks again for your sweet greeting. As always, our best wishes to you.

GF

[71] Illustrating the different attitudes of artists toward their work, Miss Farrar told of having once met Fritz Kreisler and the renowned Russian composer and pianist Sergei Rachmaninoff just as they emerged from the studio after a joint recording session. Kreisler was still aglow with the beauty of the music; Rachmaninoff, dissatisfied and unhappy, was with difficulty dissuaded from doing the whole thing over.

[72] There are three operatic versions of the Faust story. Gounod's *Faust,* Boito's *Mefistofele,* and Berlioz's *The Damnation of Faust.* Gretchen is another form of the name Marguerite.

February 28, 1948

Dear Miss Stotler:

I have just had a touching letter from Lilli Lehmann's niece. Her enjoyment of the *Musical Digest* article has been keen. Her life is dreary beyond words for the Salzkammergut is very damp at all times and the house not fitted for Winter stay. A real Tyrolean chalet, so cheerful in sunshine, but lugubrious in the frequent down-pours. She is a bright and intelligent woman, and has no human soul with whom to exchange a greeting or confidence. Wretched loneliness . . . beside that great, shimmering lake, the Mondsee, that can be so unfriendly in storms.

There is no use to hint that I might be going over someday. I could not endure the conditions that I could not alter for the better, and to see old friends in their present anguish would give me nightmares. I can do more for them, little as it is, from this vantage.

No, I did not find it confusing to sing all three Gretchens. The essence of the composer's music took care of the portraits, each one vastly different.

Yes, I did hear that Reiner[73] had resigned as conductor of the Pittsburgh Symphony. He is a gentle soul and very simpatico; now, of course, of years that prevent too strenuous a routine.

I did know Noel Coward slightly, a most talented fellow, and a keen observer, of course, in his own world, which may be a trifle outdated. Miss Lawrence,[74] who is busy with his several one-act plays, will be her usual competent self. She has a large following, is a clever showwoman . . . and everyone needs money.

Now comes a very sweet birthday message from Fremstad, in her cramped hand that shows the effort of the crippled fingers. I wish she could let enter a little more sun into her repressed soul. I will go to see her once the roads are free.

May your own birthday be a pleasant one; mine will be, though quiet, which is what I like.

No, I do not think Pisceans are especially admirable, not as I see water elements. I like fish, as edible, only moderately, have no

[73] Fritz Reiner (1888–1963), Hungarian-born conductor. After leaving Pittsburgh he was for five years musical director of the Metropolitan Opera, then conductor of the Chicago Symphony Orchestra which he established as one of the world's finest before his retirement in 1962.

[74] Gertrude Lawrence, English actress, best remembered for her roles in Noel Coward's plays.

sympathy with the inhabitants of the deep, and despise the attributes, supposed to be of the Piscean month, i.e., delicate digestive system, sensitive feet, a liver tendency, and often given to alcoholic indulgence. This last trait I have been spared, but all the others are well proven. A goggly eyed fish is so little esthetic. I hate such a slimy symbol. If there *are* more pleasant qualities, I should like to know about them!

I am reading such a simply written but eloquent book, the Alan Paton one, *Cry the Beloved Country.* It is one of the Negro problem in South Africa. The delicate pictures of the black priest with his innate self-respect, the prostitute, and the erring son, written without one word of obscenity or lapse into vulgarity, produce in this unhappy story an enormous dignity in the frame of its primitive expression.

No problem settled, of course, but that must be a matter of evolution, I fear. One hardly knows what to make of the human race, after what goes on before our very eyes, and in peace time . . . so called.

All well here and send best greetings. GF

March 15, 1948

Dear Miss Stotler:

Do not take it amiss if my letters are short and sketchy. Things here are in wild confusion with the renovations. I have moved into the blue guest room and expect to be there for another three weeks.

I heard a very interesting résumé by Kaltenborn on his visit to New Mexican work-shops for atomic energy. It takes so many departments to fashion the bomb, and the process is of such duration that he thinks the radio-activity engendered is more dangerous than the bomb itself. It exerts wide-spread influence, and is aptly called the *Death Ray.* It was quite a dissertation on man's power against his brothers.

No, I had never heard that FDR sought his own life. I do not believe this report is credible. His whole attitude while alive would disprove it to me. He had such a folie de grandeur . . . he would have thought himself invulnerable to mortal disposition . . . perhaps thinking to ride the clouds like Elijah.

I am reading *I Saw Poland Betrayed* by our ex-Ambassador [Arthur Bliss Lane] there. It is a heart-rending account of deceit and treachery, including all the big-wigs who set themselves up as gods. It hurts to see our country served by such; we shall see more of it, alas.

In the interests of our Garden Club, I drove yesterday to a truly delightful exhibition in West Hartford. We did learn there many nice things, without the pushing crowds to weary us.

One exhibit, to my mind, was enchanting. The exhibitor had taken a sycamore tree, bare of leaves, hung it with Spanish moss, and placed his orchid collection in the jungle setting. The orchids were beautifully spaced, each plant distinct from its neighbor; thus the colors came out to the best advantage. A happy memory to carry away.

The *Peter Grimes*?[75] I heard one act. That definitely threw me off any sympathetic attitude. The same goes for *Emperor Jones*[76] in which Lawrence Tibbett[77] ruined his once fine voice. And now, who hears of it?

Thank you for the Gilda drawing [of Miss Farrar in *Rigoletto*]. I sang the role as a favor at the time, for it is not of my repertoire, being distinctly the role of a coloratura to be properly effective.

Now to the attic for books to bring down to the library. They have long been awaiting this.

Our best greetings, GF

March 17, 1948

Dear Miss Stotler:

Well, the Irish have a mild day, not too much sun, but at least a half smiling sky for their parade. Its aftermath of cheer will no doubt extend far into the jolly night.

I knew Chauncy Olcott well,[78] a dear friend, and for this reason I do not care to see the movie based on his life. He was a charmer and a gentleman, with such winning ways and a pretty lilting voice.

He had, in the beginning, hoped to go to Paris for serious study

75 Opera by British composer Benjamin Britten.

76 Opera by Russian-born American composer Louis Gruenberg based on Eugene O'Neill's play of that name.

77 Lawrence Tibbett was one of the most popular baritones ever to sing at the Metropolitan. For twenty-five years he was heard in French and Italian roles and sang in premieres of a number of modern works. He was a fine actor and also worked in films.

78 Chauncy Olcott (1858–1932), an Irish-American composer and actor, was best known for his singing in Broadway musicals. The film biography was entitled *My Wild Irish Rose*.

in opera, his real love; but the voyage was so rough he embarked for Ireland, returned home and gave up such ideas for the more remunerative popular ballad plays.

I listened to the Detroit Orchestra, for I wanted so much to hear the Rachmaninoff 2nd Symphony. It is a very beautiful one, the last two movements of superlative appeal. It was composed in 1907 while he was in Dresden, a very young man of course. I did not know him until he came to the USA. A strange nature, unpredictable, and not too festive in a group. He was, like all the Russians I ever knew, very opinionated about the glories of Russia and the superiority of that land. I notice they all voice these sentiments from our safe shores, but are not inclined to return to the scenes of their earlier difficulties.

As a musician, he stood on a pinnacle; very few to compare with his gifts and his great musical integrity.

He is buried in Kensico, not far from our resting place, till his remains can be carried to Russia. I do not know what later disposition of them will be made.

Truly this world is in a sad way. The only routine I can make for myself is to do the best I can in my own little orbit, and take the consequences. The pattern has been set for some time, ever since the First World War, and an early end can be granted while the pendulum still swings in its murderous rhythm. What appalls me is the down-grading of decent, human conduct. I will try not to be a party to the general back-sliding. I hope I may keep my courage to the last, no matter what price for it. I cannot live without my own self-respect.

Yes. I do feel that irreligion plays a very tragic role in this conflagration. We are in a world of confusion and little faith—which term I like better than applied religion. I have had ingrained in me by wise and dear parents the rule that the action brings its own conclusion. I need no personal deity to crown this simple truth, for one sees evidences in everything animate.

But I also have the happy sentiment that there must have been a loving and understanding soul in the accepted Savior, whose kindness provides, I can well believe, help along difficult paths of material experience.

I do not connect so great and loving a spirit with the need for the divine birth mystery, but many do feel its import; and I would not care to disturb any thought that helps one to his life's purpose. I do believe that "There are many mansions" and many roads by which one may enter.

All good wishes, as I sit in the dust from the arrangement of my books. One feels that Spring must soon be with us . . . it will be very welcome.

GF

April 25, 1948

Dear Miss Stotler:

Another fine day with men swarming all over, this time to trim the lawn, rake and roll—if possible to discourage the moles. A handsome day, in truth.

My cherry trees are sweeping the lawn and sway in the soft breeze like a tone-poem, truly lovely to see. I drink in their beauty for it is so transient, though when the leaves cover the green it is pretty also—I have no complaint.

Miss Williams is busy as a bee, always on tour, save for occasional appearances with the New York City Opera. I am fearful that so much travel and work may put an edge on her voice, but we will hope not. She is young and enthusiastic; a good head on her shoulders, and very serious.

My comrade who died would not be known to you. My thought in contemplating such an unhappy finale is lack of serious purpose and ordered life. So many of these young, handsome creatures are gay, and, for a time, full of verve. This one married and was most happy. Then the husband died, leaving her practically on the doorstep; she did manage to keep her apartment by renting some rooms, and then this dread malady took her. Very sad.

A career is the most uncertain thing in this world. One could not count those who try and do *not* succeed . . . there must be thousands.

Yes, there is much in the area of the theater that is quite like a battle-field. It is replete with the strategy and tactics of such terrain, and one must keep a sharp eye out at every turn. I believe in fighting, that is, displaying one's equipment before the public, and letting that body judge. No argument of the press, or by word of mouth, has any value for real success. One's business is to give a fine performance, fight for it *on stage* and let the listener be the judge.

There are some stupid singers who think they must sing every role, and thus control the repertoire; there are none today who have this ability. Lilli Lehmann managed as few have done, but paid the price of envious comrades.

I have just sent off some vitamin capsules for ailing children to a friend in Berlin. Her husband, a Major in the former German army, is still a prisoner in Russia, though where is not known. She writes that, according to the propaganda of the Soviets, the Allies are leaving Berlin and turning it over to the Russ[ians]. She is frantic, along with others in the Sektor, fearing that the British and Americans just *might* get disgusted, and leave them to become a Soviet province. Let us pray not.

All good greetings, GF

April 27, 1948

Dear Miss Stotler:

A day of chill rain but I managed to get the last of the pansies in their beds between yesterday's showers. They do look sweet and friendly in array along the turf edges. I use such small flowers for the little vases to place before the pictures of my loved ones.

I am thinking of how odd it is, at least in my case, that one makes a circuit of travel and activity, only to return in later years to the haunts of one's childhood. A friend of mine, a born New Yorker, remarked that I was a country girl at heart; and I agree that this must be so.

You asked me how I studied my roles. Well, I worked wherever I found myself, and whatever the occasion. In Monte Carlo, for instance, we would sing a new opera only three times, and forget some of them (quite indifferent affairs), almost as soon as we had concluded the final performance. I usually learned all my roles by myself, and was ready well in time for group rehearsals. Playing for oneself is thus a great asset, and mental study saves a vocal wear and tear. However, many persons have to sing out every phrase in such preliminary.[79]

I heard [Senator Robert A.] Taft the other evening in an unrehearsed press interview. I sensed an antagonism in one of the female interviewers, but he did not hesitate to speak his mind with frankness and clarity re the *New Deal.* I like his observations, but he is cut-and-dried, and no doubt, with his legal mind, a better influence in the Senate than as over-all chief. I do not wish to see [General Douglas] MacArthur in that capacity either; he is perfect where he is.

79 Miss Farrar said that the great baritone Antonio Scotti could not read music and relied entirely upon his coach to teach him his roles.

I am waiting to read the latest Charles Beard disclosures on the FDR [Franklin Delano Roosevelt] regime. The reviews interest me. How long must one continue to whitewash this recent incumbent of the White House. Sickening—all this incense burning!

I heard an excellent interview, "Meet the Press," with [Governor Thomas E.] Dewey. He was adroit and would not get tangled in any acrimonious observations re [Harold] Stassen.[80] I cannot quite see the reason for *not* outlawing the Communist Party, but he and J. Edgar Hoover agree that, if run underground, they could not be handled in the manner now possible. This remains to be seen. I fear I am very blood-thirsty in this regard. Shooting is too good for them unless they scamper to their Russian lairs. Well, we can only await the outcome in this changing world.

Shall we say June 6, for the visit of you and Miss Aida?

With best wishes for a pleasant week-end, GF

May 12, 1948

Dear Miss Stotler:

I have been in a rush these last few days, shocked and surprised by the deaths of two good friends; one was Olga Stokowski of whose passing your press will have spoken. We were students together in Europe and had so many happy times. Though I had not seen her for several years due to her musical activity and New York residence, we kept in touch.

Her death was cardiac failure; she had overworked for years, but loved her teaching and lectures, and went out no doubt as she would have wished. A fine musician and a fine career. She leaves a married daughter, Sonya, by the conductor.

The memorial services were held at the Julliard school; I did not go, but let my flowers speak for our association.

My visit to Fremstad yesterday was agreeable because my friend and I made it so. It is hard to see a stubborn old woman deliberately seek the shadows. The visitor does well to limit the conversation to light and transient topics. But all went well, and I know she was pleased to see us.

I have been busy in the garden; the house is filled with pansies and lilacs; the shades drawn and a general pleasant coolness pre-

80 Dewey and Stassen, ex-Governor of Minnesota, were about to become Republican candidates for the presidential stakes.

vails. I have guests this afternoon, and we shall enjoy the shade and cozy chat over our coffee. Now to the villages and the chores entailed.

All good wishes, GF

June 2, 1948

Dear Miss Stotler:

A day in town, the city in a great down-pour, and of course no cab to be had. Miss Sylvia and I were fortunate to have dressed for such an emergency, so we skipped over the puddles and went our way. So little in the stores to buy, and not of good quality. Even an extra umbrella is of poor grain, but ours went awry and we had to invest on the spot.

The Convention harangues, . . . and "smart Alec" style of the pretty Mrs. Luce[81] (who should not demean herself by name-calling, no matter how prone the gallery is to applaud) in no wise represent to me what a fine, free democracy should be; so then, we have to do with politicos, not statesmen.

I have admired Mr. [Herbert] Hoover in his recent speeches; the one and only fine utterance, forgetful of selfish purpose and mindful of the ills that must be remedied.

Well, at last I have the three pathetic bottles of Rhine wine, sent as a gesture of appreciation for some food parcels; it has been months on the way, with no end of red tape—even to swearing before a notary that the wine was not intended for commerce!

The rain is still pouring down and the pretty plans for the 115 guests of today's garden meeting will have suffered some set-back. Our local gardens to be visited would be dripping—too bad.

Later . . . The garden meeting was happily in order, the birds came out of the woods at call, with a large chart to identify them; the occasion did not suffer too much from dull and threatening skies.

It was heartening to hear the after-comments of the radio stations regarding Mr. Hoover. He is earning the belated admiration

[81] Clare Booth Luce began as an editor, satirical playwright, and actress. She married Henry Luce, founder of *Time* and publisher of such other influential magazines as *Life* and *Fortune*. An important political figure in her own right, Mrs. Luce represented Connecticut in Congress in 1943–47 and served as United States Ambassador to Italy from 1953 to 1956.

even of his political opponents. At 73, perhaps it is not too late to tender tribute to a *real* American.

And now, all happy thoughts speed you and Miss Aida on your travels and a good landing, as the pilots say . . .

Best greetings, GF

June 19, 1948

Dear Miss Stotler:

The rain has been steady ever since you left for home. We have more planting in between showers, so the seedlings will have plenty to drink, but they do need a certain amount of sunshine if they are not to drown.

No, and again, no. Despite the pleasant thought of any scholarship donated by friends in my name, I would most certainly disapprove. I have little faith in scholarships in the main; they are too often put to small talents. It is much better for those who desire a student course to be made responsible for the outlay, which should be returned in due time.[82] There is too much give and take in these lines of late, and I am *not* for it. People should work for a career. No, do not think of this in connection with me for a second.

I am glad, for your sake, that you found Toto in good order. I love pets, not quite so extravagantly as would seem to be your inclination. Many of my friends I find inconsiderate in allowing their animals to jump all over one. I take no one's word for the amiable dispositions, having had several unpleasant experiences in this line.

One of my friends has a toy poodle which he carries in his arms like a doll. The little creature is very sweet and docile, but to see it sip water from a crystal finger bowl, and have its whiskers wiped with a fine lace napkin, quite spoils the dinner for me.

I run to the post with my letters and return to garden duty. There is much to be done and the time flies.

All good greetings, GF

---

[82] Miss Farrar was most meticulous in repaying funds advanced by a good New England friend, Mrs. Annie Webb, for her musical studies abroad.

July 28, 1948

Dear Miss Stotler:

Yes, I knew Mrs. Atherton,[83] a lively and peppery lady of great wit and attraction. She spent a Winter in Munich for her book *The Ivory Tower* and gleaned most of her knowledge of matters operatic from friends there. Her heroine was evidently a composite of her compatriots at that time singing in Munich—a certain Maud Fay of California, a handsome but short-lived aspirant, and another Californian, Marcella Craft. Both had good voices.

There was in my time much American competition in several European cities, but I fancy Farrar in Berlin, Garden in Paris, and Mrs. Charles Cahier in Vienna were the advance guard. Florence Easton was praised in Hamburg, later in small roles in Berlin. She was admirable in a large repertoire, but had little box-office appeal despite excellent accomplishment.

Did you see the newsreel in which Mr. Hoover was acclaimed? It was most gratifying—and his obvious and happy emotion.

I hope for Dewey and Warren, they would be the best we have, and certainly an improvement on the floundering Democrats. They are an unhappy band, and have limped all through this farce of a Convention. It is time they have a good spanking and remain in a corner.

Re the last services for the burial of Black Jack Pershing;[84] I well recall the bitterness caused by his choice as Commander-in-Chief of the AEF [American Expeditionary Force], when so many thought General Leonard Wood the better fitted. One never knows in this political jockeying who is the best material. What disappointments must be carried beneath an outward respect for the chief executive, in this case Wilson.

I shall drive to the Cape as per schedule on Sunday, though not in my new Ford; it has gone to the shop for an indefinite stay, dependent on the parts arrival. Mrs. G. will send her man for me. Perhaps the smash was a blessing in disguise—one has to have some solace for the disappointment . . . I waste no tears over what cannot be helped.

I travel heavy always, carrying much with me to satisfy the hours I like to be in my own company. As I always had 35 to 40 trunks in the professional activity, I am not too much concerned—of course these days I have no theater wardrobe to consider, and travel with less

[83] Mrs. Gertrude Franklin Atherton (1857–1948), American author of more than sixty novels.

[84] John J. Pershing, AEF Commander-in-Chief, died July 15, 1948.

trunk luggage. Airplanes have shaped so much of the lighter and pretty luggage.

Thank you for the Kreisler[85] article. They are old and dear friends of mine, a delightful couple. As you know, she is American. The story is that their eyes first met in the mirror of a ship's boutique when the lively Harriet was trying on a hat. They had a difficult time during the 1st World War, but Fritz made a sensational comeback. He is indeed a great artist.

I have just come in from weeding—had to give up with the sun coming down too ardently. The iris beds are thick with weeds, but it is now the time to cut their spears and allow other plants to seed nearby, notably the delphiniums.

My insect wounds are healing nicely, but the excursions into the garden have lost their charm until this heat subsides. I applied undiluted ammonia to my arms since all else did fail. I would not advise it unless one prefers loss of skin down to the third layer. This did not bother *me*. I was glad to have the smart instead of the irritation.

You must have handsome berries, but what a task to gather them in this heat. Miss Sylvia is improving her strawberry beds, has just sent off for new plants.

Our best greetings, GF

Pennywise
Cape Vincent, New York
August 4, 1948

Dear Miss Stotler:

Perfect weather here [Mrs. Gilmour's house on the St. Lawrence River] and it is heavenly to breathe the air. The river is blue as in the Italian paintings that enfold the Madonna . . . it is good to be alive.

We had guests yesterday, friends from Buffalo, who put in with

---

[85] On the outbreak of the war Kreisler rejoined his cavalry regiment in Austria, and was seriously wounded on the Russian front. Discharged, he returned to America but due to his status as an enemy alien could not perform, and was sometimes cut by former friends. Farrar told of having received anonymous letters, and even of stones being thrown at the windows when she entertained the Kreislers in her home. On one occasion when she was giving a large party, she felt obliged to warn Fritz to avoid a small group of guests who were making objectionable remarks. Kreisler solved the problem by borrowing a violin from the orchestra she had engaged, and fiddling happily away for the dancing.

their fine yacht. I accepted their invitation if there was a promise they would *not* put out to sea! We had tea and cakes, a very pleasant hour. The owners are intrepid fishers and are here for such sport.

I should indeed like to have the Lotte Lehmann book[86] you offer. I did not know she had a new one. I saw her in the picture with little Miss [Margaret] O'Brien, and could have cried at the role she accepted, as grandmother to this little moppet. How could such a warm and fine singer lend herself to this?

The folding up of the MET will come out all right. Every season they have to contend with some union combine, but an adjustment will be made, never fear; and it will *not* be put into the vulgarian hands of one Billy Rose. This little showman may be a power in his night clubs and aquacades, but is hardly the stuff of which MET material is made. Mr. Sloan's [Metropolitan Board Chairman] published reply to the effrontery of this man's offer was very suave and tactful, but I can imagine how he must have squirmed to set on paper any acknowledgment of so brash an invitation . . . even if at times the opera does not measure up to its old standards.

The MET will no doubt arrange its affairs—it always has. I have been politely deaf to any hints about solicitation. It is no longer of my era, though I do think the younger generation should have the season. The young people bring their own enthusiasm and need the visual exposition to counteract radio and screen, after all, such poor synthetic substitutes.

There are some rare old houses about here; of course a bit decayed for lack of upkeep. They were made ready for titled refugees of the French Revolution and its aftermath. They have gracious lines and are very happy attempts at rebuilding Gallic architecture.

No, I am not homesick with my dear friend. A close association of over thirty years has attuned us to more than sisterly consideration. However I still like my own walls better than any others, although this is a sweet change. I can remain quiet, while my girls are less hurried in the home routine. They need a rest from *me.*

All good wishes, GF

86 Lotte Lehmann, German American soprano renowned for her Wagnerian roles at the Met from 1933 to 1946. Her book was entitled *My Many Lives.*

Pennywise
Cape Vincent, New York
August 20, 1948

Dear Miss Stotler:

A brisk wind from the river, white caps and a hint of Fall. Goldenrod added to the other vivid colors in the fields gives the effect of a Dutch painting.

I am heartsick at the brutal news of your Wiener Tante [Viennese aunt] in her agony at the hands of the occupants of her house . . . a venerable victim to these Russian brutes. It all seems so hopeless, doesn't it? I have no word for this kind of reprisal on defenseless humans at the hands of hyenas and worse.

Mail from the Russ section of my beleaguered friend in Berlin makes the situation seem real and desperate. One wonders when we will get down to business with the treacherous ally . . . no doubt Stalin stands on the commitments of FDR and Churchill, and now it comes to light that *this* treasonable conduct—decision, or what you will, gives Comrade Joe [Stalin] all the rights he so brutally enjoys . . . what a world!

I do not suffer from high blood pressure, but it would be easy, in such reflections, to have it rise to the danger point.

I have just concluded an old book on Maria Theresa [Empress of Austria, 1717–80] and the various wars that clouded her reign. It is the old pattern, oft repeated, of territorial acquisition and material gain. After the Seven Years War the people paid a bitter price for their laurels; yet no way has been found to enforce a program for peace. Evidently men themselves are intent on self-destruction, and take the awful chances to that end be it disguised as glory or defeat.

I have also concluded a remarkable book in its study of the revolutionary soul . . . it far surpasses the Koestler volume[87] in its brilliant dissection of many complex natures; Occupied France, and those who fight for and against the Vichy pattern. It is *World Without Visa* by Jean Malaquies. It gives one to think; the pages are not easy to dismiss.

I have only a languid interest in the press and radio here. There is the more potent attraction of the river and the superb sunsets. It is quite reminiscent of the Rhine at this point, for at Biebrich where one crossed to visit Der Goldene Mainz [a famous inn] we had the

87 Probably Arthur Koestler's *Darkness at Noon* (1941), referring to the Russian purges of the late 1930s.

same lovely sky and river expanse. This house is in the same position, and when the sun sinks behind the woodlands of the neighboring islands, it is almost a heartbreak to view it.

Yesterday the Hollywood Bowl played an all Strauss (Richard) program, and in the last strains of *Death and Transfiguration* the sunset was potent sermon and prayer. I like to hear music thus, alone and in the quietude of nature . . . it is more beautiful than any spoken eulogy.

I hope you enjoy cool breezes and are well.

Greetings, GF

Pennywise
Cape Vincent, New York
August 26, 1948

Dear Miss Stotler:

The weather has turned warmer but with the hint of Fall very definite. I still have a large accumulation of letters to answer before leaving here on the 12th, though I try to dispose of them as fast as I can type.

Living alone as I do, and accountable to no one for my impulses and moods, I do not fit too readily into the routine of other households. I could only visit with this dear hostess who is aware of my propensities these many years, and who has been most understanding of them. Any other would certainly find me none too gracious a house member.

I do not think I am cold-blooded, but I am indifferent to much that seems to actuate others. I attribute this to the outpour of emotions that found their fullest and happiest satisfaction in my career. I burned away this youthful exuberance, and I like the placidity of the routine I have chosen and the home where I enjoy it.

Once when very young, I read an interesting book by Leonard Merrick, entitled *Quaint Companions.* It dealt with two writers whose chance exchange of letters led to a very tender tie. Both were wise enough to keep it in the realm of the unattainable. I thought at the time that they would never suffer disillusion, but could continue their flights of fancy with never a rude awakening. Like the Tchaikovsky romance,[88] though he had a more poignant and tragic reason to mistrust the flesh.

Of course this discourse is written at the finale of an active life, and would in no way seem a suitable program for a young spirit that thinks the world its oyster. . . .

No, the *Sunken Cathedral* of Debussy had nothing to do in my thought with the play by Hauptmann. The former had its shimmering illusion only in the play of musical colors; the play was a definite contrast between a man's material life and his wishful fantasies; as between the charming but soul-less nixie and the wife of his daily life and its hard toil. I saw the lovely Agnes Sorma[89] as the nixie, so plausible, so bewitching, so unattainable withal.

I heard the Traubel[90] program, and regret the lady's incursion into trite popular music. Also, I note with alarm the emphasis on lower notes, which habit is telling on the uneasy high register. This is not good for a dramatic soprano.

In earlier years when she was being by-passed at the MET and sacrificed in a stupid Damrosch opera, Bodansky, the conductor, argued with me that she had no true dramatic range, the high register not responsive to the demands. I fear I must agree, since later results show this in a marked manner. Up to date, to hear the Traubel voice at its best, one must choose the immolation scene [in Götterdämerung] with Toscanini.

I have remarked this lowering of the scale in Lotte Lehmann; both women of warm, luscious impulse, both loving the flesh pots, and a bit lethargic!

Best greetings, GF

September 14, 1948

Dear Miss Stotler:

I have had hardly breathing time since my arrival home yester-

[88] Peter Ilyich Tchaikovsky and Nadejda von Meck, widow of Karl George Otto von Meck, a Russian railroad magnate, carried on an ardent correspondence for fourteen years, although, by choice, they never met.

[89] Beautiful German actress who achieved her greatest fame in the portrayal of Hauptmann and Ibsen heroines.

[90] Helen Traubel, American soprano, sang leading Wagnerian roles at the Metropolitan between 1936 and 1947.

day. The heat was so severe that I remained all day in bed; the change from the Cape was most marked.

My X-ray addresses go on this week at the movie house; just some facts as to precautionary benefits and to urge all our townspeople to make their appointments. A matter of a few moments only.

Despite the heat I packed off some clothing for overseas, to the granddaughter of a very dear friend, the Regisseur of the KGL Opera [the Royal Opera in Berlin]. She is in the theater with a very meager wardrobe, but I had nothing of costumes to send, only a few dresses of civilian attire, with shoes, scarves, and a coat also.

I have had letters from the Princess Herminie,[91] but do not know her. It appears she had always been keen on the Kaiser, and her ministrations in his last years must have made his exile less dour. It is sad to know she is such a prisoner.

I shall go now to the Garden Club meeting and hope to cast aside for the moment such lugubrious thoughts . . .

Our best greetings, GF

September 28, 1948

Dear Miss Stotler:

If you like I will meet you and Miss Aida at Mr. Tode's Inn for 6:30 supper on the evening of the 13th, Wednesday, and thank you for the invitation. Then you will come to me on the following day for lunch at 12:30, and we will have the afternoon together.

I have been personally at work trimming and pruning the rose canes, and am much irritated by the embedded thorns that defy heavy gloves . . . but the place is assuming a little more order. The tangle of vines on the pergola was thick as a jungle rope.

You asked about the last act costume of [Leroux's] *La Reine Fiamette*. The dress was a lovely rose-beige velvet, trimmed with ruby passementerie, a striking combination with the red wig. The opera story was dramatic and colorful, but there was no adequate music to support it. It was not a favorite with anyone.

The MET counted more on the standard repertoire, for its season was never the full year round, as in many European houses.

---

91 Princess Herminie of Schönaich-Carolath was the second wife of Kaiser Wilhelm II. After his death in 1941, she left Doorn and returned to her home in Silesia. She was interned by the Russians but, unbeknownst to Miss Farrar, was living in Frankfurt on the Oder at the time of her death in 1947.

The well known favorites were the first considered, and the assumption of such roles placed one in comparison with a famous predecessor . . . if one had success, one was tagged with it forever.

Also the choice of a preferred singer often lent a box-office attraction. However, not even Caruso, [Emmy] Destinn, and [Pasquale] Amato could make a "go" of *The Girl of the Golden West.* It was not opera material, while other Puccini operas found success at once.[92]

As for my costume expenses, they were extravagant indeed; the opera was obliged to furnish them, but I could not bear to don the atrocities that the indifferent workshop gave out. I always had my own, from my Berlin debut.

My one anticipated enjoyment in Babylon will be a Flagstad concert on 12th December. We have a group of friends here who will attend. I admit she is worth the ennui of displacement.

All here are drinking in the Fall beauty each day before the inevitable snows close in on us.

Greetings, GF

November 10, 1948

Dear Miss Stotler:

The days are flying; we are bedding down the garden area and putting away the tools until Spring. Only two dozen more lilies to come for planting, then we are finished till next year, save for the tedious leaf-raking. I must say Miss Sylvia loves this and gets busy . . . I do nothing save admire, these last few days.

The night of the election[93] I took the girls to the movies, so the evening would not seem so long. Once at home I crept into bed and listened at ease till 7:00 next morning. At midnight I knew the issue for the votes continued to pile up for the opposition.

May they make the most of their brief glory, for me-thinks they will have hard sledding for all their seeming powerful majority. This is no time for other than hope that we shall not run into foul weather.

---

[92] Bohemian-born Emmy Destinn (1878–1930) sang at the Met between 1908 and 1921. She created the role of Minnie in *The Girl of the Golden West.* Pasquale Amato (1878–1942) created the role of Jack Rance in that opera and other roles too at the Met. Puccini's *La Fanciulla del West* was one of his less popular operas.

[93] Against heavy odds President Harry S Truman won re-election November 2, 1948, defeating the Republican candidate, Governor Thomas E. Dewey of New York.

Usually handled by incompetents, the Ship of State *must* ride the gale; it is in everyone's interest to help her. Let us hope there will be no fiasco, though we do appear to be cascading as fast as possible to the centralization pattern. A step toward Comrade Joe's dictum; his cohorts here will work for it. Ridgefield remained solidly and traditionally Republican . . . though we have no shining stars in our village.

Well, I refuse to go into sackcloth for anyone. I look around me and see such dreadful sufferings of gentle friends of mine, brain tumors, cancerous amputations, paralysis . . . one is so grateful to be spared to normal living. So why fulminate uselessly? If the great Eleanor [Roosevelt] is to be Secretary of State, it will not disturb me one whit. Better her than *me.*

Be thankful we are not in war-scarred Europe. And if the atom bomb is to be our portion (as it might well be, even here) pray only for immediate extinction—and a quick puff toward Paradise!

And now to the pleasant thought of Christmas cards and their addressing.

Our best greetings, GF

November 18, 1948

Dear Miss Stotler:

I only gathered from your letters of your mood, a dispirited one after the elections, and am glad if you are resilient to the needs of the moment. Matters one cannot change should not be deemed all important after all. I do feel that our particular times are gone; and am learning to accept the adaption one must make unless one (1) embarks on a fruitless crusade, or (2) embraces wholeheartedly the new doctrines that are fast showing themselves. I try to keep a middle of the road attitude.

As to the Hearst papers, I do not like the type of journalism they purvey, although the wealthy owner has always engaged top-notch writers. They apparently have to use the vernacular and policies of the owner. I like a conservative press, without the angle of cheap exploits, yellow tinges and horrid photos; but the object is *circulation*—so, appeal to the masses. I know many a limited reader who feels he knows the spicy side of deplorable events by reason of the lurid exposition and pictures.

Writing is a career like any other. The paying public decides the reading value, but the real question still remains unanswered, how much good does all this do? I see the same disclosures, yet the identical activities which are railed at they continue. In the end it boils down to financial support of this or that press bureau, take your choice. The biggest "blow" gets the public ear, i.e., Winchell and Co. I know something of the inside track from newspaper friends—a "scoop" has no loyalties or base of argument, save as a "scoop."

As for social security efforts, we saw this at first hand in Berlin in 1900. Our nice maids were required to give a certain portion of their wages and we were obliged to contribute the same sum to the general Kasse [retirement fund]. It still seems to me a good provision, though it was derided at the time by American friends who considered it just a move to keep the people satisfied, and the military in power.

As in our land, for so many years, private contributions, large and small, used to keep going institutions of many kinds to help those who could not help themselves. Now taxes have reduced the funds of the wealthy so that federal arrangements will replace those great donations . . . but will be, alas, in the hands of the politicians.

Re opera matters, my own first Carmen was in November 1914. Fremstad was a Carmen before my arrival in the USA. Destinn never sang it here, but often in Berlin, where she sang almost every role; a very reliable singer—she was never ill.

She created the London premiere of *Butterfly*[94] with Caruso and Scotti a season before it was presented at the MET with the two men, the lovely Louise Homer,[95] and myself. She sang it here infrequently, along with [Florence] Easton, [Claudia] Muzio, and, in later

[94] In February of 1907 the Metropolitan marshaled its strongest forces for the premiere of *Madame Butterfly*. However, Puccini, who had come from Italy to supervise the production, was not entirely satisfied with either Caruso or Farrar. He admitted the glorious voice of the former, but considered him lazy and conceited. Miss Farrar's voice pleased him less, and he doubted its capacity to fill the auditorium. (She habitually sang "half voice" at rehearsals.) Miss Farrar told us that although the opening appeared to go well, she was so exhausted by hard work and nervous strain that she cried herself to sleep that night in her mother's arms. It was soon evident that the furor created by the American *Butterfly* was such as to delight even the composer. The photograph which he presented to Miss Farrar is inscribed (trans.): "To the most intelligent artist, Miss Geraldine Farrar, this remembrance of her incomparable Butterfly at the Metropolitan offers Giacomo Puccini." The role became Miss Farrar's own property, and by the time she retired in 1922 she had sung it ninety-five times on the stage of the Met.

[95] Louise Homer (1871–1947), renowned for her fine contralto, sang at the Metropolitan Opera from 1900 to 1919 and again from 1927 to 1930. She was the daughter of William Trimble Beatty, first pastor of the Shadyside Presbyterian Church in Pittsburgh, Pennsylvania. Her husband was the composer Sidney Homer.

years, [Elizabeth] Rethberg and others, including the latest [Licia] Albanesi. Maria Gay was Carmen to my Michaela in 1908. Mary Garden sang it with the Hammerstein forces.

I do not have at hand the Seltsam book, but in each season an artist in those days at the MET was guaranteed 40 to 50 performances, so I must have been singing when our group went to Philadelphia and the Brooklyn Academy of Music. There were also tours before the Fall season, and in the Spring, when New York closed its opera season.

I had no illness that prevented the usual season, except an occasional cold, and had no trouble in the matter of repertoire. [MET manager] Mr. Gatti [Casazza] was only interested in running a fairly successful opera, and as I happened to have the luck to be "box office" there was no trouble in fulfilling my own contract, rather had to add certain gala performances.

Emmy Destinn died some years ago in Prague, her home town. Olive Fremstad is still in the nursing home. Most of the singers of my time are dead; a few still appear from time to time. Frances Alda[96] married and divorced Mr. Gatti, now has remarried and is living in New York. Giovanni Martinelli[97] and Giuseppe de Luca[98] are in New York giving lessons and are very popular figures in social circles.

All good wishes to you from us here. GF

November 24, 1948

Dear Miss Stotler:

Grey clouds and possible rain. Winter at our door. Well, well, you *did* anticipate your Thanksgiving! How nice for your friend[99] to be relieved for a time of her worrisome role in hotel management. Quite a career, I would say, but with union troubles and food shortages, one to give concern.

I agree most heartily, if just *once* we could share with all those overseas who through no fault of their own must suffer privation and indignity. I see little improvement at present in view of the magni-

[96] Frances Alda (1883–1952), born in New Zealand, sang at the Met from 1908 to 1930.

[97] Giovanni Martinelli (1885–1969) was one of the principal tenors at the Met from 1913 to 1946.

[98] Giuseppe de Luca (1876–1950), baritone, sang at the Met from 1915 to 1946, and was admired for his acting as well as his voice.

[99] Miss Delia Cooper, Executive Housekeeper of the Hilton Hotel, Dallas, Texas, was visiting Miss Stotler.

tude of the matter, although this airlift[100] may be a fine gesture and help in a certain morale.

Miss Sylvia has guests tomorrow while I go to Mrs. Gilmour. This time, Christmas and New Years, our families have been together for years. Now we are sadly narrowing down, but we keep the old customs just the same.

The real Thanksgiving is in the individual heart, and mine is the old-fashioned kind—not for what I am about to receive, but for those many blessings that are already a part of my daily living.

You ask me which I would choose, as between now and the early years. I can only say that all things partake of their time period. Each brings its advantages and handicaps, and one passes into other chapters according to the experience, discretion and evaluation. I think myself fortunate to have ended my professional life when I did; nothing for me is so disastrous as the performer who will not admit need for a change.

I read that Maria Jeritza[101] will essay several *Tosca* and *Salomé* performances soon. Frieda Hempel[102] also feels she must appear yearly. Well, chacune à son gôut . . .

My commentators are: Fulton Lewis, Jr., Kaltenborn, Banghart, and Henry Taylor. I find their hours good for my routine, and their sane comments are to my liking also.

The early morning 6–7 A.M. radio reports are only weather and local news, and a great deal of interesting farm information. I formed the habit of listening to these programs in the OPA service as they often had information prior to the general price releases, while news of cattle and grain produce was valuable.

Our best wishes for your happy holiday, GF

[100] During 1948–49 the Western powers airlifted essential supplies to West Berlin during a Russian blockade of that city. In 1950 West Berlin became a state within the Federal Republic of Germany. East Berlin was the capital of East Germany. The 29-mile wall erected by East Berlin to prevent open access between East and West Germany finally was demolished in 1989.

[101] Maria Jeritza sang at the Met from 1921 to 1932, delighting audiences with her voice and acting ability. The press called her the "Viennese Thunderbolt."

[102] Frieda Hempel (1885–1955), the German coloratura, was the first to sing the *Rosenkavalier*'s Marschallin in America.

November, 1948
Thanksgiving

Dear Miss Stotler:

The superb crisp weather happily continues; we are fortunate. The day was divine and the ride through the hills of surpassing beauty . . . a cerulean sky like an Italian painting . . . and air like wine.

I left the house at noon, where Miss Sylvia and her friends, with Margaret, were a merry group. I picked up three guests here for the Gilmour mid-day dinner, and we had a dozen at table there in charming informal manner. Coming home before dusk, I crept into bed to listen to several programs on the air, and had more of the home turkey, which is a rare specimen.

You must have had various occasions to partake of turkey, and no doubt your friends were happy in gay company . . . if only one could have given a share to every hungry human in the world. What a strange distribution; some starve, others thrive.

Yes, we are hoping to have the [Laurence] Olivier *Hamlet* once the larger centers are served. Also the *Joan* [the film *Joan of Arc* with Ingrid Bergman]. Both will receive my close attention.

As to my *Joan at the Stake*[103] costume, I enclose a small snapshot. Please return at your convenience, as it is part of my collection.

The dress was oyster white, treated so the sheen would not reflect in the lens. It was bound with rope at the breast and waist. The dress was also coated with some kind of liquid asbestos to prevent fire, while I had ammonia-soaked cotton in my nostrils and glycerine cotton in my mouth and on my lips. I wore my own hair, short, parted in the middle. It and my eyelids were treated with some kind of a mild medicament to prevent singeing, also my hands and arms. The fires were lighted and at certain intervals extinguished, to give me fresh air and deep breathing. It was not a very *comfortable* job, but it was well done, and very life-like. The smoke, too, was quite a hazard; on the side-lines ambulances and fire-extinguishers were at hand for an emergency—happily, not needed.

103 Actually titled *Joan the Woman*, this was one of several motion pictures made by Miss Farrar in 1915 for the Lasky Company. In the above letter she neglects to mention an incident that must have cost her several bad moments. Handicapped by heavy armor, a sword, and a banner that had to be held aloft, she realized during a battle scene that her horse was running away with her. Fortunately, that fine actor and rider, Jack Holt, dashed to the rescue and returned her to the battle. However, Jesse Lasky decided to engage a stand-in for such scenes in the future.

The pageantry was superb, and all the actors were legitimate theater people with fine carriage and gesture. Too bad we did not have talking possibilities then. It was quite a task to get on that horse, the armor was so weighty, but I loved every moment of *Joan*.

Best greetings as I fly to the village; it begins already to wear a Christmas air, and if this superb weather continues, we shall all rejoice.

GF

December 1, 1948

Dear Miss Stotler:

I was to have gone to Mme. Telva's to see and hear opera via her television, but the surprise of the snow was a deterrent, so I remained at home. I have not yet been eager for television, so I shall not think of buying one for the nonce.

It is a pity you are being so tormented by the hunters. Yes, we do have more normal conditions here, for the hunting grounds are all patrolled now . . . Hounds are like banshees in the chase and I know of nothing more objectionable.

I am wading through the *Remembrance Rock* of Carl Sandburg with its bleak and uncompromising history of the first pilgrims. As I was reading there came from a friend interested in genealogy some papers relating to my own forebears in which her items tally with his passenger list of the *Mayflower;* and among them is one Stephen Hopkins, the lineal forebear, a signer of the Compact aboard ship.

This friend of mine, herself of such ancestry, cannot understand why I am not alert to join the many organizations of such early importance. I am not quite so enthusiastic; however, it is interesting. . . . The first Thanksgiving dinner was celebrated December 22, 1796, at Plymouth. Here is the menu, not bad for those times.

Bill of Fare

> Indian baked whortleberry pudding, corn and beans cooked together (succotash), clams, oysters and codfish, venison (roasted), sea fowl, frosted fish and eels, apple pie, cranberry tarts, and cheese of domestic make.

In reading the account one sees cruelty, envy and spite prevailing, even among those who risked so much for the liberty they define in such rigid regulations; and consequent misery for many. Well, the old Adam still persists.

We gather here and there some idea of the folly of FDR in trusting the brutal Stalin. And perhaps (horrible thought) Stalin is acting as he has a right to do under the Roosevelt promises. Apparently Roosevelt alone is responsible for the onslaught on China, giving Stalin a free hand . . . and with results that we see wherever this pernicious villain operates. I cannot give an opinion as to what we should do for China; we know little of the groundwork, and when men are sent to report on conditions, their reports are not permitted to be made public. The Dems must have an awful smell in their kitchen to be so fearful.

Mme. Chiang[104] is a clever and fascinating woman, but this time I fear she has poor luck. Just now, Marshall[105] has retired for a check-up at the hospital, leaving his wife to act as hostess. This means, of course, no protocol. The last time she came it was as a queen. To be sure, one hears of the complete inability of her party to swing China away from the Communists, not to mention certain fantastic tales of corruption.

Now to the village and shopping.

All good wishes, GF

December 6, 1948

Dear Miss Stotler:

The delayed overseas mail is not coming along. That maritime strike was a wicked thing—and no doubt there will be more from the Commies—blast them!

One of my letters, from Ems, has some tiny seeds enclosed, from the beech trees of the Tanuswald. My friend tells me that whole families go into the forest and gather these kernels, for 20,000 make up one quart of oil. What a labor, and what ingenuity . . . one might be in the dark ages.

I have read your press item as well as other editorials re the

104 Wife of Chiang Kai-shek, Chinese Nationalist leader and herself an influential political figure. At the end of World War II, China was torn by civil war, with Communist forces showing increasing strength. Mme. Chiang came to the United States hoping for more support than was forthcoming. In 1949 the Nationalists were driven from mainland China and Chiang Kai-shek and his supporters set up a Nationalist Chinese state on Taiwan.

105 Secretary of State George C. Marshall.

China disaster. So they will go over to the Commies, no doubt. What infuriates me is the pussy-footing of our officials, who should not have tried to hide behind half-measures and tricks but have come out frankly in their refusal to aid.

I am sorry for Mme. Chiang, that her mission will be unfruitful; but one wonders if, at any time, we should have made such gallant promises, such a fanfare and propaganda. Kidney or no kidney, this was not the hour for Marshall to hide in the hospital. I am of the opinion the lady should not have been permitted to come, but no one had the guts to do this refusal. Instead, she had army transportation, and may well have imagined she would have support for her cause.

I have not seen the [Rita] Hayworth film of *Carmen*. No doubt they have given her a script in the Hollywood tradition. I like her very much, and in *Blood and Sand* no one could have been more effective. She is a splendid dancer and a mighty pretty woman.

As for reviving any of the silent films, I, for one, would not like to see them. The photography would not measure up. I had a part of *Carmen* run off at one time, to see if it could be used as a charity attraction, but it was no use.

How ridiculous if the authorities hound that Hohenzollern, August Wilhelm.[106] He made a fool of himself with his Nazi preferences, to the discomfiture of the family; it was not necessary to be so flagrant about forsaking his own kind—I have no answer for it. But he never did any harm with it all, and even our worst offenders should not be handed over to the unspeakable Russians.

The days rush by, perhaps because we have so many pleasant activities to make them seem so. Miss Sylvia and I are off to Kensico with greens from our home garden, most beautifully done.

Best greetings, GF

December 10, 1948

Dear Miss Stotler:

This morning came an express package which Miss Sylvia only announces and will give me no further news until the exciting moment of our Christmas fête. We all thank you for your thought in advance and the anticipation only adds to the enjoyment.

---

106 See note to letter of September 4, 1946.

The highlight of the week was the incomparable Flagstad.[107] I have never thought to hear from human lips since the passing of Lilli Lehmann such a performance. Like some magnificent, towering spruce of her native Norway, this truly great artiste carried the note of exultant perfection. The house was crammed with eager and adoring listeners; but with her the rapture was of the noblest expression, a true aristocrat of song. The artiste has a newer, warmer tone color in the prodigious range of her incomparable instrument. She is at the peak of the finest in singing art and interpretation. There comes all too rarely the wonder of such classic devotion, with not a false line or one cheap gesture for approval.

The party afterward was mostly of professional standing. We were all enthralled. The woman herself is so genuine, and touched at the tributes that made her happy, despite the misguided picket zealots who only fanned the high excitement of the moment.

I came home with Miss Sylvia around four, more dead than alive, but sunk in revery and memory of a great hour.

But now to your several letters and their contents. I would not have noticed the Russell Smith[108] curtain designs at the Boston Theater or Philadelphia Academy of Music, though I have sung in these places very often. The former theater has gone the way of all buildings when newer construction comes into planning, but the old theater had wonderful acoustics, as have all those of the wood era, for plaster is not so absorbing in sound. It was the scene of my first return to Boston in 1907, on the Metropolitan Spring tour. I sang four performances in a week at that time, which was not good policy, save that Mr. Conried[109] at the time rightfully felt that the box-office would

[107] Kirsten Flagstad (1895–1962), Norwegian-born opera star, was considered the outstanding Wagnerian soprano of her time. The pickets referred to later in the letter were protesting her husband's sympathies with the Nazis at the time of Germany's occupation of Norway in 1940. Her husband, Henry Johansen, a lumber and hotel magnate, initially favored the pro-German Quisling party as a safeguard against radicalism. He resigned from the party in 1941 and his son became active in the Norwegian underground. But at war's end he was seized and died in prison in 1946 without ever coming to trial. When Flagstad resumed her career, European audiences knew her story and sympathized with her. In New York, a small group of pickets bearing signs of "Quisling" and "Traitor" paraded before the Metropolitan Opera house at the time of her first appearance there. Only three years had passed since the end of World War II when this event took place.

[108] Distinguished American landscape painter of the late nineteenth-century. His work was in the romantic style and his curtain designs hung in many theaters on the Eastern seaboard. His family and the Stotlers were old friends.

[109] Heinrich Conried was manager of the Metropolitan Opera from 1903 to 1908.

be considerably enhanced by a native's homecoming. . . . How long ago it all seems!

The Philadelphia Academy is still a perfect place to perform, and hear. A lovely, gracious house. The green-room was always a source of fascination—portraits of the dear dead and gone adorned the walls and gave me thrills every time I went to sing in that city.

I never liked to go out of town during the season, however, for I usually caught cold. The dressing rooms through lack of constant use were never well heated, the stage draughts were awful, and the homecoming at 4:00 A.M. on the MET special train a nightmare. The voice is certainly an unstable instrument—at least mine was.

You asked about the whortleberry—it is a huckleberry, blue-black fruit on low-growing bushes, evidently very hardy. Those early pilgrims had to make the best of this watery fruit—it would not tempt me, I fear. I do like venison and fowl, if not too ripe.

Several of my forebears seem to have been dedicated to the ministry; Canon Farrar, of recent English date, is a well-known figure in clerical circles.

There was indeed greed, brutality, superstition and cruelty no end in the early era; that seems to be the rule of humans the world over in all centuries. One would think that only individuals stand out in mercy, sacrifice or heroism; not the general run.

No, I do not feel the strain to care for 34[110] people so much as the painful realization of its minute aid; it seems a little drop indeed, in such an ocean of misery . . . I wonder if, with all the outlay, really, there is much improvement in the condition of that desolate Berlin and the surrounding country.

Christmas cards come in while mine go out—how time does run on!

Our best greetings, GF

December 21, 1948

Dear Miss Stotler:

Your most lovely poinsettia came, and gives out a cheery note against the snow outside the window. Our warmest thanks!

Our wreath-making Monday went off well; we sent off great rounds of fragrant greens with their gay ribbons and lovely gilded

110 Presumably a reference to the CARE packages and other help Miss Farrar sent to her friends in Germany.

cones. I am now making my little mantel crèche. If we put too many of the greens about they dry and make considerable work for Margaret.

It is fortunate that before the snow came, Miss Sylvia had covered her strawberry beds and last consignment of lilies, so the garden is tucked up cozily for the Winter doze.

I am still under the impression of the magnificent Flagstad concert. The press wrote in glowing terms (indeed they could not have done otherwise) and the memory will be added to others of earlier decades, when the truly *great* were the stars of the musical firmament.

Yesterday a man in the village asked me if I knew that Mme. Chiang was going to buy a place here, specifically one of the most lovely estates on the hill, which has been a burden to the owner, widowed and with her children gone from home. One fancies the Chinese lady has come to a definite break with her husband [which turned out not to be true], a rumor that was set in motion on the occasion of her visit here. Well, one can never tell. At any rate we do not have the UN.[111] That, to my mind, had sinister portent; and in view of the present Hiss-Chamberlain fracas,[112] we want no politicos in our midst . . . what a sorry business.

My overseas letters carry pitiful Christmas wishes, with now and then a bit of Handarbeit [craftwork, embroidery, etc.] that mindful fingers have fashioned. Several friends of my age are in straits . . . the illness and heart-sickness of age and no future. What can be done to bring the world to some normal pass?

We are well and try to make our small gesture, but one has a heavy heart at the plight of humanity in an age when all should enjoy the fruits of specialized civilization. The radio report of those five scientists who sacrifice their precious eyes for murderous (so it seems to me) exploration into the world of the atom, makes me shudder. Are we then fated to destroy ourselves in this mad idea to capture the infinite and defy the normality of the species? One wonders.

Well, perhaps my mood will lighten if I carry the post to the village.

---

[111] Reference not clear, since the United Nations Charter was drawn up in San Francisco in 1945. Miss Farrar may have been referring to subsequent disagreements among the powers about the location of the headquarters for the organization.

[112] In 1948, journalist and former Communist courier Whittaker Chambers accused Alger Hiss, who had served in the State Department from 1936 to 1947, of having passed confidential documents to the Soviet government.

Since this letter may be delayed, happy Christmas Eve and Day greetings from all here. May you keep well.

GF

December 23, 1948

Dear Miss Stotler:

Brilliant days that are a joy and promise well for the Christmastide. I had the trip to my dentist in Babylon, not too difficult, as I had the town taxi come for us here, so the driving gave no concern. Our hills are not safe with the freeze, and dark comes early.

The city was a mass of humans, noisy, carols blaring via the loud speakers and bells ringing from every bedraggled Salvation Army lad and lassie stationed on the corners. We splashed through mud and slush; nevertheless, this time the sanitation department has done a pretty good job considering the problem of the packed snow. The cabs were piled with people so we did a good deal of walking; the air was crisp, and the sun shone.

Your own holiday sounds like a busy one; may it be favored with sunny weather and pleasant company.

My greens are all up and the family will open presents tomorrow evening, quietly, and without fuss.

Now to last minute shopping in the village. Oh, the blessed quiet and the fresh country air!

Merry Christmas! GF

December 26, 1948

Dear Miss Stotler:

The storm did not break here, but went out to sea; so, save for a few merry flakes yesterday, we have had smooth roads and easy driving.

Christmas Eve the three of us gathered for the exciting moment of the packages; even Mutzi had her pretty red bow, and sniffed at the rustling papers and crackling decorations.

We have you to thank for several intriguing parcels and are most grateful for the thought bestowed and their use that will endure. You sound very weary. Perhaps you have done too much with all you planned.

I have sent the [Mary] Garden[113] article to a professional friend who will be interested. Her mother was a warm admirer of mine, and often came back stage to see me in the old Hammerstein days.

Seven of us had our mid-day dinner with Mrs. G., and left at an early hour yesterday, as she is far from well and must have absolute quiet the major part of the time . . . but she was happy to see us and we made some music and sat before the glorious fire . . . sweet chat and gay musings.

I am taking the girls to the Inn for lunch, and this afternoon we are having a small tea-party to honor a guest who flies South tomorrow. With the years I lean to the smaller groups and intimate conversation.

And now to thank you again, not only for the Christmas hour, but for the many kind thoughts that have come to us throughout the year. And a happy holiday season to those at Dogwood, and all good wishes and greetings for health and content in these troubled times.

GF

December 29, 1948

Dear Miss Stotler:

Thank you for the pen fancy of the snowed-in lady. I was indeed struggling with the drifts at that time as we cut our own greens on the place.

This day is fine and frosty so I shall go over to see my friend later. She is invalided with a tired heart, as perhaps I wrote you; once the New Year's party is over she must return to the complete rest of the hospital. She has been taxed severely these last years—too many sorrows to endure.

I cannot give you details about Miss Garden; I knew her slightly, but our activities did not merge as is sometimes the case, in benefits or some such ensemble. I was present at the first *Pelleas* which was a triumph for her and the composer.[114] I have never liked the opera, though I have tried hard to find something in it at various times since. I heard her often in *Salomé,* a very sensational performance; I would say more from the dramatic than the vocal accomplishment.

113 References to the great Scottish-American soprano Mary Garden (1877–1967) occur frequently in Miss Farrar's correspondence.

114 Claude Debussy's opera *Pelleas and Melisande* was first performed in Paris on April 30, 1902.

Hammerstein[115] leaned heavily on her stellar performances and those years that he financed saw many French novelties well worth their production. Nobody was her equal in *Thaïs* and *Le Jongleur*[116] and other typical French roles. She was not a good Carmen but her name was enough to draw forth the crowd. She had fine partners, too, in Muratore and Renaud.[117] Miss Garden is *all* Scot, from Aberdeen. There is no Latin or Celt of the more melting kind in her, as far as I know.

The French schooling, as we termed it, is of elegance and plastic beauty. Fine diction and often poor singing; the reason why, after my first season of study in Paris, we chose to go elsewhere. One *must* sing well, at least. The French men come off better than the women.

I took the girls to see the amazing color film *The Three Musketeers* [starring Gene Kelly], a lush, romantic picture; beautiful scenery, riding and sword play, the men in fine fettle, the women artificial in the Hollywood manner. The place was filled with children who enjoyed it hugely as did we.

I am glad you liked the Christmas thought [a photograph album]. No, I did not go to Boston but did the ordering via post. This shop has always done nice things and I hope did not fail this time. As you had expressed a wish for photos other than those in the book I send along some that perhaps you do not know. They are none too fresh from their attic hiding place, but perhaps you can adjust them to good effect.

My mantelpiece has to be kept fairly cool—no fire in the chimney—so the candles may remain upright in the angels' hands. My upstairs study is the coziest place to sit, full of sunshine and gay flowers. How vivid the poinsettia is against the dazzling snow . . .

A Happy New Year to you, and a very merry beginning to 1949, in which the girls join heartily.

GF

[115] Oscar Hammerstein (1846–1919) was an operatic impresario who built several opera houses in New York and brought many European singers to the United States. The famous librettist Oscar Hammerstein II was his grandson.

[116] Jules Massenet's *Le Jongleur de Notre Dame* was produced in Monte Carlo in 1902 and his *Thaïs* in Paris in 1904.

[117] Mary Garden often sang with tenor Lucien Muratore and baritone Maurice Renaud. While she admired the latter's artistry she accused him of trying to upstage her.

1949

January 1, 1949
New Year's Day

Dear Miss Stotler:

I have just had your phone call and good wishes which we return in kind. The weather is really beastly, and instead of partying last night, the lady of this house went to bed wrapped in a fleecy pink cover, with her books and radio at hand, happy not to struggle with evening dress in the midst of a Winter storm. I do not wear low-cut frocks now, nor are they much the style; usually a square cut at the front, long skirt and flowing lines—this is the accepted dinner dress in the country.

More fine snow, and the wind whirls it about in a dizzy dance. This will not be posted till Monday, but the belated greetings lose nothing in the delay. I wish the troubled world might find itself once more, and its people walk toward harmony and good-will.

Our best wishes, GF

January 7, 1949

Dear Miss Stotler:

You ask me what I would wish for myself in the New Year. Well, I have not given it much thought, but first of all would be health; then courage to meet the very uncertain future which unrolls before us, and not lose faith in this great country of ours.

I used to be immoderate in the scale of real—or fancied—joy or sadness, but now I think I proceed along a certain even keel. I have learned that it is the safest course and the best calculated to go along agreeably. Perhaps too, I have exhausted my very full cup of early enthusiasms, and am content to enjoy in a milder vein.

I never knew any singer who did not suffer in some way excruciating torture before going on the stage. Once there the nerves respond to their task, but no one, I believe, ever conquers that particular Lampenfieber, as we called it in Berlin.

Audiences are prone to be kind and understanding. I recall only one time, when, in Boston, Isadora Duncan[118] really did exceed the proprieties, that they made outcry. She was at that time not responsible for even her public appearances, and should not have

[118] This American-born (1878–1927) exponent of naturalistic dance performed barefoot in a somewhat revealing garment modeled on a Greek tunic.

been allowed to go onstage. What a gift she had, and how sadly misused! Her sister, a most valuable help, and a very sweet and modest woman, died only recently in Germany. The whole family was gifted but touché.

I have had a most interesting letter from a friend who is desirous to have some film magnate buy the USA rights to a film now in the making in Munich. It presents the characters of Richard Strauss operas, with the composer in the film conducting the overture to the *Rosenkavalier*. It would be a charming documentary affair, but I fear would not find favor here, in view of our "naturalized" citizens who take it upon themselves to decide *who* shall perform for us. I have written to an English musician of my acquaintance to see if he thinks J. Arthur Rank, the top producer there, might find it advisable to sponsor its English performances.

He makes such delightful films, and since Dr. Strauss was highly honored in London, by invitation of Sir Thomas Beecham, who, whatever his irascibility, knows and performs fine music without regard to prejudices, there might be a chance that it would come under the Rank banner, and thence, to this side. There is a splendid documentary film of Toscanini that would set the pattern.[119] However, one can never know. I shall only try to send out a word.

Our routine here proceeds with pleasant tranquility. I hope all is well with you.

GF

January 11, 1949

Dear Miss Stotler:

It is really fantastic, this April mildness, while the rest of the country is either sliding apart in floods or freezing below zero. What contrasts we have in these USA!

The muted "moonbeam" frock will be worn some other time. The dove-grey crepe has a rose overtone and the passementerie catches the light and iridescence—like a moonbeam, in fact.

I had quite a shock to learn that a friend whom I thought to be a victim of the Berlin blitz is alive in her suburban home (Russian

119 Made in 1944 to be shown in Italy, the documentary celebrated the liberation of that country from Nazi domination. In it Toscanini appeared with his NBC Symphony, tenor Jan Pierce, and the Westminster Choir, and expressed his gratitude for America's role in the regaining of freedom by his native land.

sector), but in poor health and spirits since her husband never returned from the Russian concentration camp. These people[120] were friends of my youth and it gave me a wrench to know that after their lovely houses and the great wealth that they used so well, she should survive in such dire misery. . . . I am sure she would prefer death. In all countries it seems the decent and honorable ones must pay the toll of war's tragedy. The rascals go scot free—drat 'em!

I heard the Saturday opera, in many ways very good and the ambiguous speech of Mr. Sloan—a new house, or modernize the old? This is a startling thought. Too bad that the opera house interior could not be moved as it is, to Rockefeller Center, as was the proposition at the time of this conception. Then it would have had an entreé and space for all its needs, with the lovely interior, to last as our Opera House in the grand manner. But I suppose business interfered, and the hideous location now, amid the sweat shops and traffic, has complicated problems. The stage is so shallow and the dressing rooms impossible. The streets bar any expansion. I do not see how improvements can be made.

I have long since given up any auditions, for not only is the question of advice a serious one, but, if one hears a fine talent, then the problem is to indicate its future development. This means financial aid as well as supervision. We [Miss Farrar and Mrs. Gilmour] have had some examples, but the young ladies did not get far; this age is a difficult one and the various avenues of screen and radio often undo the work of serious application. I do not like to introduce aspirants to agents whose methods are entirely commercial; nor must one suppress from legitimate activity. It is something one cannot watch from a quiet country house—one must be *sur place,* and ready to battle as for one's own career. I cannot undertake this, so I have discouraged any further approaches, but have recommended those teachers and paths that could best benefit, with the good will of the student.

The position of any creative art these days is so dependent upon union cooperation, and I am such a rebel in this, I could be of no service at all.

---

[120] The reference is to the distinguished Rhenish family, vom Rath, which Miss Farrar met through the American singer Lillian Nordica. The vom Raths, parents of the person the letter refers to, arranged for Miss Farrar to give a concert at their Berlin home and invited the Intendant of the Royal Opera, Graf von Hochberg. The result was a contract for Miss Farrar (signed by her parents, since she was only nineteen) for stellar roles with the Royal Opera. She made a sensational debut as Marguerite in Gounod's *Faust* in the fall of 1901, and remained with the Royal Opera until World War I.

All good wishes. We are off to New Canaan for errands, a nice ride.

GF

January 13, 1949

Dear Miss Stotler:

I took the girls out to the Inn yesterday for lunch and a movie, to vary the monotony of taking care of me and my things. One cannot always be glued to the same chores, and they fancy a change now and then.

I believe that only the opening opera, *Otello*, was televised. It seems this is a very costly proceeding and for the nonce, will not be repeated. Then too, the combinations of cosmetics vary from those of the usual stage lighting, and I am told the effect on the stars—in this case all young and personable—was awful to see. I recall in the Summer Convention, that the most horrible distortion took place on the lovely features of Clare Luce, and she is a very *pretty* woman. I should not like to leave such a disastrous reminder—not even in the service of *art*—much less for politics.

I shall not go to the New York meeting of our Garden Club, nor any lunch at the Flower Show. I know from one harrowing experience of crowds and fatigue that it would only be a source of irritation. I recall in my childhood I had this dislike of people shoving against me. My dear mother, like all of her era, thought I should see the department store Santa Claus, ride in the Swan Boat on Boston Common, go to the circus there, and other such entertainments for small fry. I hated it and pouted all the while till she gave up when I was about twelve, and concentrated on books and music.

My mother died in 1923, Winter time. I do think that as one goes on in life one understands better what parents have tried to do for us in early youth. Mine were so fully sympathetic to our idea of song, that this, in itself, was a joyous harmony only interrupted by mother's death. My father, of course, outlived her, and thoroughly enjoyed his residence here in Ridgefield, and the very many friends his kindly nature invited.

You ask about Mutzi. She has enjoyed the holidays, but is only interested in the male visitors, human, that is. She dances and preens. At her age and with her girth, she is not likely to make a great furor among her own kind, but she is happy, and a sweet pet.

I have had a variety of dogs, but the most attached was a police dog given me by my father. We brought him up from six weeks, a great gentleman. He lived fifteen years and then succumbed to the ills of his age, and we put him to sleep.

The Peke we had was a little devil; she had a bad temper and liked only Miss Sylvia. Her lovely coat made her a beautiful specimen however, and we took her everywhere with us. She was as courageous as a lion, but I did not find her lovable. This sweet trait was demonstrated to the full in the Hansi we lost.

I have had bull dogs and terriers, but found them inclined to be noisy and quarrelsome. I think the dachshund pleases me so much because he is such a clown and so amusing, aside from having great intelligence.

Thank you for your good wishes for 1949, which this household reciprocates. With health and courage the individual will find his way—as much as is humanly possible.

GF

January 29, 1949

Dear Miss Stotler:

How attractive is the catalogue of the Steuben glass exhibit. I am sure you had a feast of beauty. I love crystal, and these designs are really superlative. After so much struggle with the care of silver, we do enjoy the crystal. So much less work, and so fresh and appealing on the table.

I enclose by way of interest my very irreverent comments on a garden club exhibit I visited the other day—a ghastly collection of strange designs. Do not return.

In re your paragraph on Rita Hayworth, that she is foolish in this silly liaison will be found out later to her sorrow. But the pompous Orson Welles [her husband] was no Galahad, and must have given her many an uncomfortable hour.

I reiterate, Hollywood life soon predisposes a breakdown of values. Few are able to withstand the pitfalls of success, more money than ever they dreamed, and the constant demands that lead to excesses of all sorts. Rest assured, no studio will defend any of its stars if there is the slightest change in public opinion. They take advantage of all the build-up of the harpies of the press, but let the unfortunate victim meet with the *wrong* incident, and he is out for good.

Hayworth, I always found warm and spontaneous. Garden, Lilli, and Sarah were of quite different caliber in their expression. They had tigerish qualities, rather hard in outline—not the winning loveliness, truly womanly, of the pretty Rita. Whether she follows the Grundy code or not, I like her.

All good wishes, GF

Winter at Low Ebb

(I went yesterday to view a garden club exhibit of Winter material. I wickedly enjoyed spoofing the results, and enclose my "review," the writing of which eased my feelings slightly.)

Dear Reader:

I crave your indulgence for this hot-off-the-griddle report of a Winter exhibit which I visited in a private home, as the club background. As an entrance fee was paid, I feel free to make my evaluations without offense to the committee or hostess of the occasion.

In the gay setting of the "rumpus" room—the modern term for a cellar arranged for cozy gatherings—the subjects were exposed in favorable position and lighting.

The objective, it seems, was to produce original designs in whatever material could be found in the somewhat bleak exterior of our country Winter. No doubt there had been much study of modernistic impressions such as those of the tongue-in-cheek Dali, by ladies responsible for the display.

Being an ignoramus, and thus free from any painful need to conceal lack of knowledge in these matters of measure and arrangement, I would disagree with most of the highly-prized blobs that sported the gay ribbons of the judges.

Here and there a weary cabbage lifted a none-too-proud head of purple knobs on a bare branch, or was tucked into the crotch of a prickly viburnum.

One large seashell held a mélange of wilted contents with protruding spikes that dug sharply into my posterior.

An odd effect, winning first prize, was a graduated clump of straws, unevenly shaved to create the impression of an overturned drugstore container of such things, with two wisps, daintily pointing to the East . . . bone-meal or saw-dust, I could not tell which, since my glasses were not available, was lightly sprinkled at the base. Whatever symbol intended, escaped me—those conical piles doubtless had some meaning? Mighty curious.

One sizable piece embraces a large hornet's nest, among bristling branches and fungus, limp reminders of decay, and the abortions of a Winter's rock garden.

A fantastic pyramid of fungus appeared to entrance the beholders. That sprouted wings, nicely pinned into a soaring movement, of raspberry canes.

One lone exhibit (very choice) resembled the swirl of a not-too-happy hair-do. This evoked cries of admiration, and the repeated phrase, common to garden clubbers, "Such purity of Japanese outline!"

On another table stood a modest collection of pampas grass; this displayed a feathery arch, similar to a well-ripened grainfield, implanted in bits of green broken glass; a portion of the beach at Waikiki, perhaps?

I noticed several appalling festoons of slightly decayed fungi, and in consequence confess that I had little appetite for the delicious sandwiches and punch served; in fact I was fascinated to watch a timorous footman trying to work his way among the chattering ladies, no doubt fearful that he disturb, ever so little, the correct tilt of twisted bark, dried berries, or viscous mass.

So I sat awhile, my accompanying friends pursuing their own speculations. Once in the entrance where normality was restored, it was comforting to observe potted primroses, orchids, and white spirea . . . so simple and lovely.

I still wonder why any one goes so far afield in the creative gesture to obtain the ugly, distorted and unnatural. Meanwhile, dear reader, you may assume that I shall *not* be invited to further exhibits; my humor (probably misplaced) and foot fatigue, powerless to find compensation in the results at hand.

February 18, 1949

Dear Miss Stotler:

A brilliant, crisp day, with enough snow on the ground to resemble the light mist of a dewy morn. It is good to breathe deeply and be able to enjoy with our five senses.

I went to our local Fashion Show yesterday, mainly to glimpse the pretty girls who did the modelling—such lively youngsters, prancing about like frisky colts. They wore Summer cottons of delicate colors, cart-wheel hats and smiling faces. My own wardrobe is a special one for the matronly figure, and I could not hope to indulge in these designs that are more and more feminine, thanks be, with little touches here and there of lace and frills. I wish I had six daughters to dress and spoil!

I ordered a book for your birthday from Brentano yesterday; at last it is on the market. It looked from the reviews to be a welcome addition to anyone's musical library [*My Many Lives,* by soprano Lotte Lehmann]. I know the authoress, a charming and intelligent lady.

The 28th I shall be among women friends; a lunch at Mrs. G's. We shall sit about the huge fire and retell some of our amusing experiences, since, with her exception, the ladies have been my professional friends. These reunions see spaces vacated for one reason or another—it is best to enjoy each day with not too much thought for the morrow.

Miss Sylvia has built a second house, besides the one called Les Miettes; a little darling, on one floor, and planned with great care. It will be ready for Spring rental. There is no thought of our separation, but some day it might be a good thing to have this little place. I hope never to leave my present home, but it is wise to have another "egg in our basket." Who can tell what may come to us in health and finances? If I live overlong, and have to husband my forces, a one-floor house might be very desirable. For the moment we are having fun in its completion.

Yes, our Red Cross branch is under the chapter in Danbury; this in turn is under the North Atlantic Area, and under military orders in time of war or disaster. Like all organizations, it depends on the personnel. I have worked with a fine committee always, both here and in Danbury; this puts a happy complexion on the matter. Our women have been tops.

The tree man is here. It is good to have an inspection of the lovely things from time to time. All the trees in New England have something or other the matter. The white pine blister has wrought havoc; the chestnuts are almost extinct; the elms have to be watched for the dread Dutch elm disease and scale; with bug infection over all. Sprays are not DDT but some milder solution to encourage the leaves and bloom. One does what one can.

You are kind to think of my birthday coming; it is a fact that I have so many delightful things that I would not know what wish to express. It was in this fashion, in the early days, that I built up my collection of songs and opera scores. In those days they were more rare than now, with the multifold printings of such. As a matter of fact I should be about sending this material to its promised destination [The New England Conservatory] . . . but somehow it is hard to part with these scores and song books . . . perhaps I might not do so, but bring them down from the studio at Miss Sylvia's and keep them yet awhile.

Now to the village for some ingredients desired by the butcher who is cutting up our steer in the cellar. A magnificent beast; my mouth waters at the eventual delights at table that he will offer. I call them all "Henry" . . . I do not know precisely why, but I do.

Best greetings, GF

February 19, 1949

Dear Miss Stotler:

As predicted, we woke this morning with the snow pouring from Heaven. It looks like a day of impenetrable curtain. I hope the postman stops for his cup of coffee, then he can take my letters with him. There will be no driving for this household today. A pretty, soft landscape, with it all, and I feast my eyes on it.

Yes, I too, have a very difficult stomach—one reason why I prefer home fare, a quiet routine and early hours. What I suffered during all my professional career, much travel, nervous excitements, food changeable . . . when I think back, I shudder.

I can recall, as if it were yesterday, the first visit I made to Boston for an audition with the lady who became my first singing teacher. I did not sleep all night, could not hold my breakfast, and nearly collapsed from excitement on the old-fashioned brownstone front. This agony of preparation never left me. It was dreadful until I actually got on the stage, when it disappeared as if by magic. There was nothing to be done, only keep as calm as possible, and accept it as part of the performance—only the toll came before, not after.

The tree men did a fine job in the orchard yesterday, cutting out the dead wood and the suckers. We shall hope the fruit will be encouraged. Some feeding with a little spraying, alas, this seems to be a must if we are to continue the good work done last season at such expense.

The American Garden Guild has just brought out a fine book of our wild animals, most effectively illustrated; I am delighted to add it to my own nature studies. An *Encyclopedia of Horticulture* as well, a most handy volume, excellent reading for the layman. The new Spring catalogues make one yearn to invest, but I am firm, knowing that nothing comes to bloom without requisite care, and this we cannot give in undue proportion.

And now, a "Merci" French line of cars to return the compliment of the food train, so artfully publicized by one Drew Pearson . . . it is so silly . . . why must the French people have to return anything of this kind if it was a gift? Why not be more punctual in a business transaction? But this would not rate a medal for *humanity*, I dare say.

Our good wishes to you. GF

February 21, 1949

Dear Miss Stotler:

I have already 100 letters ready for the Red Cross drive, and 30 more will see this task completed. You are so good to do the posters; the official ones make no impression on the eye or memory.

Yes. Regarding my youthful participation in funeral services—I loved to sing, and there must have been some latent dramatic feeling even then. Then too, the $5.00 was always welcome, put aside to add to the sum for my later lessons. I did not care for the preaching for there were so few ministers who were really eloquent and the somber note seemed to belie the Sunday School teaching of the loving presencc of Christ, even more understanding and approachable than one's own father. I was never saddened by funerals, only a great wonderment prevailed, and still does, where are they now?

When we laid my sweet mother to rest, the sun was pouring through a stained glass window; the organ played a soft melody; there was nothing gruesome or hysterical in those last hours. My father also had this last peace, he lay in a merciful coma; we could scarcely tell when he left us.

As to faltering in the choice of a singing career, that never happened to mother and me. It was only when I retired that I realized the cost to her. Mother was not of my opinion in this; her child did not grow up for her. So many mothers nourish this singular determination; it makes them restless to *have* to note the passing of time. She would not have borne the declining years happily and God was good to her to let her spirit soar elsewhere.

The Mindszenty[121] affair is a scandal; life imprisonment might

[121] Cardinal Jozef Mindszenty, then Primate of Hungary, was sentenced to lifelong imprisonment in 1948 for his opposition to the Communist government. During the 1956 uprising he found asylum in the U.S. legation. In 1971 the Vatican negotiated his departure from Hungary.

just mean some future time when his sorely tried country resumes its normal state, that he may emerge a white-haired wreck. My thought is, his first letter explaining the possible "relapse" at any trial, is the estimate he put upon the treatment likely to be inflicted upon him by his gaolers.

But people are so divided; even the religious will not, as you say, become united for their own protection; and Communism is a growing cancer affecting all the world.

The little pen fancy of my leap into the new bed is perfect. It is wonderful—I could almost emulate [the great ballet dancer] Nijinsky!

Greetings, GF

February 25, 1949

Dear Miss Stotler:

The wealth of talisman roses and the breathtaking mimosa are here with my breakfast tray, and are like a field of Spring gardens. This is only a hasty word and a special merci for the lovely flowers that bring me so much happiness.

May your own celebration be one of cheer and goodwill, wherever you elect to spend it.

GF

February 29, 1949

Dear Miss Stotler:

So you have invested in diamonds. I believe they are always of market value in any crisis.

I am reading an amusing little book [*The Family of Grammercy Park*], the boy-language of a youngster whose family lived at Grammercy Park. The author, Henry Noble MacCracken, later became president of Vassar. The book was given to me by reason of the fact that when I first came to New York, I too, lived in this section and was given the key to the park, where the families sat and talked or aired their children, while the busy life of the street went on outside.

Regarding *Amico*[122]—the usual blood and revenge plot is the musical frame. *Navarraise* was somewhat better than the Mascagni

[122] *L'Amigo Fritz* was one of Mascagni's less successful operas.

opus—Massenet was the better workman, and the story a lively one of the war between Navarre and Spain. The heroine offers herself as ransom for the life of her lover-Captain, who is fatally wounded but lives long enough to repudiate her for the sacrifice. Calvé[123] first brought the latter opera to the MET and was a sensation in it. Our later one was a mediocre production, I thought.

Toscanini begins his NBC concerts. I am not partial to Berlioz and could wish for other selections, but since he has played almost everything written in the symphonic field, there must be some gesture for material less familiar.

Best wishes from all here, GF

Later:

Such enchanting memories are evoked by items re *The Merry Widow.* It would seem that such musical offerings now do not measure up to the lovely ones of an earlier era. . . . I recall the thrill of those first performances.

I have just concluded the Billie Burke[124] book, *A Feather on My Nose,* chiefly enjoyable because of the wonderful pictures; beautiful girls in stunning costumes. The musical numbers of the *Follies*, too, were always pretty and catchy.

I suppose after all, the generation itself creates the effect, which lingers long after its own passing; but today's "string beans" have nothing like the allure of the wonderful women then.

Pennywise
Cape Vincent, New York
August 10, 1949

Dear Miss Stotler:

The beautiful cool days roll on, such a comfort after the previous heat. The sunsets are rarely lovely, flaming across the broad expanse of the river; the finale of the *Götterdämmerung* indeed!

One hears that two thirds of the pigeons at St. Mark's— Venice,

[123] Although Carmen was one of Farrar's most popular roles, she always regarded the French singer Calvé as the Carmen par excellence.

[124] Billie Burke starred in the *Ziegfeld Follies,* and was married to Florenz Ziegfeld, the producer.

of course, have been killed by hail-stones; while nine deaths by freezing have been reported in Chile. The vagaries of climate!

Yes, that amazing and beautiful young woman bull-fighter [Peruvian-born Conchita Cintron] whom I have applauded in Mexico, is indeed unique. Her first bulls are played by her from horseback, her every movement grace and color, then she dismounts and fights the last half on foot, also a splendid spectacle.

It is a curious occupation for so slender and delicate a woman, but her skill and elegance are unequalled in the arena. She must have a wrist of iron, and untiring manipulation.

Of course one either does or does not care for what this represents. I agree it would be nothing for Miss Aida.

Your letter arrived this morning from Bedford Springs. I have friends who have taken the waters there and speak highly of their effects. I know pretty Frederickstown and the Fritchie home; have often sung in Hagerstown too, and taken the lovely drive over the Cumberland mountains. Of course, many years ago.

Our routine is very quiet. We drove to Ogdensburg in the breeze along the river; charming scenery, and the country full of legend and the story of the early settlements. We visited an antique shop of two sweet sisters; such pretty things, but I am not adding to my home treasures; Margaret has more than she can handle now.

My room here is a gay and lovely nest: the wallpaper of French design, gardenias on a rose background; highly polished early American furniture; darling crisp curtains; flowers everywhere. My desk overlooks the river and I write in the grateful shade of the trees which extend to the water's edge—an enchanting place for reverie and quiet.

Toscanini will give his concert in Ridgefield[125] on the 7th of October. The committee will have their worries; at 82 one cannot be too certain of the Maestro's resistance, but we shall hope for his proverbial good luck. It is most kind of him to honor our little village again.

In re Gustav Mahler, he was a most sensitive conductor with whom I sang a few times at the MET. He was very neurotic, and of uncertain temper and manner. I did not care for his monumental symphonies, and I fancy the fact that he could not measure up to the immortals played no small part in his striving and moods. His blond wife [Alma], lovely indeed at the time of their marriage, afterward

[125] For love of Farrar, Toscanini brought his NBC Orchestra to Ridgefield for several years to play for local benefits.

married [Czech novelist] Franz Werfel; both small men, but they appeared to have some strong attraction for her. . .

The horrible accident that resulted in the death of the author of *Gone with the Wind* [Margaret Mitchell] was shocking. One hopes the driver will pay the penalty, but I doubt if it will affect any of his kind.

Speed, Speed and more *Speed!* One would like to see a symbolic painting such as Franz Stuck used to do, of the demons who whip human beings into their ultimate pit of hell . . .

I remember in the Munich Art Gallery, a most impressive painting by this artist, entitled *War*. It was of a gaunt horse, blood streaming from its nostrils and bearing a skeleton rider picking its way over thousands of mutilated bodies. No *glory* there; only the writhing of torn limbs and hideous faces. It chills me now to think of it.

Yes. One wonders, "What is Glory?"

To a happier theme—I have been pleased to see the various editorials about Mr. Hoover, and his fine birthday address. At 75 he is to be praised for going his patriotic way, with only the best advice to offer.

My father would have been 88 had he lived, for he shared the 10th as his birthday. I recall how we teased him, for he loved parties, and the weather at this period was often hot and uncomfortable, with thunder storms to intimidate his guests; but we had wonderful fêtes, just the same.

I will keep well and enjoy the cool at last. GF

Pennywise
Cape Vincent, New York
August 12, 1949

Dear Miss Stotler:

Our ducks are growing big and beautiful in glossy plumage. They will soon be flying to other shores, prey to the guns that will begin to roar. I wish they might continue their happy, innocent pilgrimages up and down the river, but that would not seem to be the way of any living things on this globe.

The season has been so gay here, with many guests attracted by the fine fishing. It is hard to realize how quickly the waters are replenished, so that the catch is generous and satisfies all sportsmen.

The law sternly regulates the limits however, and thus the game life is protected from too voracious killing.

I understand Mr. [Cecil B.] De Mille is busy with a story re *Samson and Delila,* with Hedy Lamarr. At one time he was hoping to make the *Ring* and *Parsifal,* but no doubt he realizes the cost would hardly be justified. He is a wonderful director, even if he does err on the sensational side. His wife is pure-bred New England, a clever and most charming balance wheel for one of his exuberant temperament.

If I can prevent it, there will be no public acknowledgement of my own 70th year; there would be few, if any, of my generation who would have a particular interest in the accumulation of my years. Miss Barrymore is still in the public eye, so her management are correct in keeping her name before the screen audiences.

Mr. Hoover is active in the sane promotion of public benefits; his fine efforts *should* be brought before the people, who are too often ungrateful and indifferent.

The Toscanini concert will again be a gala affair; that sprightly 82 year old never wearies.

The luncheon bell is sounding, so I bid you good morning, and hope you enjoy the same glorious weather. It hints at Fall, and the gentian filled meadows with their blue cast, and the helianthus, tall and golden, make a handsome picture after the too arid Summer.

Pennywise
Cape Vincent, New York
August 17, 1949

Dear Miss Stotler:

We are having a terrific gale, hail as big as moth-balls, and the river lashing out in waves that could easily cradle an ocean liner. It is thrilling to watch from this safe vantage point, a big fire burning brightly and flickering on the pretty walls and appurtenances of the home. My young ducks have taken shelter in the woodland, I hope.

I do not doubt that the marriage of the daughter of the Kronprinz, the younger Cecilie,[126] will be a happy one. Why not? She is freed from the home poverty and the unsafe position of the

[126] The Princess Cecilie, born in 1917, was married in 1945 to Clyde Harris, a young interior decorator from Texas, who was serving as an officer in the U.S. Army's occupation of Hesse. Their wedding at the ancestral castle, Burg Hohenzollern, was the last great gathering of the Hohenzollern family.

crowned heads. The young husband will have much to offer her in this land. I can only see a much improved position for her. God grant it. After what has been the experience and aftermath of the war, I imagine this will be a haven of happiness.

Referring to my riding days in Berlin, I rode side-saddle, wearing a long, silky broad-cloth habit, with a small, gay Panama hat—no stiff beaver. Berlin never saw any lady riding astride, or attired in trousers, or jodhpurs, as I believe they are now called. My habit was draped softly and was very pretty, though perhaps in an accident it might have presented difficulties not encountered at present when legs are free to slip out of the stirrups.

As to my dressing room in Berlin, we all shared the same there. It was sparsely furnished, for the usual gathering place, as in Paris theaters, was a general hall where the singers remained, waiting for their cues. One side of the stage was for the ladies, the other for the men. Underneath, on the ground floor of the Oper, there was a flourishing business in edibles and beer, an excellent Bier Stube, which the artists and chorus could patronze when intervals permitted. In the foyer of the promenade hall there was the usual cafeteria with small tables, which the public visited during the entre'acte, until a bell rang for the continuance. No German theater is without its concession for edibles, a pleasant interlude.

At the MET, Sherry has done a good business, though there are few accommodations, and the food has to be brought over from the Park Avenue restaurant in heaters, a rather awkward arrangement which of course makes for a very light menu.

No callers backstage at the Berlin Oper; the performance was a serious affair. No encores, and no acknowledgment of applause which was discouraged until *after* the curtain was lowered. No presentation of flowers; everything was sent to the loge.

My dressing room at the MET was another thing. At first I shared a huge drafty room that had seen many a fine singer come and go; but it was so much trouble, every performance bringing my own personal belongings, so I did obtain from the directors a small room just off the stage, and fitted it up like a boudoir. It was sweet, and commodious enough for my wants. I had the key at all times; it was my personal retreat, and no one else was allowed to use it.

I had it draped in chintz, with special lighting for stage effects, and cupboards where my garments and shoes could be cleaned and kept. It caused much envy but I did not care.

When came the holidays or my birthday, the men back-stage always had it wreathed in flowers, and the gifts could be sent there to be opened after the performance. Of course we could, and did, have time for all sorts of callers; this was more tiring than the performance, but it was the custom. Some two hours after the opera's close, I would stagger to bed, quite exhausted . . . so many hands to shake, so many people who pressed one, all taking with them some of one's waning energy. It was an ordeal, but of course, part of the career.

The luncheon bell rings, so off I hurry.

All good wishes, GF

Pennywise
Cape Vincent, New York
September 3, 1949

Dear Miss Stotler:

The heavy rains have freshened the fields and the prevailing green is lush, and takes care of the large herds of cattle, grazing contentedly beside flowing waters.

I have not been on the river this year; a large yacht is at anchor belonging to friends who extend a hearty invitation to us all, but I shall not accept. I feel unhappy in the constricted area of any boat—even the *Queen Mary* would not tempt me.

I have had a happy surprise from a German friend, USA sector, Berlin, in the first cable greeting allowed to be sent. She was all excitement, but the poor lady will have had much to pay, I fear, from her meager funds.

Your reference to the German blood of the would-be Indian lady makes me think of a friend of early Berlin days. Her family were Nordic to the last degree, but she fancied that there had been a Slavic strain somewhere in the annals, therefore she appropriated the most outlandish name she could find (in the estimation of her circle), Ruano Bogislav. I call this going far afield indeed, but she was a musical personality, talented in languages, and who knows what odd vibrations sounded in her ears to offset the more homely Klambach of her parents!

As my own name was always sweet and euphonious to me, I selected such poetic names for my dolls. I recall a favorite when I was about six years old named Ethelinda Montmorency.

A long, sad letter from Lilli's niece, in solitude at Scharfling. She laments, as I would do, fiercely, the insistence on the Max

Reinhardt[127] réclame [publicity], when the whole musical world knows that the Salzburger Fest was inaugurated by Lilli Lehmann [1901-1910] under the patronage of the Archduke Eugen, because he honored her for the great artist she was; with such names as Muck, Mahler, and the opera personnel of the Vienna Oper to sustain the stage and orchestra plans.

It makes me angry to note that the charming Bijou Opera House, that is the true home for the Mozart operas, with the Mozarteum for concerts (the corner stone laid by Lilli herself), should give way to the renovated stables for the Reinhardt plans. The Domplatz will suffer the all too frequent rains, and make performances impossible. The band of mountebanks and inflated poseurs who soon surrounded Reinhardt with their Broadway money bags is still a hard mouthful for me to swallow. Ah, well, I am thankful to have memories.[128]

May you have a pleasant weekend, as shall we here, much gaiety and then au revoir till next year as people go their various ways.

GF

Pennywise
Cape Vincent, New York
September 8, 1949

Dear Miss Stotler:

The rain pours down in a cold sheet and we have started heat and fires. Even the intrepid fisher folk have thought better to remain at home, and this goes for our circle. We shall have some neighbors

[127] The Austrian theatrical director (1873–1943) was known for his lavish and colorful productions. While he is usually credited with the founding of the Salzburg Festival in 1920, he was joined in this undertaking by the poet Hugo von Hoffmanstahl, and the composer Richard Strauss. Miss Farrar objected to his getting the sole credit.

[128] One memory was of the handsome Antonio Scotti, bowing right and left to the delighted populace as he drove through the street to the Oper attired in his Don Giovanni costume. He was at this time known to be in love with Farrar, a situation that added to the excitement of their fans when they performed together.

Miss Farrar said that nothing recalled those days so vividly as the recording of the duet "Là, ci darem la mano," which she sang with Scotti. She was the Zerlina in that production, while Johanna Gadski sang Donna Elvira and Lilli Lehmann, Donna Anna.

in this afternoon for tea and a cozy chat. Most of us are preparing for flight . . . my boxes are being filled gradually.

My ducks are full-bosomed, and ride the waves proudly. Some hunters will have fine birds for their tables, thanks to us. They were just babies when we came, and looked so charming sailing up in a flotilla—39 of them. They are amusing pets, and come at my call; indeed I shall miss them, but must content myself with the smaller interest of the dog and canary.

I know quite a bit of the young Cecilie from a god-parent at present here. She and her young man have known each other since the war's end. I fancy this is no mere romantic attachment but a serious tie, which, according to the god-parent, both young people are well qualified to enjoy. In any event I make no wager with you, for you have, indeed, a cynical view of marriage; on this subject we shall neither agree nor argue.

I listened only a few times to Father Coughlin [a controversial radio preacher]; I do not care for rabble rousing from anyone, so am not sympathetic to his exhortations. I think the church should concern itself with matters spiritual not political; but since all do become involved, such addresses carry little weight in my mind.

I start now on a round of farewell visits to my friends. The weather continues cold and windy, so I am glad of my one wool dress, which Miss Sylvia insisted on packing. When I have a free moment I will write you from home; meanwhile, best greetings.

GF

September 20, 1949

Dear Miss Stotler:

At last home, after a most delightful trip off the much travelled roads. The weather is cool and pleasant; my desk is piled high. So many foolish people write me, and some I deem impertinent: to wit, a woman who sent me a check for a ticket for the Toscanini concert with the request that I buy a seat *with me* for her son, a youth who is interested in music. She felt sure it would be an experience for him to accompany me. She said she would drive her son to my house from Philadelphia, and leave him with me. Pretty picture.

Yes I would like to know what van Paassen[129] has to say. I

[129] Dutch by birth, Pierre van Paassen was reared in Canada. A Unitarian minister, he spent much of his life as a correspondent and commentator on world affairs and writer of books on a variety of subjects.

understand he is an out-and-out *Red* but I have read some of his war observations which impressed me with his human touch.

Thank you for sending Mr. Lissfelt's report of Richard Strauss. This great composer—for he was that—could be a most sympathetic conductor. I liked to sing with him on the podium, and his piano accompaniments to his beautiful songs were like poems. He did drive a hard bargain, and his singing (?) wife [Pauline] was pretty hard to accept, for she was not gifted . . . but they made out, he being the dominant factor.

May I suggest October 20th for the visit of you and Miss Aida? At this time you should not have to contend with icy roads, as might be the case later.

This month is full of pleasant activity. I went to lunch yesterday at the new and beautiful Fox Inn, the re-modelled home of an old friend here. A handsome location on the mountain drive, and done in fine style.

I have friends here to lunch today; a god-daughter whom I have not seen since her baptism, she is now nineteen! It seems but the flick of an eyelash, for those of us on the downward slide.

A happy weekend to you. GF

September 1949

Dear Miss Stotler:

Yes, there are so many incidents that come to mind of those early days. 4th Klasse cabs, with four of us, as students in Berlin, taking a Sunday drive through the Tiergarten [zoo], having pooled our spending money. Three comrades of that time never did anything in the song world . . . but what high hopes then, and how gay we were!

As for musical research, think of the task of a friend of mine to collect if possible the scores and musical matter in the Russian zone, Berlin, of the archives that were stored there, which have been scattered to the four winds, God knows where. My friend is off on a wild goose chase to my mind, to locate the Wagner scores[130] among

[130] Much earlier, Wagner materials had been collected by an Englishwoman, the Hon. Mary Burrell. Her closely guarded collection was later bought by Mary Louise Curtis Bok (Mrs. Efrem Zimbalist) for the Curtis Institute of Music in Philadelphia, which she founded. On October 27, 1978, the Burrell collection was sold at auction for $1,353,000, to be used for the benefit of the Institute.

other valuable data. Much, of course, must be left to the ashes with only the memory to serve. If the data has been carried elsewhere I envisage a hard task to locate and buy for the conservation.

Now to village chores before we start packing away the Summer dresses.

Our best greetings, GF

September 29, 1949

Dear Miss Stotler:

I was up in Dutchess County all day yesterday, to view gardens and lunch with an old time dear one. It was a drive of breath-taking beauty, the mountain slopes a mass of vivid and exciting color.

Tomorrow three of us of the Garden Club have been asked to suggest some new planting for the recently opened Fox Inn. The management is eager to have a plan outlined for the coming Spring. This will give us three a real pleasure, but will not be easy on my feet, for there is to be quite a bit of walking over undulating property.

I see by the paper that Miss Garden has arrived on the *Nieuw Amsterdam*. My *Tribune* gave a pleasing report of her. I hope to hear if she is speaking in New York. I have read nothing of her plans so far, which seems odd, for advance publicity should have come out by the 15th of September if she contemplates a Fall and Winter season. However, she is a canny lady, and needs no advice about her business affairs.

I have nearly finished the van Paassen book [*Why Jesus Died*]; it is certain to provoke controversy. I do not agree with John Haynes Holmes, the New York minister, that "He has written an exciting and exalted interpretation of Jesus." This splurge, which tears down all concept and imagery as we know it, seems to me to be of very coarse fiber. It will not detract one whit, in my estimation, from the splendid figure that most of us believe to be above the usual human pattern, and that has withstood the test of time.

I have so simple a feeling about the divinity of the Christ. In my credo He did not have to be of mysterious birth, since His innate goodness spoke for His source of being. But if it gives comfort to millions of people to believe in the Immaculate Conception, and they need the assurance, why tear it to pieces?

We shall all pass the same portal, no matter what our chosen avenue, and how many need to be taught not to fear the journey!

I never did know the name of the author of *Elizabeth and Her*

German Garden.[131] How charming it was, also two later books, one about the marriage of an English girl to a Pomeranian farmer, the other called *Love*, a semi-humorous account of the pursuit by a youth of a lady much older than himself, his insistence on bringing about their marriage, and the lady's eventual departure with the inevitable letter left behind. She could not endure the youthful spirits of her husband, who had no notion of her need for a more quiet companionship. Really a pretty study in ebullience versus middle-aged reflection.

At this post I have a gesture meant to be kindly, but I cannot approve the reason.

It seems that many years ago, at a performance of *Bohème* in Philadelphia, the basso became ill in the last act, whereupon Caruso offered to undertake the aria he was to have sung. He made the error in my opinion, to sing it in recording; collectors have had copies printed, and one was sent to me.

What ghouls people are to applaud such a stunt, that had *no* value, and is at best, a dubious joke.[132]

Planting time will soon be upon me, though I am waiting for colder days, for the mice and moles would doubtless nibble at my bulbs.

Now to the village for shopping.

All good wishes, GF

October 7, 1949

Dear Miss Stotler:

A light drizzle that may make our Toscanini concert going a little soggy, but will not affect the general gaiety of the hour.

The men have some crowding on our small area, but perform with right good will.

I cannot lunch with you re the Fox Hill invitation, as I have an appointment, but thought you might like to take lunch there the day after you come to us, and walk around the lovely grounds. Then we

131 Mary Annette Gräfin von Armin (1866–1941).

132 Miss Farrar, herself, was responsible for an unusual recording, the original of which commands a high price as a collector's item. On one occasion Caruso turned up very late for a recording session. Miss Farrar detected the scent of liquor on his breath but said nothing. However, in the love duet of *Butterfly*, instead of the phrase, "Si, per la vita," she sang "He had a highball!"

shall have supper together as we agreed, on the evening of the 21st at Mr. Tode's. I can well understand your disinclination to stop at the Savoy as I know the city has little charm for you.

Saturday afternoon

It was not possible to send out the letter enclosed yesterday, so many phone calls and last minute affairs, until it was time to dress and speed my way to the [Toscanini] concert. The occasion has been a brilliant one, the gratifying return now over $15,000, a huge sum for this community, though the patrons made it possible by generous response.

Now as to your letter of Wednesday; the pen fancy is quite like the original scene of those lovely 90's; my pretty span of Schimmels and the nice little coachman, it being long before an auto became so usual.

I recall in Paris seeing one crawl up the Champs Elysées and wondering if *ever* one could convert it to actual use. It was only a little later that I owned a superb touring Mercedes and a town Renault, both left over there, while I brought here a seven passenger Renault . . . what an era of novelties!

In those days I always used a car for travel in Europe, and it served as a nice vacational activity, the while I saw sights that the train did not permit.

As to the costumes of the royal family while at the opera; unless it was a state occasion or visiting royalty, uniforms for the men and light silk or velvet for the ladies. My impression is of light colors and much glitter, as the style then was for dresses spangled with paillettes of all kinds. Usually hair ornaments but not crowns, were worn.

The cut of the ladies' décolletage was measured by the Court Mistress of the Robes; usually off the shoulders with a light fall of lace to finish off the bodice in lieu of sleeves. These could be in semi-toilette, both puffed and leg of mutton . . . High pompadour coiffures, the hair drawn up from the back of the neck to quite towering dimensions in front. The Empress [Kaiserin] had strings of lovely pearls; she always wore these. Long gloves to the shoulders also. Orders [medals], of course, were worn by the men.

Visits to the royal loge were made between the acts in the costume one happened to be wearing at the time. These receptions were screened from the public, in the spacious antechamber of the loge itself.

A Chicago friend writes me that the young Princess Cecilie passed through that city on her way to her new home. I fear she will find the broad lands of Texas a little intimidating; let us hope there will be good friends to help adjust.

I have had to haul out Summer frocks again in this heat. No planting till cooler air and harder earth and fewer insects!

Our good wishes, GF

October 10, 1949

Dear Miss Stotler:

The village is slowly coming back to normal after the exhilaration of the gala. . . .

No parties before the concert but plenty after. I attended none but came home at once; I felt as if I had sung five operas and been kicked in the solar plexus by a mule. Quite an emotional aftermath. But what a glorious memory! Now my friends have dispersed to their more mundane duties.

I can find no announcement of a Garden appearance, though we are in touch with the lady's manager. But really, if she intends to make something of her visit to these shores, she should be about it; the season will be booked. However Garden has always been a bit uncertain.

This is such a day of languor, due to the brilliant sun, I shall not go far with my plans for clearing the garden . . . one works better when the air is crisp.

All good wishes, GF

October 14, 1949

Dear Miss Stotler:

No, Mr. Kreisler is not ill that I know; only had to undergo a serious eye operation that will allow him some measure of sight for a few years though not a cure. He has some form of glaucoma.

I have cancelled my seats (8) for any lecture of Miss Garden. I was so unhappily affected by her inane and commonplace air interview, though in earlier days she knew the right kind of sympathetic publicity. Friends who saw her on TV report a disaster. How could it be otherwise? This harsh medium is not for the aged.

Yes, the [Berlin] Royal Opera was a lovely house indeed. The royal loge and the entire theater were hung with red velvet and gold. In the Hitler years, many remarkable improvements were made in the underground machinery to permit fine stage effects. The theater was a very old one and had undergone quite a few transformations over the years.

The sweetest little theater was the Munich Residenz Theater.[133] There, the decors were like a picture book. It was mostly for Mozart and chamber music. Ah well, such baroque delights are gone forever, I fear. It was my preferred style.

All good wishes for your journey, till we meet, GF

November 5, 1949

Dear Miss Stotler:

Your little sketch of the reception in the royal loge is very good. The Empress had very blue eyes, blond hair (quantities) and a fine, fair complexion. Her [eldest] son inherited the intensity of the blue eyes, the blond hair, a long "alter Fritz" nose and a small chin; a very marked resemblance to his ancestor [Frederick the Great].

The Crown Princess, quite as you have her; fair skin, pretty expression, but not actually handsome; châtain [auburn] hair in high style off the forehead. Tall and slender . . . a really charming, gay person, as I knew her.

Yes, I liked those drawings of Kahlil Gibran [poet and painter] that illustrated his books; something elusive and delicate in their outlines. He was a Syrian, a friend of a friend of mine. I heard him speak in most interesting fashion about the Bible parables and what had transpired in the different translations. In several cases I got quite a different meaning from what we read in our usual versions.

I did not like the first choice of the NBC concert program. I am not keen on Berlioz and have never been an admirer of Debussy . . . so while the Maestro was his usual impeccable musical self, I could have wished for other selections. But perhaps the somewhat moderate pace best suits him now; after all, with the exertion of rehearsals etc., there must be a few moments when "Homer nods."

Yes, I have had a correspondence over a long period with the

[133] This enchanting theater was designed by the dwarf architect, Cuvilles, under the Elector Karl Albrecht. It survived the bombs and reopened after World War II in all its mid-eighteenth-century splendor.

Pittsburgher, Matthew Frey. He should be an accomplished musician and teacher, though he is habitually modest about his own efforts.

A professional friend tells me she ran into Miss Garden at one of the candy shops in Manhattan, both indulging in a soda. My friend remarked that her face and body were extremely thin. Probably she has had her share of austerity programs.

We saw the picture *Mme. Bovary.* Miss Jennifer Jones would not have been my choice for the lead. I thought the whole production lacked taste and real feeling. Commonplace Hollywood.

The old flickers now and again are shown in various movie houses but usually to stress the comic side, with comments to illustrate the quick action and the melodrama that was considered so thrilling in other times. Vide Pearl White [star of the nickelodeon era].

I once saw a revival of *The Birth of a Nation.*[134] It was unbearably comic and I was fearful to see anything else of that period. At the time this was the cream of the screen crop and no doubt pointed the way to later improved focus. Griffith was the first to have the "close ups" depict facial expression; till then the scenes raced through in violent action.

Later:

The recent airplane tragedies linger in the mind. Why do such horrible things occur, and so many? A touching incident about the ill-fated French plane that crashed in the Azores was related over the radio. It seems the bodies were so charred as to be unrecognizable, though aids were doing their best by means of jewelry and such matter as did not suffer the flame. The young violinist, Ginette Neveu, who had opened the last concert series here, and was loudly praised by the press, was recognized by her tight hand on the violin case, that article being quite untouched by the fire. . . Is this not weird? Poor girl, she and her brother were on their way for professional engagements here. Not a soul survived the crash.

The wreck of yesterday at the DC airport is a calamity one cannot understand. An alien pilot mistaking the signals, the collision, and 55 persons catapulted to their death! The search is still going on, on land and in the Potomac.

Our very favorite resident in Wilton, Helen Hokinson, the clever wielder of the pen in the interests of the dowager figure, was

[134] The 1915 film epic about the Civil War era in the South by pioneer American film director D. W. Griffith.

burned to death on her way to speak at a meeting in Washington. It seems that the meeting had convened and was waiting for several guests who were due to arrive by this plane when the tragic news was given to the committee and made public, the audience standing at silent attention at the shocking narrative.

Violence and disaster, the order of the day in so many avenues.

I am going to be interested in the daily column beginning today in the *Herald Tribune* by Joseph Newman, who is back from Russia with a fund of information. It is given front page billing.

I now apply myself to the stuffy business of paying bills. One is always surprised when they arrive, though on scrutiny, the purchases are in order.

Our best greetings, GF

November 12, 1949

Dear Miss Stotler:

Just back from Kensico where we took our beautiful greens. The sun is brilliant; the languid young men are raking our lawn in desultory fashion. I wish I could put a firecracker under them . . . such lazy bones!

The sweeping Democratic victory in all the land, save New Jersey, that has finally thrown out that rotten boss, is but following the trend that has been obvious for many moons. We are now told via the air, that with this consolidation, we can expect Franklin [Roosevelt] Jr. for eventual New York governor, and his brother, James, California governor. I refrain from comment.

A huge convention of the Hoover Committee meets in Washington, December 12 and 13. I could not possibly undergo the confusion and excitement, and must await the printed report; but the ideals are good, and the speakers, with counsel for future activity, deserve a good hearing.

You ask about the procedure before royalty. In the case of the reception at the opera, or the palace, it was formal, and one curtsied with *Hand-kuss*. At smaller functions, when the royal family gave the cue, one could be more informal, but mindful of etiquette.

The conversation in the royal loge was in English; the Kaiserin was rather stiff though not unfriendly. One had the impression that her more voluble spouse held the stage and she subsided in such moments to a reserved Hintergrund [background]. There was a strong attachment between her eldest son and herself, and during the last years of her exile in Doorn, he was there much of the time, trying to make the event less painful. . . . Hitler had offered certain amends if the royal family, meaning the Kaiser and Kaiserin, cared to return to Berlin. It was a very wise decision to remain where they had been installed . . . there was not certainty of anything in the Nazi regime, and there would have been plots and counter-plots.

In passing through Holland every precaution was offered to protect the royal couple and nothing disturbed their last days there. At the death of the Kaiserin there was general disapproval of the second marriage; but no one need blame the old gentleman if he chose to avail himself of the devotion of a young and worshipful woman. Nothing about the situation was other than tragic, and could not finish otherwise than it did.

I have had other articles regarding the services for Richard Strauss. I suppose all the honors were done that could be, under existing circumstances and the disorder of the country. After all, what matter these attentions, if, during life, one received appreciation?[135]

Now off to village chores; all good wishes, GF

November —, 1949

Dear Miss Stotler:

I shall drop this in the post as we go to view *Christopher Columbus,* which should be an interesting movie. There is a hint of snow in the grey sky, but so far no errant flakes.

I spent a very busy day in New York, the special mission to see a friend who is sailing for a year in Europe. We lunched in the excellent restaurant in Grand Central, thus saving time and motion. Now the next trip will be on the 11th of December for the incomparable Flagstad.

I came home in time to catch the most lovely Toscanini concert; a delicate bit of lace-work in Boccherini—the Ravel Suite had dizzy orchestral effects.

The lowest form of morbidity came over the air today; a program entitled, "Voices that Live." There were half hour recordings of earlier fine singers, among them a charming song by Calvé, beautifully sung, and then, 36 hours before her death, a spoken farewell

[135] Famous both as a conductor and composer, especially of operas, Richard Strauss (1864–1949) was first courted, then harassed by the Nazi authorities. In 1947 he was honored at a Strauss Festival in London.

that was painful, old and broken, with no real meaning. I was sick at heart. What *is* the matter with people these days?

Now I have heard Garden's cracked phrases, Alda's similar ones, the bass Caruso record, and this last gasp of Calvé. Why can they not remain in the frame of youth and lovely singing?

Yes, I have read that the mother of Paul Draper (that able tap dancer of the Communist tinge), one Muriel Draper, together with Paul Robeson's wife, have gone to Moscow. Mrs. Draper comes from an old and respectable Salem, Massachusetts, family; I knew them well. The Robeson lady, a very intelligent but utterly radical person, must have some odd appeal. The world is certainly cock-eyed.

I am reading a most disturbing and provocative book by Lillian Smith called *Killers of the Dream*. It gives one to think, in its brutal exposure of the cancer of the South. Her chief resentment seems to be fastened on segregation. I still have to find out what would be *her* remedy.

Well, I shall go out and try to think of the lesser evils, and contemplate the smiling heavens. They at least are beyond cavil!

All good greetings, GF

November 29, 1949

Dear Miss Stotler:

The soft snow fell all day yesterday, a pretty sight that gave me pleasure to watch; a feeling of coziness pervaded, music and reading were the interests.

Now that the turkey is being enjoyed in piecemeal left-overs, always so good, we must think of Christmas preparations; albeit ours will be of the simple kind, my mantel offering the usual green arbor to the crystal Madonna and her attendant angels, with here and there a bit of fragrant green at the doors.

No parties, for it is too much effort for my girls; but friends in at odd times for a cheering cup, until the snow falls in such amount as will imprison us . . . then we shall sit to our chore of making curtains to match the lovely upholstery work of the couch in my study.

I did like the film *Columbus*. I like English productions; much attention given to costumes, decors and casting. It is good for the girls to get something other than constant care of my wants, and our Playhouse is conveniently near.

I am glad your eye trouble will yield to stronger lens . . . but frankly, I should hardly think the [Burton] Holmes film would be the rest you need. Is not your attitude a trifle flippant?

The redoubtable Muriel Draper does come from a fine New England family. She is no radical, but a very tough bird, as you say.

Your letter of Tuesday asks me, "Was I a flirt?" Well really, I could not tell you. You will have to take Mother's word for it, as she was often moved to remonstrate when I was gay and spontaneous; for though she was lively, she was always cautious—and I never was. My impulses have been nicely curbed by time and experience, however.

I recall many tales by the gifted Marie Corelli [writer of dramatic fiction]; but the odd and impossible trial to accommodate a personality to glands that have actually been rejuvenated was most eloquently expressed, I thought, in Gertrude Atherton's *Black Oxen*. Her writings always carried a hint of her own personal reactions; perhaps the reason they had such spirit of genuine feeling.

This subject was also dealt with, in a very simple but thoughtful manner, in a play, *Mrs. Moonlight* [by B. W. Levy]. An airy fairy creature, granted the wish to remain forever young, in the end became an odd and suffering intruder into the natural development of the rest of her family.

Now to lunch and my portion of the home bird. Miss Sylvia's party was a gay affair, and I came home in time to greet her friends. Mutzi had a red ribbon after a sweet-smelling bath, and was fêted also.

All good wishes, and I hope no bad effects of the holiday. GF

November 29, 1949

Dear Miss Stotler:

I must go to the village after all, so will drop another note.

Thank you for your pretty pen fancy of the *Hand-kuss* episode. There was an ante-chamber back of the loge, a more intimate one, that gave the impression of being on the stage; very much nicer when one wished to see the details of a production. Such loges also exist in the Paris Grand Opera. When there were very formal and large groups, the huge Hof Loge, in the center of the opera house, was used, and an array of aides-de-camp were at the portals.

It was all so lovely, and because of one's youth, no doubt doubly precious in retrospect.

I have just had a letter from an old comrade of those days, who writes with such pathos, "Our good Kapellmeister, Leo Blech[136] is back here, and at 72 has lost none of his fire and *Schwung* [verve]. A recent *Carmen* with Gianani [Giannini?] was a huge success, and others under his baton." Then the singer goes on to say, "Alas, the Kapellmeister can well continue in energy, where the unfortunate singer of like vintage cannot compete." How true, indeed!

I have just read in *Town and Country* a very amusing article by a man dressmaker of the mode, certain souvenirs of the once fabulous Lady Duff Gordon (sister to Elinor Glynn—she of the *Three Weeks* book of sensational sale) who made lovely frocks, mainly for slender fairies like Irene Castle,[137] and could not resign her crown to the later Lanvin and Schiaparelli who lifted the dress to knee length, and lowered the waist-line below the kidneys . . . a most distressing distortion. Duff Gordon fumed to no avail; fashion is a jade who follows the latest crank irrespective of taste and individual appeal.

Just now I read that moleskins are colored tomato-red and broadtail is purple hued. What next?

A friend from London writes that [Salvador] Dali, of all people, was allowed to stage the local production of *Salomé* and that [soprano Lubja] Welitsch had hard work to overcome his silly quirks . . . .

We once had such a *fou* in *La Reine Fiamette,* a Russian with perverted ideas of the Italian Renaissance; but I got hold of the aquarelles, and was ready with colors in my costumes, and a fiery wig that set his ridiculous effects to shame. Also, with the aid of my trusty electrician, *two* spotlights never left my person! There was many an argument, but I won out!

Sorry to say the opera was not worth our time and efforts.

I recall one time that Urban, a fine artist when he wanted to be, was utterly depraved about opera after the stark colorings for the *Follies.*

In the garden of Marguerite [*Faust*], I sat under a dark chestnut tree which was dripping with huge purple grapes . . . this, too,

136 See letter of September 4, 1946.

137 American dancer Irene Castle (1897–1969) and her English husband Vernon (1877–1918) were a greatly admired couple who brought new refinement to ballroom dancing in the years immediately preceding World War I. They popularized the Argentinean tango and invented several dances, including the Castle Walk, that became all the rage. Vernon died in an accident at a Texas airfield, where he was serving as an instructor.

needed an entire revision of my costume; but happily there was also Gounod's lovely music . . . of immortal memory.

Best of good wishes, GF

Later:

The Saturday Toscanini concert was exceptionally beautiful, I thought. It gave me great pleasure. That lovely Beethoven . . . so sure, so calm, so inspiring.

I heard Kreisler last evening with the "Telephone" group. Much of the luscious tone was present, though I trembled with apprehension, for he is not well, and not too young . . . but has been *such* a fine artist. I wish he would retire for the sake of his luminous career. So few however share my feeling about retirement, that I fancy I am alone in it.

I do not mean to discourage you, but I cannot see the interest in breasting opinions so divergent to your own; inviting expressions that may or may not be genuine in the art circle, and will only cause you emotional disturbances. If several of you feel so strongly about present management, why not withdraw and form your own chosen group? There is no law against that, is there? I hate strife and do not seek it.

My appointment to the title of Kammersängerin [court singer] was conferred on me by cable, as at that time I was a member of the MET and busy on these shores. There was no Orden [medal] connected with it. The usual Orden, for those of the music or theater world, was given instead of actual fees. If one sang enough one could go jingling to quite a loud clang, with all the little medals pinned to the lapel.

One had also presents of jewelled objects, and of these I have quite a few, but I do not expose them. They are in their cases in the safe deposit box.

I did not count your roses, but they filled three vases, as I told you on the phone. They were a glorious yellow that brought sunshine into my study. You need not worry but that Mr. Martin will give you value—indeed they are most honest people. I expressed the wish for the yellow color since he was good enough to inquire my preference.

December 8, 1949

Dear Miss Stotler:

Winds are howling and the snowflakes fly. I shall try to get to the post before the dark comes on.

I love the music of *Rosenkavalier* so the indifferent radio performance of last Saturday did not distress me too much. The cast was not distinguished, and the Reiner direction in the pit was heavy; none of the enchanting details were present, and that lovely women's trio of the last act entirely unbalanced.

What a joy to hear, on the "Firestone Hour," the aristocratic renditions of Marian Anderson; even through the ether waves the nobility of the woman permeated every phrase.

Strauss *was* a great composer, and those ridiculous observations in the first entr'acte were insulting. I wonder what bird-brain writes for the others to read aloud? One can dismiss these chatterers with scant courtesy.

In re throat operations, I could speak of much experience in the matter, but if you do not mind, we shall let what I have written in my book be the ultimate; it is not a pleasant memory.

I knew of Chevalier Jackson; he has treated many a singer for the aftermath of vocal strain and incidents of professional vocal cords. He has a high reputation.

It is a delicate and most annoying treatment at best, nor do the results always bring perfect success. While these little bands of tissue can resist great impact of tone and breath, yet once the delicate and ill membrane is removed to permit a new imposition, there is need of great care to gentle it. It will not bear the same tension as the original tissue. I suppose, actually, we are not intended to constantly subject the process of speech and singing to hours of artificially induced response. It is a nightmare to have to worry about these things.

Our greetings, GF

P.S. If you would really like to know what would give me pleasure for Christmas? A large size pen sketch (such as you do so well, and the usual size of the Red Cross posters) that I could put outside my entrance door and wreath with greens. A jolly smiling Santa Claus, with swirling glittering snow behind him, in the sleigh, or only his laughing face if you prefer. I leave the decors to your fancy, if the idea suits your time and energy.

December 12, 1949

Dear Miss Stotler:

I do not know when I can get out to post my mail; we are befogged and I have to use caution in driving. This fog along with the ice kept me from going into New York yesterday, greatly to my disappointment. I did not attend the Flagstad concert or the reception to honor her. It must have been another fine treat. My friends reported the same fabulous ease and graciousness. I shall content myself with her latest London records, the next best thing.

Regarding the Reiner conducting of *Rosenkavalier,* it appeared to me that it was a heavy handed performance, but then again, to be fair, I think I have mentioned previously that the position of the mikes, as well as stage movements, often give a very uneven effect in singing as well as in the orchestra. Mechanics are wonderful in their way but not fool-proof yet.

Yes, this is an ugly press photo of Garden; but then such "candid" effects are never flattering. Old bones and brittle ones undoubtedly caused her injury in the fall. She has courage to want to continue the dreary round. She is said to sail the night of the 26th, but this may be a rumor. There will be no exchange of cards; the once I did so and received the courtesy in return, was only to hope for the publication of her book. Whether or not she has one in the making, I would not know.

Mrs. McCormack [wife of tenor John McCormack] is bringing out one of her husband. I hope for her sake there are no disappointments. There was one during his lifetime, no great seller.

Dorothy Caruso has one of her husband [*Enrico Caruso*, 1945] consisting mostly of very personal anecdotes and letters, pleasant enough reading. It may be this book will be the basis for a film *Life of Caruso.* She is said to be in negotiation with the Hollywood agents. . . . This is easy. They write anyone who has material; then you might have years of waiting before it comes to the screen; and when this auspicious moment *does* arrive, dollars to doughnuts, the genius(?) script writers have given it their own peculiar interpretation.

I recall my disgust when MGM acquired the Kreisler operetta, *Sissy,* based on the life of the lovely Empress Elizabeth of Austria. The original music was played as *Appleblossoms* with nothing to do with the Empress text. Then the composer reworked the music into another text about her. This version was played in Vienna, Munich and Berlin, where I heard it. A most charming piece.

When the screen had finished with it, as a vehicle for Grace Moore, it was so changed and the text so commonplace, I could have wept. It was called thus, *The King Steps Out,* and the opening scene was of Elizabeth milking a cow at Possenhoffen . . . so it goes.

I heard only some portions of the *Manon Lescaut,* which is the true slancio [enthusiasm] of Puccini and has not a hint, for my money, of the exquisite French élégance . . . the Puccini music soars always and is so grateful for the vocalist, but the Gallic touch is nowhere evident. It is such a truly French picture that one easily grants the supremacy of the Massenet work as the veritable tableau.

The French text has its own particular grace; heard once, it is not possible to accept less. I assure you this role in German is fully as incongruous as *Tannhaüser* in French—which is almost effeminate.

I do not agree with Mr. Lissfelt re Maggie Teyte [English soprano]. She specializes in the French repertoire. For me, the voice is brittle, cold and very stylized. A pupil of [tenor] Jean de Reszke, I had the feeling (as with many of his pupils and those of [coloratura Marcella] Sembrich) that these past masters of song had grafted onto their aspirants the methods by which they had to a certain extent defied time; thus the natural ebullience of a young singer was founded on the older *art,* not the individual spontaneity. Also there is little use for extended range in this genre of French singing, so one never knows if the singer is really endowed with a normal range and dynamics . . . however this is my personal reaction.

Did you hear the excellent and at times humorous address of Hoover at the Citizens' Conference? He did not mince matters, but the 22 million odd leeches on the government payroll, alas, will not be eliminated. I have no confidence in the Truman intent to the right kind of economy. If he has it he should begin with his own circle.

Fulton Lewis, Jr., is indeed a crusader. One wonders if the delay in pursuing the [anti-Communist] material is not another clampdown from the powers that be. Washington must have been crawling with Russ spies and home Commies all through the FDR years. Shame on him!

I gather Pegler has some inside information about the lady present with the artist at the Warm Springs house [where FDR went for treatments]. What difference does it make, all this hinting at a little scandal? All water under the bridge, and pretty stagnant in view of so much that is rampant in the news and more important for public information. The other is really a concern of the wife, after all.

My 500 Christmas cards are addressed; some rainy day we shall sit to close and stamp them—a good chore indeed.

Our greetings to you, GF

December 18, 1949

Dear Miss Stotler:

The two wonderfully fine Santas came in last night's post and are to be hung today. Many thanks for your kindness and prompt execution. They will give a warm spot of color and greeting to my friends who are due here for an informal tea-party.

As to the bestowal of my musical material to the New England Conservatory, the trustees did everything they could to induce me to come for a reception for they were truly grateful for the donation. But such affairs do not appeal to me and I "regretted" with the best alibi that I could. I did assist at the presentation some years ago of many such memoirs of an American singer, Marcia van Dresser; the donations were brought from her home in England by a trusted friend, and it seemed a courteous thing to do at the time, since I was going back and forth on errands connected with the institution.

Later on they shall inherit other bequests from me if they wish. If not, they can be disposed of for the general fund I intend to give to Roosevelt Hospital, in memory of my parents.

Yours of Saturday at hand. I thought *Tristan* had many dull moments, due to the performers, and also—tell it not in Gath—because "der heilige Richard," in all his operas, has the well-known Teutonic insistence on lengthy explanations that bring to a standstill the dramatic action; the long harangues of Wotan, Fricka, the Norns, the dying Tristan—and very objectionable a picture is the present incumbent with his Gargantuan silhouette [the tenor Lauritz Melchior] that heaves mightily across the footlights—and the cursing Ortrud, to name just a few erratic moments.

So *very* much phraseology!

I agree that the pageantry of the Catholic Church has much to recommend it in the warm, lovely impressions and color, the emotional swing, where the colder Protestant worshippers have to sit out so many dreary sermons with no appeal to the senses. In the end it is probably more easy to sway the group emotionally, than to convince one separate individual fighting for his own thought. The Catholic Church has also great flexibility and understanding of human nature.

And it trains its neophytes in organization with one thought . . . it works for them well, in the main.

I understand an invitation *was* extended to Flagstad to join the MET, and she refused. She does not need this present institution but they could do with the box office she would be for them.

How very good to know that your eye trouble is gone. I have all the pen fancies labelled and dated; they recall so many pleasant activities, thanks to your talent and interest.

My Christmas dinner, midday, will be with Mrs. G. in Stamford, if the roads are clear.

And now, may your Christmas Eve be a happy one, and ensuing holidays as well. Health and humor are the best qualities I know and cherish—may they be yours in abundance!

Our best of auguries for 1950. GF

December —, 1949

Dear Miss Stotler,

Well, the gay times are over and the aftermath is a birthday party for a dear friend to close the holidays.

Now to your Christmas parcels . . . we had our gifts Christmas Eve in quiet enjoyment. Thank you for the amusing garden gloves, the smiling angel, and the pretty bowl. You have been much too generous, so perhaps you should be scolded!

I did not listen to the opera broadcast; I was busy with other matters. I believe Miss Garden was to have spoken during the entr'acte. Her New York lecture comes on this evening. I can imagine the French singer with her—formerly of the MET—will have the task of "eating time" with his songs. Heaven knows what she will say; so far there has been no properly prepared address, just a series of quips.

I have just been regretting several requests for public appearances. One is to be the recording program at the Metropolitan on the 17th of January. The very amiable gentleman [Milton Cross] who does this hour on the radio has taken the opera house to give an evening of recordings, hoping to have costumes of the singers on young models to enliven the occasion.

I have tried to make my refusal as gracious as possible. I cannot picture myself rising up in a loge to receive plaudits (perhaps too well drilled, as in radio) like a relic of old—or a ghost, albeit a plump one! These affairs where one must present one's self in the legend of other days are a mistake to my way of thinking . . . perhaps those who go are happy to bask once more in a warmed-over wave of admiration.

My tea party was a gay and informal one. I do not sit down, for two friends usually handle the table, while I mingle to see that everyone is well placed and knows her neighbor. I wore a black velvet gown with a low neck and black lace cut-out; a pretty frock it is.

My New Year's greetings, and may all go to your wishing. GF

1950

April 25, 1950

Dear Miss Stotler:

A busy day in town yesterday, to say goodbye to my friends; then home in the usual inundation of the prevalent April showers.

I begin soon the third Churchill book, *The Grand Alliance,* another résumé that I take with caution, knowing the doughty power of the Englishman and respecting the same; nevertheless, I have never understood why we are swung to any side save that of our own best interests.

I have concluded the Hoover book [*Our Unknown President,* by Eugene Lyons]; it is factual and makes me wrothy to see with what vicious manners the succeeding officials went out of their way to smear him. He is no doubt a God-fearing and patient man, who will reap the results of forbearance and proper conduct.

Mme. Eames,[138] as I told you, disapproves of my *America First* attitude, which is her privilege, but some who share her viewpoint may come to find it not a bad idea. I have so little patience with those who react more strongly to European affiliations than to their own country's welfare. I still feel that I am a better patriot than she, for I did not forswear America to return to these shores only when there was no other comfortable place to finish existence.

It is unimportant, anyway, but she was born in Shanghai (her father was captain of his ship at the time) and she actually stems from Bath, Maine. I do not know her politics; I should imagine that they are the same as mine.

I did like her, though she had a sharp tongue and was never over friendly to people in general. We never had any feud in the opera; it seems to have been the recent war that changed her. Well, no matter; she has to make peace with herself as we all must.

What a hard time it is! Mr. Hoover has more trust in humans than it is my fortune to share. I only perform the personal duties to the best of my ability. Now to the Garden Club and another Blood Bank meeting.

138 Admired American soprano Emma Eames sang leading roles at the Metropolitan Opera between 1891 and 1909. Miss Farrar related an incident that occurred during Eames's farewell performance in *Tosca.* During the dinner scene with Scarpia, the audience noticed to its horror that the tablecloth had taken fire from a candle. Without missing a note, Mme. Eames snatched up the cloth and rubbed it briskly together until the flame was extinguished. Needless to say, the applause was deafening.

Shall we set June 14 for your arrival in the village with Miss Aida? The weather should be fine by then.

Best greetings, GF

Pennywise
Cape Vincent, New York
August 9, 1950

Dear Miss Stotler:

Cool, sunny, cheery days—really an idyllic time on this broad river. If only one could ignore the horrid headlines and this ugly Korean business.

Now we have undertaken the stupendous job to police the free fronts. I fear it will come to a showdown—stupids that we are.

Meanwhile, the skies are clear, nature smiles. I must try to emulate her.

Later:

Our first shower, rather hot and muggy in consequence. The farmers will not like it, in view of their grain just ready to cut.

The book of San Francisco is of too early a date for much opera comment. It carries it to the time of the earthquake[139] with Caruso mentioned, 1906, Spring. I did not return to these shores until that November, and save for one brief opera tour with the Scotti Company my appearances there were on the concert stage. Other volumes have been confined to the movies, and therein full compliment paid us all.

Yes, I knew Clyde Fitch [playwright] quite well; a "precieux" and very advanced for his era. I was devoted to Belasco,[140] too.

And now to join dinner guests,
Best greetings, GF

---

[139] At the time of the earthquake, the Metropolitan Opera Company was on tour in San Francisco. Sembrich, Scotti, and Plançon assembled in the lobby of their hotel and waited anxiously for Caruso. When he finally appeared his head was wrapped in a towel, and he was clutching a silver-framed autographed photograph of President Theodore Roosevelt. Members of the company and orchestra were unhurt, but all the instruments were destroyed. Mme. Sembrich made a most generous gesture in refusing her salary until these could be replaced.

[140] David Belasco, famous theatrical producer, who at one time offered his theater to Miss Farrar for dramatic roles. She did not accept.

Pennywise
Cape Vincent, New York
August 14, 1950

Dear Miss Stotler:

A very cool day that requires woolens and coat; the river a frosty blue. Our gaiety here is informal; there is no great effort at dressing or table service. Many gatherings with buffet, at the edge of the river under the trees. I am not partial to this, as the insects like me too well, but for the present the cool winds keep them at bay.

General [Lucius D.] Clay is warning New York State and vicinity of plans to meet any emergency.[141] I think I did mention that our village might have to share in the care of evacuees . . . I fear that a rush of Manhattan aliens would be highly distasteful to me; not at all to my liking. But if such an eventuality arose, one would have to do what one could.

Yes, I have always thought that [General Douglas] MacArthur is too much of a *man* to have patience with the politicos in Washington. He is needed in his present role, but he would be ousted in a minute if that crowd could do without him.[142]

As to the Korean mess we have only ourselves to blame since FDR and his cohorts at Yalta and Potsdam gave open-handed to the Russ. Now we pay a hideous price, that hardly has begun to demand its dividends. Never doubt, it will.

Later:

A breathtaking day of blue sky and the river like a mill-pond. After church many will take to the fishing boats. I am told the lampreys have been so savage and numerous that the bass are having difficulty to survive. Killers are everywhere, it seems.

We have charming guests from down the river. The porch is a perfect retreat from the cool winds that incline one to shelter of this kind—and screened.

All good wishes, GF

---

141 An attack by the Russians on the eastern seaboard was considered a possibility at this time.

142 MacArthur, who was in command of the United Nations forces fighting in North Korea, wished to pursue a more aggressive policy than the Truman administration was willing to support.

September 27, 1950

Dear Miss Stotler:

Last minute donors for the Blood Bank are signing up. Some have been away, others were suffering from colds; we are hopeful now of our quota.

I have out my pretty yellow uniform, my nurses' aides are getting together, the motor corps is ready and the canteen service will be on hand. All Thursday and Friday we shall have our hands full. We have the Odd Fellows' Hall by courtesy of this organization. The village groups are never laggard in cooperation. A small locale is known person by person, and carries a pleasant sense of general interest.

Your posters are here and are most effective. Thank you for getting them to me so promptly. I know of your indisposition and fear I should have refrained from asking you to take such pains . . . but *Blood* for the saving of lives is our immediate objective, and though this Korean tide has apparently taken a turn in our favor, it is not without great loss of life—alas, alas.

You ask what my Red Cross work is? Well, as Chairman of Voluntary Services I have five units to supervise.

1. Staff Aides—to which I belong, a purely clerical group, who have all the typing, correspondence etc., to handle.
2. Production and Supply—which is for the peacetime Veteran Hospitals to provide attentions not furnished by the Government.
3. Motor Transport—Mostly active for blood banks and such group needs. Now we are not in surgical dressings; otherwise we do all the service of delivery of material, raw and finished, to whatever chapter is designated, though not farther than New York.
4. Entertainment and Instruction—Has to do with making life a little more pleasant for incurables (veterans) and to give them some hobby or activity of therapeutic interest.
5. Blood Bank—Canteen Service (only on tap when the Blood Bank is in action, perhaps four times a year).

I have a monthly report to make for the Danbury Chapter, but this is not tedious. All will depend on how many Blood Banks we must offer per year, and if or when the surgical dressings demand cooperation, as in the last war. One hopes Korea will be the turning point and engender no further combat . . . but . . .

I suppose we shall have another National Chairman for Red Cross, now that General Marshall[143] is accepted to replace [Louis Arthur] Johnson, as Secretary of Defense.

The heavy smog, reports of which the radio and press are full, does, indeed, emanate from the forest fires in Canada. They must be dreadful to cast such a pall in the heavens. Friends who arrived by plane from England were detained hours on their approach to our shores. So thick was the smoke that the passengers could not discern the wings!

This occurrence evidently spoiled the effect of the eclipse. One lady called in to the press, "At what hour would it be resumed?" Evidently thinking it could be turned on and off at will.

No doubt you had fun with the inventory of the old Singer mansion in Wilkinsburg. You say it reminded you of the house in the *Circular Staircase,* of Mary Roberts Rinehart. A good story, that.

I took the girls to see *Sunset Boulevard,* a most painful but well presented story of the aging Gloria Swanson. It made a very sad impression on me. So many professionals refuse to accept their years, and labor to the point of exhaustion in the furtherance of their ego. Many of the older players were like corpses; the presence of Henry Warner was quite inexcusable—once a likable and talented actor. Mr. De Mille seemed dreadfully feeble and aged. It was not a happy moment for my taste. Several of the chorus extras who had worked with me in 1914 tottered in and out—pretty gruesome!

My best greetings, and no more indisposition! GF

October 2, 1950

Dear Miss Stotler:

The most heavenly day of June warmth and sunshine. We take out the Summer frocks again and lay aside the wools; it is nice to bask in this cheery moment.

This is a busy week; all the donors for the Blood Bank will be on hand for the great day, Friday. Your posters are admired by all; they carry a more personal note than the official ones.

Perhaps I told you I was asked again if I would serve on the Price Control Board, and have signified my willingness. Since I am

143 A five-star general, George Catlett Marshall (1880–1959) served as Secretary of State from 1947 to 1949, during which time he organized the European Recovery Program known as the "Marshall Plan." This earned him the 1953 Nobel Prize for Peace.

entirely sympathetic to the civilians, I can further their interests better than a paid and over-zealous agent, all too happy to bring in "heads" at the slightest provocation. We shall see the results of such tactics once the election is over.

The textile shortages are becoming obvious, gently, in the pencil and sheath skirt, and other restlessness of women's fashions. I am not buying other than simple sports frocks, and an occasional afternoon dress that will do duty for the infrequent dinners that I attend. Evening parties I try to avoid, as they tire and bore me.

Today I am off to acquire shoes in Danbury, as shortages in this line are to be expected, and this family will profit by early purchases.

Sunday

The great event is over, with surprisingly good results. Thursday we prepared the hall and its rooms for the equipment, scrubbing and sweeping. I took down white sheets to cover unsightly walls, and the place was spic and span. Miss Sylvia was a glutton for work; I could not have done without her. We placed all the posters around the walls; they were bright and cheery, thanks to your efforts of recent years.

We had 158 acceptances, but so many were afflicted with the prevailing hay-fever sniffles and high blood pressure, that we could only take 110. This number was greeted with such jubilation by the Danbury chapter [of the Blood Bank] that we were not too disappointed; but those rejected were really mortified, as if it had been something of a stigma.

I would much prefer activity along other lines; this is a nasty business and everyone is uneasy. We have many boys being inducted and the parents are far from agreeable to the mess we are now obliged to confront, thanks to the stupid follies of previous officials . . . however we must do our best now.

All good wishes, GF

October 14, 1950

Dear Miss Stotler:

The shades of a lovely, luscious twilight are falling over our hills. One is happy to have eyes to feast on it. I have been busy, as usual, all day, but this hour brings truly a most restful quiet and delight.

I am not too familiar with the outline of Pittsburgh. When I came, it was to sing, and to guard, if possible, against the smoky air, which always troubled me. I was at the [Hotel] Schenley, which offered a pleasant atmosphere, then down-town if I had to catch a train immediately afterward. I daresay now, with no professional responsibilities, I should not so much mind the heavy, fog-like atmosphere. This always colored my waking hours.

I must thank you again for the grapes; they are like a rich perfume in the dining room, where they graced the center table at a tea I offered some committee ladies.

Miss Jeanette MacDonald[144] had very pleasing press notices in her Carnegie Hall concert here. She should be happy about her Metropolitan appearances. She is a hard worker.

I think you will be amazed at the announcement here enclosed. The older members who have stood loyally by the opera and given generously when asked, are now excluded from the traditional opening night, always a great event to usher in the Fall season; and have to pay an extra subscription if they care to go. Two other performances are in the same scheme—no one seems to know what it is all about.

The opening opera, *Don Carlos,* an old fashioned thing, has been given twice in my memory at the MET. It needs stars even to sing the phrases that are truly Verdian.

We keep well and are busy with small chores in house and garden. Bulbs will soon go in . . . happy thought for Spring.

Our greetings, GF

October 23, 1950

Dear Miss Stotler:

Here rallies are the order of the day, and the usual pre-election antics are in full swing [off-year election of November 7]. I shall vote with none too sanguine a heart, for the trend of the times is worldwide, and we are not of the pattern that is forming.

Mr. Hoover was not far wrong when he warned of the trouble likely to result from pledging our resources all over the earth. I see no point in ramming down our procedures when it is obvious they

[144] Extremely popular in Broadway musicals and films, where she was first partnered by Maurice Chevalier and then by Nelson Eddy, Jeanette MacDonald (1901–1967) also performed as a concert artist.

are in great need of revision directed to home affairs if we wish to set a shining example.

The indecision and general conduct of the UN, as well as that of Truman, are maddening. A grim outlook for Christmas. What do the beaten soldiers think of retracing their hard-won tracks to hope for safe evacuation by the sea? Now the blame must be pushed on MacArthur, which is as cowardly a thing as has come to light in these many days. The desk generals and advisers are trying desperately to make him the scape-goat, but the general public is not so gullible.

No, I do not believe I gave the impression that Miss MacDonald considered the MET. I understand that Patrice Munsel replaces [Lily] Pons when the latter does not care to appear. Munsel's voice appears a thin, tight one, but I am told she is adept and graceful on stage. One really should never judge by radio—no true medium of expression.

Flagstad is in San Francisco where there is a season of opera with stellar casts recruited from the MET. Her New York concert will be on the 10th of December, for which we have our tickets as usual. I hope she is rested and in her finest estate. I do not care to sit through *Fidelio*, it is symphonic, not opera music.

Now to the village and its chores,
Our good wishes, GF

November 8, 1950

Dear Miss Stotler:

I was absent all day Sunday with friends, and yesterday I went to listen to the TV opening [of Verdi's *Don Carlos*] at the MET.

It was quite an improvement on the first performance; the camera men were careful of angles, gave the stars the best lighting and frame possible, and the close-ups were more frequent, thus allowing the facial expressions to carry. The only thing that disturbs me at present is the non-flattering conveyance of the vocal quality. There is plenty of volume, but all sounds nasal and tinny . . . I feel it fair to reserve judgment of the singers until I hear them in person at the coming Saturday matinee . . . I thought the contralto [Fedora Barbieri] by far the finest, very spontaneous, generous in the tonal outpour, and with a fine sense of the dramatic . . . even in this rather stilted opera. The Schiller tragedy does not come off well, but there are some fine parts; only too many memories evoked of a more potent *Aida*.

The house was evidently jammed; the cameras caught the so-called social high lights . . . but the women were, none of them, beautiful or alluring. They all looked, in their daringly cut frocks and slicked hair, like the filles-de-joie, with much of the *joie* left out. Heavy, big mouths, squinty eyes, greased hair . . . all the Hollywood gloss. This pancake foundation gives a mask that is far from attractive.

I am glad you enjoyed the Burton Holmes lecture; he is a remarkable person and a charming gentleman. Long may he live, if he wishes to do so.

No, I never knew the late King of Sweden, but his predecessor, Oscar,[145] was also a delightful gentleman who loved opera and the theater.

I have always been at war with G. B. Shaw.[146] He is a contrary cuss, and some of his works were timely and amusing. However I like a richer soil for the theater; not to be bombarded with a constant stream of ironies and sarcasms.

Now to the village to judge some posters for the school children, though what good I shall do is problematical. I shall go by the pleasure afforded, if any.

Our best greetings, GF

November 9, 1950

Dear Miss Stotler:

Dull skies with menace of snow; but our spirits are considerably lightened by the surprisingly good results for the GOP. We got rid of [Democrat Chester] Bowles, though I could wish a change in the Connecticut senators, too; however, with Taft, Warren, Dewey, and some others, Uncle Harry [Truman] will not have it all his own way. The Red menace and the war have perhaps awakened the too easy citizen to the perils this country can expect at the hands of its native sons.

I still claim that the America First without any entangling alliances would have been the best policy for these USA. FDR was

---

145 Miss Farrar enjoyed greatly her guest visits to the opera in Stockholm. King Oscar never missed her performances and honored her with Sweden's Order of Merit.

146 George Bernard Shaw (1856–1950), Irish-born playwright, music and drama critic, and social and political commentator, is best known for his plays, many of them highly satirical, including *Pygmalion, Man and Superman, Major Barbara,* and *Joan of Arc.* In 1925 he was awarded the Nobel Prize in literature. Proclaiming his disdain of public honors, he is quoted as saying, "I do not wish to sit in the House of Lords and I have already conferred the O.M. (Order of Merit) on myself."

certainly a sick man to have allowed himself to be jockeyed into the position for which we now have to pay so dearly.

A letter from a dear friend, the excellent doctor in Munich whose clinic I frequently attended, says that were it not for (1) his profession and (2) his music—as the whole family including in-laws and grandchildren are regular performers in string quartettes etc.—he, too, would go mad.

This is in relation to your cousin, the [German] artist Bernhard Mosl's reference to keeping one's eye and heart open to beauty . . . in some form that the spirit may grasp.

All well after a strenuous housecleaning.

All good greetings, GF

November 15, 1950

Dear Miss Stotler:

Crisp and sunny days, always a good omen for activity.

The matinee of *Don Carlos* had its points, though the work is an old-fashioned one, and needs good actors as well as singers. There was only one, the mezzo, Fedora Barbieri, who had fire and spontaneity. Miss Margaret Webster, new to opera direction but born and bred in the theater, no doubt labored to the best of her ability to bring some idea of stage conduct.

The conductor, Fritz Stiedry, had impossible tempi and no clear understanding of Italianate feeling. The new decors and costumes were pleasing and Miss Webster gave a most felicitous TV interview. Mr. Bing,[147] so far, has not been inspiring in his several discourses; we shall see his results.

You will have seen by the press that the lovely Marlowe[148] has finally passed to her rest, much to be desired, as the last few years she has been invalided and without much realization of the passing scene.

Before coming home I saw in the New York papers the unhappy incident of a demented Ridgefield man who nearly killed his little son. The parent has been committed to an institution and the child is on his way to recovery. A horrible affair made all the more

---

147 Sir Rudolf Bing, manager of the Metropolitan Opera from 1950 to 1972.

148 The distinguished actress Julia Marlowe (1866–1950) had died in New York on November 12. She was said to have appeared in more Shakespearian dramas and before a larger total audience than any other actor or actress.

sad for the little one was his father's favorite and even now he asks for his parent. The mother and two other children are also being cared for by public contribution. Our village is always very generous for our home people and their troubles.

Our Blood Bank is due here October 6th. It is *not* in Danbury but in our own village as usual only now we have the added state equipment in the machines, and medical attendants joining with our local aids. We shall probably use the Odd Fellows' Hall as a very convenient place.

Now to a meeting. All good wishes and I hope the knee is better.

GF

November 25, 1950

Dear Miss Stotler:

I do not know when this letter will be posted; the wind velocity has suddenly overwhelmed us here in the night, and is now screaming and raging. The rain has turned to hail, and alas, my lovely trees are crashing all about us. I hope it will not be the roof-top that sails away in the storm, that does not seem to abate since early last evening. Blizzards and snow are the news from the North. I hate wind—it is impossible to do anything in its evil force. I am watching with trepidation if the big pine tree over my front porch will crash on our roof; it would be a real disaster, for no workman could possibly help us while this gale is on.

No electricity, but if the walls hold tight we are not too badly off. We did our week-end shopping yesterday, and we can put on enough woolens to be comfortable.

All good wishes. Miss Sylvia and I keep house while Margaret is warm and cozy with her Jersey family—we hope.

GF

November 27, 1950

Dear Miss Stotler:

We read of deep snow and bitter cold in your region, and perhaps your papers have carried our hurricane results. The toll of trees has been high; my evergreens crash as I write you and there is great damage in the woodlands. We are still more fortunate than many; 1,000 evacuated in New Milford. I shall replant only the low evergreens, thus saving such loss in future. I shall order the large pine cut down as it could easily have crashed into the rose room. We watched it sway onto the roof with great surge.

As yet we have no heat and light; the dog and the canary are well wrapped in their woolens. We drove about an hour in the village to enjoy the heat of the car, and are going to the movies—to keep warm.

I can well appreciate your regret at the decision to move from your present home, but it would after all seem a wise decision with times as they are and no one ready or willing to companion one. Yes, I think Miss Aida is courageous in building now; a house of any size brings such cares to keep it in good order. This home that we love takes so much money, strength and time for its upkeep.

Later:

We saw the picture *Red Shoes* [with Moira Shearer and Robert Helpmann] at our movie house. Save for the old man cobbler, [Léonid] Massine, was not too impressed by the highly touted cast. Two full hours of ballet, with continuous acrobatics, bored me after a while. Certain scenes at Monte Carlo were agreeable in retrospect.

I do not know if or when operations were performed on the throat of the lovely Marlowe. To the last I found her voice delightful and of great sweetness. Many now speaking on the radio have a harsh tone which seems to me like affection [malady] of the vocal cords themselves. That little huskiness that is not pleasing to the ear—note [Tallulah] Bankhead, and the Barrymore's murky tones. To me this represents overtired or misused cords in the vocal production.

I knew the Puccini *Manon Lescaut* many years ago but never sang it. The music is lovely and sensuous, passionate and haunting. The Massenet work is replete with charm and elegance, as are the French singers who perform, as against their more uninhibited Italian confreres. Italians are fundamentally vocal . . . they have *the* precious voices.

Thanks for the article on Caruso . . . vivid as of yesterday, I can still hear that impeccable voice, in its unique velvety quality. In addition to his great natural gift, the greatest, I believe, that I have known, he worked unceasingly to perfect his breathing, technic, and the building up of his roles, for he was an emotional and intelligent actor.

We all loved him, and he was devoted to my parents, especially my mother, whom he called "Mammina" in the Neapolitan manner.[149]

My Mutzi will have to be put to dodo, as the French have it. She is blind and her legs so stiff, it is not possible for her to move about well. She will be better not to struggle, and I not to have to watch her. We will look out for two brother dachies afterward—babies to raise in the Springtime.

Our best to you, GF

December 4, 1950

Dear Miss Stotler:

The rain is pouring down but one is grateful to be spared high winds and snow. The elements are as much at sea, one thinks, as those idiots in Washington; they are truly criminals, with their long-winded debates at the UN, or from easy chairs at the Pentagon—or from their favorite bars—from which they dare to judge MacArthur and our struggling lads. How easy for them to sit at home in comfort and deliver "hot air."

I shall take refuge in history; [William James] Durant's *Age of Faith* is at my bedside and I remark that all ages have had their terrible crises, with their human defections and no betterment that I can see. The old *Adam* is the same, only now his tempo is faster, and his lust for conflict seems to be handled from laboratories, rather than by force of personal daring.

Yes, I have last year's recording in London of Flagstad and [conductor Wilhelm] Furtwängler, the finale of *Götterdämerung,* a wonderful rendition. They are obtainable here as the London group works with RCA-Victor.

I have the [Lubja] Welitsch [Bulgarian soprano] record of *Salomé* . . . a good reproduction of the voice, but one must see this primitive creature to enjoy her completely.

Among other pleasant activities, I have been compiling a part of a catalogue for some record collectors who wish to commemorate Caruso's passing, just thirty years ago next September, 1951. The

[149] When Caruso came to New York he was accompanied by singer Ada Ciachetti and their two sons, to whom he had given his name. When she left him for another man, he was heartbroken and went through a period of great depression. At one time he suggested that Mrs. Farrar would make a good mother for his younger son, a beautiful boy of about six. She was startled, but countered by asking if he did not think she had her hands full with Geraldine.

record collectors are developing in droves all over the world it seems.

Flagstad is a very sweet person, very forthright and natural, not spoiled by her prodigious success. She has no taste in dress, alas, and does not make the most of her fine skin and pretty hair. The style of the usual dress she wears does not flatter her figure. She is amply but well proportioned, with small hands and feet, a wholesome figure at all times. She is inclined to drab colors. Her first concert dress was her very best, a sweeping black velvet with a wide lace collar; she looked a picture indeed.

I hope she delivers herself of the torrential outpour of voice when she comes to Pittsburgh. She is not a Lieder singer per se; she needs the stage and the orchestra to be heard at her most fabulous.

Now to the village for shopping chores, best greetings. GF

December 11, 1950

Dear Miss Stotler:

Dull and rainy. I drove with others to the city for the Flagstad concert, and noted the happy absence of any picket line. One wonders if word has gone forth from the MET, in view of her later appearances there. Perhaps this accounted for the peaceful entrée of the listeners. They jammed the house and were, as usual, long and loud in their acclaim.

I did not care for the program, truthfully, for this gorgeous voice has to be unleashed to fulfill its highest potential. The lady is not an interpretive Lieder artist, her glory is the hoch dramatische [highly dramatic] . . . her choice of material, therefore, did not bring these qualities to the fore. The English trifles were not worth her effort to sing, or ours to bend an ear. The Grieg was all of one color, and not too attractive in this native tongue.

We stopped in for a little supper at Mrs. G.'s. Home at 3:00 A.M.

We learn that Eisenhower will be supreme commander abroad, on this mission of salvation from the Russ . . . well, that eliminates him from the 1952 campaign and Truman can breathe easier, perhaps.

My Berlin friends are petrified, and why should they not be? Europe is drained, uneasy and mystified.

There is no reason for you to return the Berlin program of the play. I was stupid not to explain why I sent it. The lad named in one of the roles is Ulric Busch, grandson of the once admired singer,

Johanna Gadski. His mother, at present in Berlin, is an excellent teacher of opera repertoire. I only wish her health permitted her to extend her activity in this country.

A dear person, but like many, a victim of the war; her beautiful property depreciated, her family scattered . . . whether this boy has theater *Blut* remains to be seen.

I presume the new-fangled vier-zeitig [four-sided] stage allows the audience to partake of the stage action. Several such performances have been given here in Summer stock productions. I did not go—it might be amusing, however.

Most interesting letters from some musical friends who live in Japan. Their comments are very enlightening. It appears that the young people have a very delicate appreciation of the finest in Western music, and are more familiar with the great masters than many of our own youngsters. There is a very fine violinist who gained excellent reviews last Winter. She had the fullest approbation of General MacArthur. But shut in that little island, and under present conditions, these young people have small chance to develop.

You ask me about the story of the great Lilli; well, I only know the one she told me herself. She borrowed a pair of stockings from Nordica when they were both singing in *Don Giovanni,* and afterward, carefully washed them out and returned them. It would never have occurred to her thrifty German soul to invest in a new pair.

She was never too proud to be what she was, carrying her own meager childhood habits into her later life.

When I bought her a most handsome Parisian hat, plume laden (her picture with it I have on my dresser with those of my parents), she was loath to accept it; said I had paid too much money for a present for her. Likewise the episode mentioned in my last visit to her in Salzburg, when she looked so regal in the beautiful silver fox I had brought her. She told me with much simplicity, but it seemed a heart-ache, that she and her sister were so poor in their youth, they could not accustom themselves to other than privation, even when they did not need to be so "Sparsam" [frugal]. Poor great souls—they did, indeed, die in poverty, despite their happy fortunes in their song land. The war saw to it.

Keep well. Best greetings from us here, GF

December 13, 1950

Dear Miss Stotler:

No, the Fremstad organ had nothing like the sweep of Flagstad. Fremstad was a true mezzo forced into soprano by careful study and great ambition. One can understand it, for *Isolde* and the *Ring* beckon to all who have emotion and the grand gesture. She too, did not dress well, though she had a fine body that lent itself to the carriage and pose of her personality.

I had a card from her for these holidays, written in a trembling hand. Her mania to remain in one room without seeing any one is pitiful.

Mutts? Well, I still think, from my own experience, they are my preferred; my highly bred canines were not so gay or intelligent as some who found their way to our door, or were a cross breed.

My thought for you would be to take possession of your apartment you say will soon be free and give up this nerve-wracking business at Dogwood. It is not going to become easier; especially if we have again those OPA controls that I foresee once the New Year comes along. Gas will be a commodity hard to come by.

Now to the village. I should need hip boots, for the down-pour is unceasing.

All good wishes, GF

December 15, 1950

Dear Miss Stotler:

A fine sunny day, though bitterly cold. The men are at work on the large pine at the doorway, and by this evening it should be prone, and no longer a danger in the high winds.

I have just looked again into the collection of Wagner letters. The thought persists, why should such unhappy bickerings between man and wife afford material for special attention? The English collector has spent so much time and money toward this end. I know, of course, that the gifted man could not always be portrayed as the Swan Knight in the daily routine, but why does he have to be presented in such odious human light?

Well, his works live on, and his dust and that of Minna [Wagner's first wife] belong to the other dusts that are equalized in the final analysis.

I am glad that Dewey got in his "say" a night before Truman.

This latter should know that the temper of the people will not always be so malleable, and there are distressing signs that he should read. Marshall, it is reported, will soon resign. With Eisenhower off to Europe, Truman has spiked *his* chances for the 1952 election. Meanwhile the attempt to smear MacArthur goes on, so far, unavailing.

I heard a crash; the pine is on the earth—a fine giant, but now I am without fear that it comes into the house uninvited! Vale, indeed.

Our best greetings, GF

1951

January 10, 1951

Dear Miss Stotler:

At last I am on my feet some part of the day and the nasty flu is going away; one feels so mean, for such a trifling ailment, that only becomes serious if neglected.

Thanks for the two letters and the fetching pen fancies depicting good times in Monte Carlo. A new world for me, and a glimpse of the lovely Riviera after the cold, grey North of Berlin; a gay season of cosmopolitans and fascinating people of note . . . such lovely women and handsome men, many of them in uniform, from all over Europe.

Well, it is nice to have had such early memories. I had a letter from a friend today, who, after a visit to Paris, opines that it has become a tired replica of its old self, with no gay faces and only the unfortunates who remain from the two wars. He much preferred the musical and theatrical life in Rome and Seville, although he complained of the *dirt* in those old cities.

Letters from Germany but express the terror of the Russ and the fear of his entering into Western territory . . . I was not reassured by Truman's speech; he is still too vague as to foreign policy. We all want to know *what* our partners can offer for our cooperation. I am not complaining of their attitude (insofar as we can know it via press and radio) for they have had two major wars to meet and are now hardly able to rise fresh and enthusiastic for another. But how can one get an ensemble on this very difficult program, since each people has individual problems and needs? Perhaps now the powers that be in Washington regret their Revanche [revenge] program. We could use the dismantled industry, and also the well-trained officers who were so summarily dismissed for having been their idea of good soldiers.

Odd, is it not, that former enemies who went down to defeat should be the force so desirable for survival? How do they like to serve under a general who smashed them? Can we trust their co-operation? How far will Communism infiltrate into all Europe if Marshall [Plan] monies cease? And how is the USA going to carry on a global war with indefinite support, failing the required tax sustenance? It is all horrible to me. Whatever we do we shall be hated and tricked.

I would offer no harsher criticism abroad than I reserve for the dolts and traitors of my own land. We need a good housecleaning *first;* but it will take a tragedy still more obvious than the useless Korean blood-bath . . . God rest the lads who lie there, its victims.

Yes, I knew Bidú Sayão, a delightful artiste, entirely Latin in origin. She is quite a favorite, though not so frequently heard now in Bing's roster.

I did not care for the *Don Giovanni* with Reiner, one of my prized operas. The women were all out of line and the conductor greatest at fault. I have such heavenly memories of earlier performances with painstaking care on everyone's part; delicacy and refined style. The orchestra was definitely coarse in texture. Welitsch still is unequalled in *Salomé,* to date her best role; but she is sorely undisciplined and does not always sing true. This is carelessness.

I did not have the pleasure of the New Year's party, being already ill of the flu. I resent such an ailment when I have been so virtuous in good hours and care!

I hope all is well with you. Our best greetings, GF

January 15, 1951

Dear Miss Stotler:

Wretched weather again, rain and sleet; roads too icy for comfort; yet overhead now and again, a glimpse of blue that might well presage an April day.

We shall be a group of friends to hear Flagstad on the 22nd; driving in from here, unless the roads are impossible. I shall wear the black velvet that is a standby these days when I want my upper torso covered at all times.

I hope the conductor will be a better choice than Reiner was in *Don Giovanni;* he may be a good stock man but he imbues no one with life or nuance. But no one there is a fine musician to my mind . . . we shall depend on *Isolde* to furnish the requisite thrill.

I regret to see the begging for continuance of the opera . . . I believe the answer would be a chain of smaller opera houses all over the country; and the MET season should be eight months long with nightly performances and a large standard repertoire, thus really representing a house of music.

I am no friend to huge auditoriums, though the radio appeal evidently dictates this thought. Why one should have to rely on the mike, except when actually conveying singing par distance, is inconceivable to me. One spends years to bring a voice to proper expression, in nuances, color and volume, only to have some dim-wit use *his* idea of the dynamics intended. It may be a paying career in money and réclame, but the radio is no real development (at present) in the school of fine singing and acting.

Thanks again for the cheeses, such a delicious treat. I have some every evening for supper, the hour for eggs and salad.

Our best greetings, GF

January 17, 1951

Dear Miss Stotler:

We are once more free of ice, the roads are easy. We have still two Winter months, and let us hope they will not be too severe.

You asked me if I became dismayed or indifferent to criticism. I can truthfully say I seldom found the most adverse review without some idea upon which to build a future performance; but I did not always agree with the thought of the writer, because the one who performs has advantages (or disadvantages) that are not within the province of the listener to judge. Thus, I have heard Caruso bring forth the most heavenly tones, with great care for the text and style—especially when singing in French—not too easy for his luscious outpour, only to read the day after that he had "saved" his efforts, "no doubt not being in his best estate." Critics are as vulnerable to vanity as performers and fancy themselves as the ultimate criterions . . . I have often been infuriated but never dismayed, because I knew what I hoped to accomplish, and I had a clear enough vision to know that this never did come to the peak of perfection, since the more one studied and probed, the less inclined would one be to be satisfied with one's efforts. One could be *happy* in song, but not often content . . . do you understand the difference?

Then too, I had a delicate throat to consider, and a very emotional giving; this was hard to bring into complete focus . . . one seemed to outrun the other.

I did not hear the *Trovatore,* but the Rigal soprano is nothing to induce me to hear; on the other hand, I note a critic refers in disdain to the mezzo (whom I have liked for her frank, dramatic display and generous voice) while praising the soprano to the skies, mentioning her elegance and dignity . . . she is stiff as cardboard, and has no appeal at all—my opinion—so you see how one can differ . . .

At present the most enjoyable music that comes over the radio, to my mind, is the 7 P.M. Longine Symphonette, a half-hour of delightful small orchestra selections, daily fare.

I am all well again. I stopped into the MD yesterday; I am sure he will not have had such a patient ever, for he laughed all the time. I told *him* about myself—so we are quit for a time. At 69, next month, I do not expect the resilient arteries of my young days, nor care to emulate the dim-wits who haunt the beauty salons, who starve and purge, slap poor faces and dye hair in a vain hope to recapture youth. It cannot be done by any miracle save perhaps to be born again, and that is problematical . . . if one feels well and has only minor handicaps, there should be no grumbling!

All good wishes, GF

January 25, 1951

Dear Miss Stotler:

Well, the great evening is over; words really inadequate to express the success of the Flagstad re-entry at the opera. The night was cold, but clear, so there was no difficulty in attaining the portal. The house could not have held even an extra sardine, and it was all "hers." One felt the entire loyalty of those present.

The standees had been hours waiting, and when we went in at 7:30, masses of excited people were pouring in. A gay mood and happy smiles—a nice way to start the evening. Once the curtains parted, such a roar went up—people sprang to their feet shouting welcome. It seemed a long time before they quieted down. The artiste never acknowledged by a sign the usual "prelude," and kept her position of the half-turned face of the heroine [Isolde]. When that glorious voice rang out, and with ensuing phrases, attention, tense and breathtaking!

The curtain calls were delirious. After sharing many with the others she rightfully was left alone to receive the thunder of welcoming shouts. It was an occasion no one could forget, and in which we all could partake with something like a feeling of vindication. How the woman went on, building up her role to the most tremendous climax, effortless, but steady and true! Till the last transfiguring solo that closes the opera, it was truly great in all respects. She looked like a Viking queen.

While I was waiting for the car to drive me in, I sought out some records of ten years ago, the very *Tristan,* for comparison. In them the voice was magnificent, crystalline and rich in compass; but the interim had deepened her color tones, and matured this magnificence into heart-warming and heart-breaking beauty . . . the phrasing was like speech, so beautiful in diction and intention.

I have not recovered yet from its magic; her nobility of movement and simplicity of gesture . . . the truly grand manner that no one has these days. The era of the golden age, in her case, was indeed present. I hope she was happy after the rightful vindication over the vile scandal mongers.

I asked very specifically of some one who knows, *who* had the courage to brave these dirty elements, and this person said, "Mr. Bing." And when Bing was protested, he replied "Whatever the sentiments, think of the box office." It is apparent for once, the dissenters had the sense to let this material advantage weigh properly—all honor to Mr. Bing therefore!

I must here note that Reiner followed every intention of Flagstad, in the most sympathetic manner; he is not the most inspired leader, but he did his best for her and the others, who were without distinction, save the tenor [the Chilean, Ramon Vinay] who could be good material with more work and hints about acting . . . a young, virile man.

Well, so much for this eventful occasion. With the coming Saturday of the Maestro, one can have memories to cherish forever.

I wish you could hear Flagstad in opera. She is at her glorious best and has no peer.

Our best wishes. GF

January 27, 1951

Dear Miss Stotler:

To revert to previous observations of your letter, yes, I had plenty of adverse comments. They stem sometimes from actual good will and interest and some musical knowledge; at other times from spite or frustration, especially if the critic fancies himself as composer and wants his songs sung by certain artists.

Then too, when a performer is young and about to engage in new interests, some of the older critics fear for the older artists. In fact, one singer was so perturbed she came to me with apology on behalf of the critic who had resented my assumption of a role she had sung. We remained very good friends, but the critic was not to be propitiated, although I believe he did me no harm.

As in any career, the beginning is hard when one must attain a footing. Then comes the trial of retaining it, with the constant work for perfection, till comes the time for a new voice to usurp the place of the older singer . . . and so it goes. One is fortunate to have more than one facet to polish, come the day of abdication.

To reply to another query, one *never* comes to the ultimate in a role, so it does not present a stale task so much as a challenge for betterment. I so loved to sing that it was the same in essence for five or five hundred or five thousand. The current is so variable between the listener and the singer that each contributes to the other. The mike is, to me, no worthy conductor of one's best efforts.

All good wishes to you. GF

January 29, 1951

Dear Miss Stotler:

Snow and cold; the roads were not too favorable for the New York trip, but I had a good driver. Another memorable occasion, the Toscanini benefit for the Verdi Home in Milan. This Verdi *Requiem* is of great, rather austere beauty, and tremendously difficult for the voices. I think the radio will give you some idea of its great effect. A packed and respectful house.

I came home with friends and was tucked away at midnight, not too tired for having had such a happy excitement.

I understand that the opera matinees will have the consecutive *Ring* performances, a joy I shall prepare for, with the Toscanini broadcasts afterward. A rich offering to enchant us for many weeks.

You will be busy with the exhibition on the 4th. Your subject, *A Picnic Corner,* sounds gay and attractive. What a talent to be able to draw and color!

Our knitting for the Red Cross is active again. My girls here are expert and are busy turning out sweaters and gloves.

We shall have a meeting tomorrow with many pressing matters to discuss. The Motor Corps is to work with the Disaster Committee for Civil Defense. We have a quota of 120 cars and drivers to furnish, by voluntary offer, for emergency. My name is on the list, of course.

I daresay we shall also have the questionnaire re the number of evacuees each dwelling can house. I serve also on this committee, so know about what to expect; the plans have yet to be worked out in detail.

First Aid and Home Nursing are being promoted. The excellent course which we all took in the last war does help the immediate situation and relieves the hard pressed MD for serious attention. Our committee is well established and some younger members make our routine less arduous.

Well, we shall do our best.

I am so sorry that Miss Aida should have the concern, and her husband suffer more hospitalization . . . hard on both, indeed.

Yes, I think I would like the Abigail Adams letters which you mention, and thank you for the volume, in anticipation.

Our best greetings, GF

February —, 1951

Dear Miss Stotler:

The days have been busy ones at my desk; many letters for Red Cross and Civil Defense.

I should not have made the observations of our Mr. Frey re Flagstad. He evidently had in mind a more illusive model for Isolde . . . though one cannot be a wisp and carry out the musical intention. This was marked in the Brangaene, the lady was of Hollywood meagerness, with corresponding inadequacy.

I think perhaps this is why he did not recognize me, on the aisle, for he could not have missed me if his eyes had been attuned to my years . . . one must, however, recall that he was no doubt looking for a black-haired siren(?).

The *Walküre* of Saturday found the soprano [Flagstad] in fine fettle. I liked also the tenor [Günther Treptow] as the voice came over the air. The Maestro's concert, now sponsored by Squibbs was shocking. To hear Beethoven punctuated by commercials was more than I could endure. *Too* bad, for at least this program was unique in its devotion to music per se.

The next two Saturdays of the *Ring* will have Traubel as the goddaughter. I am sorry, for Traubel has been behaving so badly of late, in vulgar radio and TV programs, that I cannot accept her as a serious artiste, which at one time I hoped and believed she would remain.

In regard to Mata Hari[150] I can give you no more information than the brief summation in my book. She was at all times in our Monte Carlo group, a shy, retiring, pretty figure. Her dances in

[150] Dutch born Margaretha Gertruida Zelle performed Indian dances under the name Mata Hari. During World War I she was accused of spying for Germany through her association with high-ranking Allied military officers. She was found guilty and executed.

Le Roi de Lahore were given more to posturing than to the conventional steps.

Massenet was present there, and I often called upon him in Paris. A gentle soul, typical musician of the dream world . . . not too robust in those later years.

I am afraid your weather conditions are truly perilous. We keep well, but are chary of our strength and do not venture out in the excessive cold except for the brief shopping needs.

Our best greetings, GF

February 7, 1951

Dear Miss Stotler:

Your comment about the diamonds was illuminating. Some friends in the business have told me that diamonds are always a good buy. It seems they are now in great demand for precision instruments, and that the market for pearls is very poor at present. Is it not interesting to note the rise and fall of such lovely things, as pertains to commercial valuation? I recall the time when a finely matched string of pearls was the dream of every woman, for their beauty and the distinction they carried. I am told, however, that in stones and furs the cheating is fabulous unless one is well aware of their values.

You will tell me what you think of the [Ingrid] Bergman *Joan* [*of Arc*]. One Hollywood friend considered it greatly reduced in poignancy by reason of overemphasis on the color schemes. I have not seen it yet, but shall await it with pleasure.

I like the sincerity of Bergman in all she does, though at times I think she is miscast . . . she does not suit, thank heaven, the dubious fast women that now and then she has graced. Thank you for sending me your program. The *Joan* photos do not carry my idea of the maid. There is something rather gross about them, which I have never noticed in the usual facial expression of this admired actress. Even when she played the Lady of the Camellias, in the radio adaptation, I could lay aside the early surprise at the heavy Swedish accent, the intonations were so genuine, though I always think of this charmer in terms of exquisite French.

The tree men are here, always a sign of Spring pruning and general order. My big elm is fated to carry a tube release always to eliminate the poison sap. The man said they were of the opinion at the laboratory that the Dutch elm disease started with this type of sap.

They are trying a preventive treatment, all of course in the experimental stage.

We are hoping to get fruit from the orchards since the trees bore such abundance of bloom. They, too, have to be watched. Nowadays nothing seems to prosper by reason of normality . . . so much for our education and science.

Yes, a steer, grainfed and kept in the finest condition, is quite expensive. They are usually killed at about 1,250 pounds; your estimate is correct, and I pay five to six hundred dollars for the beast, delivered and ready to cut. Perhaps it is not now so imperative, but one cannot tell what odd regulations may come about. If we are to feed the world it is wise to have some home products on hand. The meat one buys cannot, of course, compare with what I have.

I am off this afternoon to hear some young musical aspirants in Norwalk—happily as a guest; there is nothing official connected with this effort.

All good wishes. GF

February 8, 1951

Dear Miss Stotler:

I am sure you enjoyed the watercolor exhibit. I do wish I knew how to do these charming things. I am quite without talent for anything of the sort. One Summer in Brittany with artist friends, I essayed to combine some colors. The landscape was so lovely with the rolling sea, for we were within easy distance of St. Michel, and often rode over the sand bar at low tide on donkeys. But color and form escaped me and I inevitably turned to my piano and song . . . that was my paramount urge at all times.

At the American Women's Volunteer Services meeting, plans for caring for possible evacuees were discussed. The auxiliary police work with the state authorities to this purpose. I think the committee have made excellent plans, considering the food, shelter, sanitation and water facilities. I believe we could handle, and make at least comfortable, some 3,000. Decontamination in case of bombing is also a possibility, which will be strictly enforced if necessary. Ambulances and private drivers will be called upon to assist.

Our plane spotting is as yet indefinite. The little observatory of the last war was quite the best place; a stove and comfort, with a wide expanse of sky. The house we now use is not in any way right. If the service is to be a daily one we must seek other quarters.

Yes, I knew about the RCA "immortals"—did I not write you about the grandiose luncheon that was to collect all those who have still escaped the cemetery in one group for publicity, speeches and awful candid camera shots? Well, I regretted twice, for such occasions are anathema to me; but many of the tottering ones turned up, with Miss Truman, via the camera effect, between Kreisler and [tenor Giovanni] Martinelli.

Toscanini is to give his last concert. The knee injury bothers him and his MD insists on a complete rest. I am sure the Maestro is fulminating for he hates to be idle; but he is soon to be 84 and must stop sometime. He is driven, indeed, by a daemon.

No, I prepared nothing under Massenet. He only sat and nodded approval at what he saw, so one went ahead with what one wished to do. He was at that time an elderly gentle soul, not in good health.

I sent a wire for her birthday to the 83 year old Fremstad. I was very much minded of her at the Flagstad performance, for she too, had the noble classic line. A queenly carriage.

I enjoyed the scenic effects of the movie *King Solomon's Mines.* The story was ineffectual, and the leading lady [Deborah Kerr] was shown first with flowing red wig, then a crisp, short permanented thatch, which did little to make her the struggling heroine. Why must these ladies always look as though fresh from a beauty salon dryer?

I have to differ with you about the shopping exploit in lamb. First of all you should know that the feet of these animals provide delectable gelatine when boiled, and the extra bone makes the most nourishing soup stock. These parts are always included in the price, so why should you refuse to take them and waste all that good energy?

Best of weekend wishes, GF

February 14, 1951

Dear Miss Stotler:

St. Valentine's Day. The good saint has been a frequent visitor here, so that I have not so much minded the turn of the weather with sleet and cold.

The lovely hyacinths came just as I returned from the village, so fragrant, with hints of Spring. The Winter at this time is a bit dull and unfriendly . . . I am reminded of that haunting "Treibhaus" song of Wagner, the Vorspiel to the *Isolde* music . . . a memorable incantation.

I have the Memorial Service to attend for the Martin boy, the young flyer who was killed recently in action in that D—D Korea of evil repute. This lad had such promise—life scarcely begun, and now, over the border . . . what a mystery it all is.

Flagstad sings the entire *Ring,* but as an extra series, for box office reasons. She closes this series tomorrow, then I believe, has five *Fidelio* performances. These do not interest me at all, with *any* singer; a static theater piece, heard best, in my opinion, on the concert stage or in a symphony.

Do you know *Vienna Golden Years* by Hanslick? A collection of his articles at various times, and most interesting.

The phone just advises me that my new car has arrived, so I rush to Danbury to complete last details.

Best greetings, GF

February 16, 1951

Dear Miss Stotler:

I am too full of the superb Flagstad performance of yesterday to think of much else. The day was fine and the ride in from the country most enjoyable.

The matinee *Götterdämerung* lasted five hours with one short entr'acte. The decors were not good. The Rhine looked like a poor edition of the Hudson Palisades, narrow and out of perspective, with too much emphasis on the middle stage, rather than down front. This worked badly for the Rhine Maidens and the finale of their singing.

The Siegfried, [tenor] Set Svanholm, was excellent, youthful and buoyant, but the great star was, as usual, Flagstad. How this woman pours forth such torrents of purest lyric melody is something we may not hear again. Her classic line and economy of gesture again made the nobility of the role apparent, where others swirl about the stage with much tossing of drapery. I am exhausted; but the harmonies linger with persuasive beauty. I can relive them all with the inner ear . . .

So frantic was the enthusiasm for her, that should anyone voice the slightest difference of opinion, I am sure he would be mobbed. How easy it is to climb aboard the bandwagon when all is once again safe!

Now to chores in the village—but I confess I am walking on air, and far from matters mundane.

Best greetings, GF

February —, 1951

Dear Miss Stotler:

I was utterly done up at the Memorial Service for the lad who died in Korea. The service was so simple and genuine; all the townspeople (Norwalk) there, with much sympathy. The military stamp, of course, was not lacking, but these young men were all visibly moved. The officer who presented the tragic gold star to the mother, could hardly voice his message. One wonders the "why" of all this dreadful business. I left with a heavy heart and an inquiring spirit. No one has any answers that make sense to this global war and our role in it, alas.

The Maestro has concluded abruptly the last Saturday concert. I could have wished he had gone out in the blaze of last season's glory, but then, he must fulfill his destiny; and few professionals admit their horizon's limit.

We are waiting impatiently for the Spring's arrival; one does feel a quickening of verdant hope in the air, sharp as it is.

Our good wishes to you. GF

February 18, 1951

Dear Miss Stotler:

The pretty blue car is now installed in the garage, where it will remain this wet day of rain and sleet. It is quite a lady's car, roomy and easy riding, of a lovely shade of blue, lighter than my last. It should prove a staunch friend for the next ten years; a real Valentine gift to myself.

I had a touching letter from Fremstad after the birthday wire to her. I fancy her childhood was dreary and poverty stricken. There was much sternness in her father, and a desperate religious discipline, so she told me. Then too, she must have had this intolerable yearning to sing, and obtaining the education for a career was a problem. She sang abroad as mezzo soprano, then essayed the soprano roles, not always suited vocally, but with superb understanding and dramatic fire. A nature such as hers seems to be at war with itself . . .

I am reading, simultaneously, the stories of two warriors, MacArthur and [German General Erwin] Rommel; both impress me. I wish such men were a part of the pressed-pants brigade that surround Truman and [Secretary of State Dean] Acheson; but men of action and resolve do not naturally revolve to desks.

As for Hoover, here is really a fine soul, dignified, and with that excellent judgment and restraint. It was the fashion to pillory him; however he is a proof that the law of compensation does work out.

All good wishes, GF

Back from the village, I shall add a note to my letter of yesterday. We are beginning preparations for the Red Cross drive; and it means a little clerical attention. As my dear friend of the operated eye is not able to fulfill her usual post as chairman, I have taken over some of her work, just right for someone like myself, with free time at my disposal.

I am so happy in my walls these Wintry days. The blue guest room has been refurnished with delicate painted pieces, a soft off-white, with the grain running through, and decorated with little brass handles. A French provincial desk was needed and looks very attractive before the window.

My own room is maple, very mellow in tone, and with a high gloss, also French provincial. The bed is too large to suit the room, but is in itself a most comfortable one. I bought everything at sight at our excellent New England Furniture store in Danbury. The same factory supplies the big New York stores, but the price is almost double. Danbury knows just what the traffic will bear and I consider that I have good materials at a reasonable price.

Regarding [Giordano's] *Andrea Chénier,* it is a pleasing opera, mainly by reason of the story. The composer always chose good theater, but his melodies, while effortless, have no particular value for a humming public. The story is the usual one. The poet, Chénier, an actual figure of the period, condemned to the scaffold, in love with Maddelena of a noble family. Neither is safe from the jealous Gerard, erstwhile gardener on the estate of the girl's family. He vows and obtains revenge by reason of his affiliation with Robespierre. It remains dimly in my mind.

In Warsaw it was received with such tumult from the students we did not venture it a second time. The Russians were in command of the tri-part Poland, and the opera functioned under their aegis. Such demonstrations foretold the later wild disorder of the local riots.

At the MET it needed a Caruso to have it on the roster as a new performance. The female lead, I believe, was [Claudia] Muzio.

I too, thought *The Family of Gramercy Park* rather thin, as coming from the pen of a gentleman so highly placed; but it did bring to mind many a time that I sat on the park bench to study and read. No bicycling in New York for me, I was too busy with singing and study.

Mother went nightly with me to the opera, and I was a very tired little girl when we got off the street cars—cable cars on Broadway, horsedrawn on the crosstown lines.

There was also the time I auditioned for a church choir position. The board liked my singing, but felt I was too young, unless I put my hair on top of my head. Mother would not consent to this and we really did not need the extra money too much.

I do not recall your offer of the [Mary Roberts] Rinehart book; perhaps a letter went astray. I knew the lady slightly. She, with others of that period, came out to Hollywood to supervise their stories but found themselves to be entirely superfluous, save as decors at parties—and to draw their not inconsiderable salaries.

Their efforts to shield the children of their brains were distinctly without success. I recall Gertrude Atherton was so wrothy that she withdrew a book she had written. The firm had bought only the title. Then she retitled it and published it with great success; whereupon these stupids bought back the same material under another name.

I have completed at last all the Red Cross correspondence, and the parcel will be delivered to the Chairman for his signature tomorrow.

I am keen to see your posters, always a happy spot of brightness.

Our fine Angus is now reposing in the two freezers. He was the most beautiful beast, so firm and rosy. Today his bones and certain fats go into soup bouillon; tomorrow the rest of him will be converted into soap! We do not lose an ounce—he is too expensive.

So many friends are ill, in the hospital for one reason or another. I am sorry not to visit in person, but cannot run in and out of New York on these mercy errands. They will have to get well and come home!

Best greetings, GF

March 5, 1951

Dear Miss Stotler:

The woes of two opera heroines are in progress, but I must get on with my many letters, while the music clangs and the blizzard rages outside. What a change from the Spring-like mildness of the 28th. The lion of March is here in verity!

Thanks for the milestone card, very apropos—truly a pilgrim's progress—and a happy one with each year's arrival.

I had ten very close friends to tea. The table, a paradise arranged by loving hands and thought of by Miss Sylvia, pink roses and Kaiserblumen entwined with ground pine, a most lovely effect. The same, in roses all over with porcelain additions, and tall blue candles.

We gathered at 4:30 and at 7:00 were still busy chattering; a most enjoyable fête. I was not too fatigued after the dear guests had gone.

You ask me a difficult question—"Is there a present MET singer with a voice resembling mine?" I cannot answer this, you must judge from your own listening.

I do not know the book you mention, *Troubled Sleep*. No doubt one of those unpleasant Freudian affairs, so do *not* send it. I am not over-fond of this pathology . . . the present French writers seem determined to exhibit their own odd departures from the accepted pattern. Such does not make agreeable reading, and should be their own private business—a clinical picture.

All well and busy here. Spring housecleaning in the offing; no very restful contemplation, but it seems it *must* be done.

Our best greetings, GF

March 15, 1951

Dear Miss Stotler:

Cold and windy, but the cheerful sun makes matters pleasant. One yearns for Spring without another snow avalanche.

Flagstad has just announced her retirement here. I hope she will firmly keep to it no matter what the insistence. Let her go on concert tours, if she will, perhaps less arduous; but for my part, I hope she will retire in her glory. Too many critics are waiting to pick flaws.

I liked her concert attire at her first New York appearance, of black velvet with wide lace collar—she was queenly in it. Recently she has not been too happily gowned . . . poisonous green and dull brown—no reflections in the stage light.

I pity all parents in this Korean mess—or any other that may be cooking at present. There is no magic name of president or general that is going to heal the heart when a boy is killed or missing in action.

There is a Home Service of the Red Cross that is admirable in such circumstances. We have a wonderful chairman here. The family is sustained while waiting for matters of insurance, etc. to be settled, with food, clothing, and such comfort as can be given. But it is still heart-breaking, and will be more so I fear.

Eastertide will soon be here, and it will not be a joyous one for many in our land, or in others, for that matter. One can only hang on, keep well and busy.

Greetings, GF

P.S.

I am sure Flagstad would welcome your flowers when she appears in your city. Usually the singer likes to have them at the hall and presented on the stage at a given intermission. As one is likely to check in late, rush to dress and sing, and often leave the same night, the flowers are most welcome at the concert hall.

The MET is sending on tour their *Fledermaus* version.[151] They hope to raise some needed money for the coming season, as well as pay off some of the present obligation. After Flagstad, this offering was a sell-out.

I hope you will have a pleasant Easter, despite the indisposition of the Factotum [Naomi Lyons, Ilka's devoted maid].

April 5, 1951

Dear Miss Stotler:

I am closeted with writing materials in the sewing room, as the house cleaning has driven me from corner to corner . . . the merry hum of the vacuum is going full tilt, and there is much hustle and bustle.

I note with regret that Flagstad has been persuaded to recon-

151 During the Metropolitan's Spring Tour the leading soprano role in *Die Fledermaus* was shared by Patrice Munsel and Roberta Peters.

sider, and will remain at the MET. She probably has her reasons[152] . . . they would not be mine.

I heard a very beautiful Sunday Symphony, a Wagner program with Eileen Farrell.[153] I have noted this young singer for some time, and she gave a noble account of herself in this offering. She seems to be more of a radio than a concert artiste, but the voice and her use of it, could not be surpassed. However the hour is awkward, 1:00 to 2:30 P.M.

The Garden book[154] is soon due; a friend is making me a present of it. I confess, after reading the first magazine installment, I would not have invested in it . . . only a gossip column spun out at great length.

Now to the village chores. I am glad I still have my snow tires on and have not removed the Prestone.

Our best greetings, GF

Later:

I did not care for the superficial Wagner rendition of de Sabata; it takes a profound musician to obtain perfection in the magic of the orchestration.

Mrs. G. and her friend are off to South America; I have withstood a warm invitation to accompany them. Things here are too interesting. Besides I hate the water, and this cruise will find them about to enter Winter. But she loves travel and it will do her good.

The Scouts are doing well; all will be excitement till after the Fashion Show on the 14th. The choice of pretty dresses keeps them happy; they really show off the frocks very well. If we could *ever* get them all together for just *one* rehearsal, but there are so many classes . . . however we shall do our best.

A happy weekend that now looks a little more sunny.

Greetings, GF

---

152 Mr. Bing had promised to mount a production of Gluck's *Alceste,* in which Mme. Flagstad wished to sing as a change from her Wagnerian roles.

153 Eileen Farrell (b. 1920) owed her entire career to radio. This excellent soprano began with popular music but went on to her real forte, Lieder and operatic arias, singing regularly with the Columbia Concert Orchestra conducted by Bernard Herrmann.

154 *Mary Garden's Story* by Mary Garden and Louis Biancolli.

April 11, 1951

Dear Miss Stotler:

I have been in a hectic mood, as has most of the country, over the MacArthur affair.[155]

Mrs. MacArthur got the news of her husband's dismissal via radio before their lunch. Twenty minutes later the *Flash* official message came.

What an odd observation from Eisenhower, "I hope he does not return to become a controversial figure." I do not see how else he could return since the general public wants to hear first hand from him. He can well afford to present his side of the shoddy business.

Colder weather; much to do about repairs here. Roofs, windows, pool painting, constant hammering—most confusing. Wages are shamefully high but with it all people are having a hard time to pay for food and living expenses. Who can understand inflation except as a wicked trick to exist for a time on the intangible that turns out to be a zero?

Our best greetings, GF

April 12, 1951

Dear Miss Stotler:

I have sent off a personal cable early this morning to General MacArthur although I do not know him at all. Somewhere at Lexington and Concord there must have been forebears who have transmitted to me their burning resentment at injustice. . . . They, no doubt, waited for no order to "fire" but lunged forward from the fields with pitchforks ready. I feel the same urge now but bare hands will have to suffice.

All good wishes at this hectic moment. GF

---

155 In a surprise order, on April 11, 1951, President Truman removed General Douglas MacArthur from his posts as Supreme Commander, Allied Powers; Commander-in-Chief, U.N. Command; Commander-in-Chief, Far East; and Commanding General, U.S. Army, Far East. Lieut. General Matthew Ridgeway replaced him in all these posts.

Copy

General MacArthur . . . Tokio Japan

Sir: As a private citizen may I express to you personally my contempt and indignation at those forces that have bowed to wretched politics and thus relieved of command a superb officer in whom resides this country's admiration and confidence for Far East affairs. May God bless you and yours whatever the future holds.

Signed Geraldine Farrar
Ridgefield, Connecticut

April 20, 1951

Dear Miss Stotler:

I am off now to Mrs. Gilmour's in Stamford whose TV will carry everything we wish to see and hear on MacArthur day in Manhattan. The estimated crowd is 5 million. The speech of the General yesterday will provoke the investigation that long should have been available to the citizens. Just before the historic event we had an hour of recapitulation on the TV.

The scene in Congress was breath taking. As the officials filed in they looked so commonplace—so "jaunty" if one may say it. But when the sergeant at arms announced the General—ah, there was a *man* who walked proud and erect to stand before the lights and the cameras for his address.

With quiet emphasis he unfolded every vital point on which he based his program . . . there were tears in many eyes, certainly in mine, though there was no appeal for pity. The old soldier stood by his colors to the last, certainly a great figure in history of which any nation can be proud. What happens to his great administration program in Japan is no longer his concern. Well, we shall see how his enemies go about their undermining . . . but if the people have any memory they will listen to what he has to say.

As to Lady Astor's comments[156]—she is a wisecracking puff of

[156] Nancy Langhorne (1879–1964) of Danbury, Virginia, married Englishman William Waldorf Astor in 1906. When Astor took his place in the House of Lords as the 2nd Viscount Astor in 1919, his wife won a seat in the House of Commons, the first woman to become a member of Parliament. She was also famous as a hostess, entertaining lavishly at Cliveden, the Astor mansion in Buckinghamshire.

hot air. She knows nothing of this country and has only the narrowest outlook upon which to base her cheap quips. I know something of this as she is a cousin of Mrs. Gilmour.

All good wishes, GF

April 21, 1951

Dear Miss Stotler:

I shall try to settle down now after a week of excitement. Yesterday the parade in Manhattan was beyond my poor power to describe. The TV carried it beautifully over an hour of frenzied welcome.

2,800 *tons* of ticker tape almost obscured the sky and the *seven and a half million* glued to every available space shouted themselves hoarse. The General was composed and smiling all through the long drive. At the City Hall ceremony he made a brief address, never controversial but firm and clear in its message of patriotism. Shame on those who try to dislodge him from his niche in the Hall of Fame!

I think that Harry Truman is in for a boomerang—not that the General will be reinstated, but by the bitter politics playing into leftist hands; and above all from the surrounding evils which swamp this inept person . . . the [corrupt] Prendergast [political] machine [which had supported Truman] expanded from Missouri locales.

The broad statement that "Courage was imbibed with Bourbon and Benedictine at midnight," does not fall on inattentive ears. A tragic happening that should awaken our citizenry to the traitors who instigated the affair and throw them out on their posteriors.

I heard nothing of the suggested bells here but the New York whistles, bells and sirens spoke for the nation in no uncertain terms.

My home flag has hung for three days at my door, proud and solitary, unencumbered by the bunting of the UN that betrays unity while it sullies peace.

Fremstad died last night, very peacefully in her sleep. I shall not attend services but send flowers of course.

Our best greetings, GF

April 25, 1951

Dear Miss Stotler:

Spring days come on wings and the tender green is a delicate veil through which to see something lovely, and for a moment lay aside the shadows and strife of the political hour. Still the repercussions are loud and many.

I hope you listened last night to Henry J. Taylor. This General Motors' commentator is a frank and fine reporter. Taylor grabbed a plane and had a personal interview in San Francisco at the time of the General's arrival there. He told this shocking tale. That same evening, General Albert C. Wedemeyer (the officer whose China report was never allowed to be made public) gave MacArthur a message from Washington that he was *not allowed to make any speeches.* Upon this MacArthur replied that he *must have a written order* to this effect at once. All through the day of the tumultuous parade in San Francisco the General waited for the order that never came. Can you imagine his state of mind? Trying to prepare his speech before Congress under such conditions?

He was clever—they dared not risk an order that would shut him up for good. To date, save for the press, he has *not* been advised why he was relieved of his command. This man can hold his own in any tight place, and will. Those in the State Department are no match for him, indeed, thank God.

The war *is* a war in Korea. Yesterday a customer came into the Martin flower shop, and in talking made the observation that of course Truman did what he had to do—after all we are not at war, etc. The same old protocol alibi that deceives no one.

Little Mrs. Martin reared herself angrily, pointed to a picture of her son and his buddy, killed two weeks before, and in a scathing tone said, "Do you think those boys are at the bottom of the ocean because they were playing tiddly-winks?"

I have been reading many items from parents whose boys were killed in Korea—although of course, "There is no war."

I enclose a tribute I wrote for Fremstad. The paper printed it today. Do not return.

To the Editor of the *Herald Tribune*:

May I offer a last tribute to a fine American singer who has just passed away?

Olive Fremstad was a valued member of the earlier Metropolitan Opera, principally noted for her splendid Wagnerian repertoire, still remembered by admirers and colleagues.

She was the first Salomé, a classic figure in *Armide*, an Olympian Venus, and spanned the *Ring* to a triumphant Isolde, to mention a few of her acclaimed roles.

I saw her in later days, semi-invalided, living not too far distant from my own home. Her fondest memories were of past musical glories and her oft repeated "dream wish" to sing just once more, Isolde, under the baton of Maestro Toscanini.

Her most cherished possession was his photograph, adorned with the inscription that recalled electrifying performances with him.

As she treads the stairs to Valhalla, may a friend and colleague offer here the laurel of remembrance for her devotion and achievement in the field of the great tradition?

Geraldine Farrar

I have rejoined the *First Aid* class to refresh myself. *Civil Defense* is hoping all who can will do so. I can always learn.

My planting is now done—young and small, due to the chronic depletion of my purse in such matters. It will grow in time.

All good wishes, GF

April 26, 1951

Dear Miss Stotler:

What a heavenly day, the earth sparkling and scrubbed to perfection after the heavy thunder storms last night. The garden begins to look pretty now that the debris is out of the way, and the general air of clean tidiness does my heart good.

I have written about Fremstad. She was cremated and the urn will be taken to her Western home.

Her vocal ability was nothing like Flagstad's. Hers was a mezzo voice of warm color, but not the clarion call of the Flagstad. She worked hard and did accomplish fine effects with the soprano roles of the Wagner operas, but there was always careful preparation for the range that was not hers by nature. Her splendid figure, stately bearing and grace were of the Viking style. Indeed, she was of the great tradition.

In re Eisenhower, he is not my man. I hope for [Robert A.] Taft as the Republican nominee, and that our General may remain apart from Washington. His value will be greater so.

Not having the missionary spirit, I shall always remain a nationalist, a one flag woman, and respect the right of others to do the same. The best thing for freedom loving people is to decapitate the UN, that unwieldy, dishonest bunch of thugs. We are always the losers; I see no reason to assume the role of Messiah. Other countries have their own gods—we end by having none.

I enclose another pamphlet on the Maternal Health Bill we are working to have approved in our Connecticut Legislature. I have been busy in this field also, having for years been a modest contributor to the sad institutions that house all kinds of unfortunates due to unplanned parenthood, impoverishment, and the ills that follow. If all could have a beginning of health and decent living we would escape some of the penalties that breed under opposite conditions. As it now is here, we send our troubled mothers to a legal clinic for information across the state line in New York . . . educational progress is so slow.

I had six copies of the Windsor book[157] given me, so was able to furnish volumes to some friends. An excellent, well written story, that will, no doubt, disappoint the sensationalists. I hope the decision that cost him so much is well repaid in the lady, not to me a very sympathetic figure.

Now to the village and shopping.

All good wishes, GF

May 16, 1951

Dear Miss Stotler:

These heavenly days fly by; I keep busy with many things. It is for this charming season that our city friends wait through the grim Winter, and all of us here try to have guests at the time of bloom and sunny days. I have been out every afternoon for tea, and to see the wonderful gardens—poems in themselves.

Would Thursday, June 14th suit your plans to come to us here? It should not be too warm at that time.

I shall like the finance chairmanship of the Girl Scouts. The young people are nice teen-agers; our camp is here on the village mountain and there are no disorganized forays into alien grounds.

I did not go to see the Hoover portrait hung; such a trip would not repay me for the effort entailed. The artist is Richard Marsden

157 *A King's Story* by H.R.H. the Duke of Windsor, published by Putnam (1947).

Brown. I have not seen a reproduction but I was happy to contribute my check. A fine gentleman is Mr. Hoover.

I read the journal of Katherine Mansfield when it first came out. As with her prototype, [poetess] Edna St. Vincent Millay, I found nothing to swing me into this pallid orbit. I do not find such nebulous matters of any particular interest, and am perhaps the only human who can say with truth that *Pelleas and Melisande* is the most boring affair in opera. I was present at the Paris debut (Garden) and have tried on several occasions to listen with receptivity . . . it is a dull moan of monotony. So much for Maeterlinck[158] and his many poses, no matter how he was acclaimed for the vague works he threw together. Like the sexless Tagore[159]—one lecture from *him* was all I could endure.

Well, to the village, and another train of thought.

All good greetings, GF

May 30, 1951

Dear Miss Stotler:

The sun has shone for the various parades. Our household has attended none, having need of relaxation. I envy your planting activity but have had to forego most of it, having decided that it is the better part of energy conservation to let the men do what has to be done.

Miss Sylvia and I, with another friend, drove to New York to meet Mrs. Gilmour's ship on arrival there at 8:00 A.M. so we left these parts at 5:00. But it was a nice surprise for her after six weeks of absence.

I believe that our General is to take an important position with Remington Rand, so reported by friends who have an interest in that group. This would mean his domicile in this neighborhood as their offices are in South Norwalk. It would never occur to me to want to meet him or his family. My enthusiasm for him is quite impersonal and I need no nearer approach to consider him our finest example of a gentleman and a soldier. It is the principle.

The farce in D.C. still goes on. I have written to Henry J. Taylor for his report on General Wedemeyer whom he visited recently in

158 Maurice Maeterlinck, Belgian dramatist and poet.

159 Sir Rabindranath Tagore, Indian poet, novelist, and educator.

San Francisco. I smell a rat there, from his recent analysis of that frank speaking officer.

I understand that Ike is dodging any recall home as he does not wish to be involved in the imbroglio.

As to your question concerning an audience with the Pope, I never had one, so the matter did not rise, what one should or should not wear. As to the recent case of Dawes[160] at the English court, I do think there was much unnecessary to-do about his thin shanks as a theme to serve the knee breeches; a court procedure. He could well have avoided criticism in conforming, else why accept the post?

Now off to village chores. Best greetings, GF

June 15, 1951

Dear Miss Stotler:

It is still cold and the sun is pale; I am glad of a coat. Such a hectic time, three funerals followed by a wedding and no end of general meetings that eat into time and energy.

I have found more attic treasures that have been very happily received by the Thrift Shop here. They plan an auction soon. This is the excellent organization that takes care of many of our local needs.

You are quite mistaken about my interest in baseball;[161] I never played it, do not care for it, although it was my Father's Summer profession.[162] I can remember nothing that deviated my thought and action from the field of music.

The furious political debate goes on and General MacArthur has his followers even in Democratic Texas . . . It is now a matter of principle, more than anything else, to get back on the road to reason.

I hope your trip home was pleasant and not too tiring.

Do not bother to see *The Great Caruso.* The cheapest thing to

160 Charles Gates Dawes (1865–1951) had been a brigadier general on General Pershing's staff. He served as Vice President to President Coolidge and as United States Ambassador to Great Britain from 1929 to 1932. In 1925 he shared the Nobel Prize for the Dawes Plan proposing the reduction of Germany's reparations. He apparently did not follow the conventional style when presented at court.

161 However, Miss Farrar once umpired part of a ballgame between Lowell Thomas's team and one from Danbury, Connecticut.

162 Sydney Farrar had played first base for Philadelphia in the old National League.

come out of Hollywood, save for the young man [Mario Lanza] who sings too loud and too much in it. An entirely inaccurate script.

Our best greetings, GF

June 27, 1951

Dear Miss Stotler:

The heavy showers have devastated the blooms; happily the gardens of the several hostesses were in full beauty for the showing, as it was fair yesterday and not too warm.

The auction preparations are going on merrily. I have had many phone calls about the various items offered for sale. People have called from a distance and I have put them in touch with the committee. I shall indeed be at home and incommunicado. I hope results repay the ladies who have been heart and soul for the affair. I shall send Miss Sylvia to help.

Some of the fans and feathers are truly lovely; most gracious reminders of a day when they were the essence of feminine charm and appeal. I think, off hand, that the little fan I gave you was acquired in Paris before the First World War. It is supposed to be a genuine Henri Martin. The case for Miss Aida was also a Paris fancy which I often carried on my concert stage.

I seem always to be dashing about on Civil Defense business. These last days we had test spotting, and now are setting up a control center over which I have agreed to take charge; a personnel manager so it seems. The outline at hand involves all the areas, our Fairfield County being our own province in charge of a retired army colonel, very pleasant.

Yes, I too am afraid that the unions are going to be the death of this country and one day there will be a catastrophe for them. I believe many workmen are not happy at the arbitrary methods of their leaders, who act like little Hitlers. It is as your friend says, the public who pays. Someday they may *not* pay . . . but en masse people are not very intelligent.

We would enjoy the raspberries if you wish to take the trouble to send them; but the picking is such as task; you should be careful not to invite sunstroke.

Our best greetings, GF

July 5, 1951

Dear Miss Stotler:

We had almost another hurricane! High winds and tossing trees, a bit too violent for comfort.

I'm off to chores in the village. Never did see the Summer take such wings! Or is it perhaps because we travel downward from the life peak?

At any rate, I have much to do, and want to have my Autumn plans mapped out, so my August holiday will be mostly free from routine matters of local interest.

I hope you had a happy visit in Cleveland with a pleasing home trip.

We put Mutzi to sleep—the heat had made breathing an effort. Now she lies under the roses . . . probably already sprouting canine wings, dear little beast, in her new realm!

In haste, GF

July 6, 1951

Dear Miss Stotler:

Thanks for the pretty cards from the museum. I have kept so many of my early loves from the European areas, and now find them priceless, for no one knows where so many of the originals might be, stolen or worse. What a pleasant nostalgia to review them in a collection by means of these prettily tinted cards.

I was quiet at home on the 4th, no guests, and enjoyed complete relaxation. I have learned that as one can never depend on the weather for gatherings in mid-Summer the wisest course is to make no plans, which thus relieves the household the fatigue of preparations.

The auction made $1,800 as perhaps I told you, to be distributed among our local charities. I think it is a goodly sum for the village. The committee are jubilant.

I shall go this weekend to view the operation of the Civil Defense post. Ours will not be ready till September. I think I wrote you of this.

My rooms are filled with the overwhelming beauty of the Regale lilies now in bloom. How lovely they are!

Our best wishes, GF

Ilka Stotler and her mother Elise Stotler, 1904. Ilka was reared in a rather formal atmosphere.

Dr. Stotler in Munich, drawn by John W. Beatty, later the first director of the Carnegie Institute of Pittsburgh.

Dr. and Mrs. Fulton R. Stotler.

Ilka loved the outdoors. *(right)*

Ilka Stotler with Cricket. *(below)*

Aida Truxall with Miss Farrar at Fairhaven, 1948. *(above)*

Aida Truxall at home around 1940. *(left)*

Farrar in *Königskinder*. Toscanini later recalled, "Yes, she was beautiful; she was very beautiful." *(above)*

The role of Manon was Farrar's alone in Berlin.

MR. AND MRS. SYDNEY D. FARRAR

Sydney D. and Henrietta Barnes Farrar, Geraldine's parents.

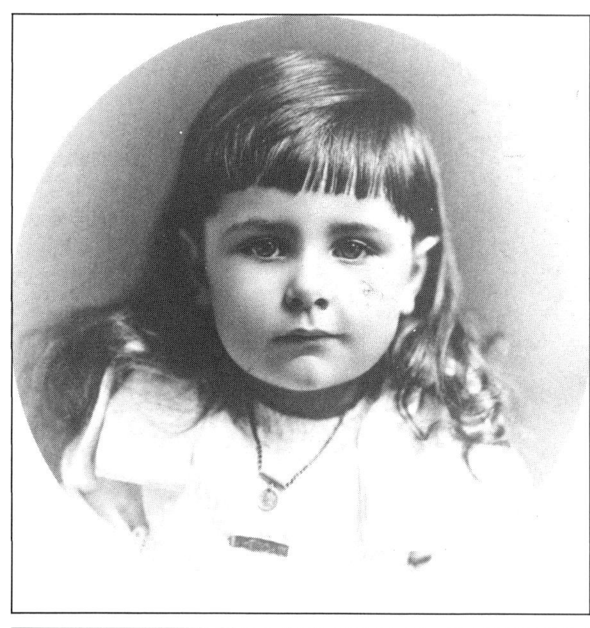

Geraldine Farrar as a child.

Kaiser Wilhelm and the Kaiserin showed great kindness to Farrar during her years in Berlin.

The Crown Prince Wilhelm (left) and his wife Princess Cecilie remained Farrar's friends for life.

Lilli Lehmann, Farrar's revered teacher, to whom she often referred.

To Farrar, Toscanini always remained "*The* Maestro."

Mary Cobb (Mrs. Howard) Gilmour, Farrar's dearest friend since the opera years.

"My precious Sylvia" Blein, Farrar's companion for fifty years.

Geraldine and her mother leave Berlin, November 1906.

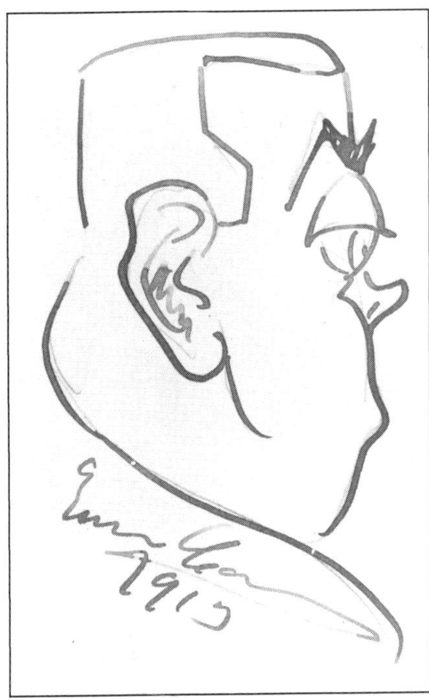

Enrico Caruso drew this sketch of himself. Farrar commented, "I think he was as happy drawing as when he was singing."

Enrico Caruso as the Chevalier des Grieux in *Manon*.

July 10, 1951

Dear Miss Stotler:

We have had such freakish weather; high winds, broken branches, dark skies. Today the heat is intense . . . the old earth must have her own travail, with so many devilish pin pricks from the active humans!

I have had the *China Story* [by Freda Utley] for some time. Every one should read it to know what perfidy has been committed in the name of the American people.

Now Dewey finds it imperative to make a Pacific trip. Why does he not stay at home and act the Governor for which he was elected? These politicos are like ailing prima donnas—they never want to give up.

Reds are indicted and convicted, bailed, and then disappear. Pretty business, why arrest them? It deceives no one of the thinking public.

I spent four very interesting hours at the "test" rehearsal in a nearby locale Saturday; one had quite a good idea of the intentions. It pleases me to see preparations for transitory comfort and food only; the evacuees will be moved on and out of the immediate area. Food, shelter, and clothing were on hand, churches and schools at the disposition of the committee planners. The installation is yet quite simple, it can easily be enlarged if need be. This would be our system, I think, for we are on the path of New England traffic, and liable to be pressed from New York as well as our own industrial centers.

My overseas letters require time and thought these mornings. I have to choose my words that the discouragement of those who envisage coming to our shores may be firm but not brutal. Several refined women are madly arranging their schedule to include secretarial work in English, French, and Spanish. This is not hard, but the conditions they would find here are another matter. I realize they are unsettled but so are we, with the same menace hanging over all of us. There is no escape from this crucial era of two ideologies . . . better stay home and fight it out where conditions are at least recognizable.

I am interested in anything that will allow me service, with the limitations of my years, with which I have to cope. Certain strenuous matters would not be my province, but I get along with people in general, and an air of harmony is to be hoped for. Indoor activity, desk work, etc., are perhaps not inspiring, but if the service is needed that is enough for me.

St. Stephen's is the lovely white church on Main Street, nearer the town center, almost facing the bank; it is the Congregational Church of stone that faces the street fountain. This marble erection provides at its lower base plenty of water for thirsty dogs and wading children. It was a gift to the town from the noted architect, Cass Gilbert, whose remaining family live a bit further down the street in the so-called "Cannonball" house. There are many accidents centered about this fork of the roads and every once in a while there is a clamor to have the fountain removed, likewise, the magnificent old elm under which its sparkling waters play; but so far we have been able to overcome the minor voices of this wish, and I trust we may continue to do so.

I sent off yesterday sketchy ideas of the four Blood Bank posters and leave their execution in your able hands.

All good wishes, GF

July 20, 1951

Dear Miss Stotler:

Hot, humid weather, and in consequence there is little activity in our house today.

Yesterday we went on a long and fruitful ride, way North of Danbury, in search of the dachsies. After much inquiry we did locate a kennel that deals only in this breed and had males for sale, the brown color, and just six weeks old, nicely weaned.

We sped to this lovely old place, excellent kennels, and the most ingratiating canines you would want to behold. We picked a pair of brothers, the sweetest little lumps of fur . . . babies that nestle in one's neck and love to be held tight and warm. They stood the long motor ride well, and are now bathed and fed, running about in the laundry yard until their play indicates rest.

I call them Bubi and Luka . . . such adorable scamps. With the two canaries we have quite a pet shop. My older canary, Pepi, is in the sunny bathroom, and Coco, the second acquisition here, in the study at the front window. Both are cheerful singers. Margaret is their warden and is regular with offerings of orange, lettuce, tonic, bird biscuit and so forth, to supplement the seed cup. Every one in my household has a hearty appetite.

We are well and send best greetings, GF

Later—

A couple here for lunch plan a most interesting trip. He has business in many corners of Europe, but means to combine it with certain novel expeditions in the company of some Athenian gentlemen; Athens, Crete—the history of this island has intrigued him since his college days—then Egypt and the Nile, with the loitering that is productive of speculation and stimulates the imagination. He is my lawyer, and glad to eschew for a time the routine of a successful métier and the pressure of our hectic tempo. His wife is a dear friend, talented and musical, with the same elasticity of perception . . . they should have a very unusual vacation. I could go along, as they hinted, but the thought suffices, with my thanks for inclusion. I could not make the transitions that conditions would entail . . . I do like my home ease. The journey to the Cape, with its simple routine to which I am accustomed, will be quite enough for me.

I feel deeply the passing of my friend of these fifty years,[163] a long time to surmount wars and such changes as have been his lot . . . I knew he was not well, but did not dream to what extent his health had been latterly undermined. His own letters spoke little of his plight, but were mostly concerned with events that meant little happiness for his country. His daughter and her husband came to visit me before taking the plane to attend services; a nice young couple—they will make out well. She is in good hands.

---

[163] On July 20, 1951, Crown Prince Wilhelm of Germany died in French custody at Hechingen, Württemberg. At the close of World War I, he had renounced his right to the throne. In the days of Geraldine Farrar's early success in Berlin, much was made of her friendship with the Crown Prince, then a slender youth of nineteen, her own age. On one occasion her father "beat up" an editor whose paper was circulating especially scandalous stories. The American press in Berlin also staunchly defended Farrar. In truth, she had neither time nor inclination for dalliance; it is clear that her career was all important to her.

In 1906, when Farrar requested a leave of absence from the Royal Opera, the Intendant refused to take up the matter with the Kaiser. She then spoke for herself, explaining her desire to try her wings in her native land. The Kaiser granted the leave, to be repeated in succeeding years, on condition that she return every spring for a season in his capital. She did so until the outbreak of war in 1914.

All her life Farrar remained in close touch with the Crown Prince and members of the royal family, who had always treated her with great kindness. After World War II, she assisted them with CARE packages and other small comforts.

Yes I have been refusing all suggestions to film my book. Really it would mean a large sum to sell my name, and God knows what would ensue—though I can pretty well guess.

Caruso was a generous and lovable human, warmhearted and a good comrade. The film is inaccurate and cheap . . . his own life offered far more interest than the trumped-up stuff portrayed.

All his friends rejoiced that he found so much happiness in his marriage to young Dorothy Benjamin, although it was destined to be so brief. The birth of his daughter was, he said, his crowning glory, so he named her Gloria. The mother has not been happy in succeeding marriages. Caruso was her idol.

Please excuse the many typing faults; I am in a hurry and still drowsy from this wonderful air and the delight of *dolce far niente* [it's sweet to do nothing].

Best of good wishes, GF

Pennywise
Cape Vincent, New York
August 2, 1951

Dear Miss Stotler:

Reports of heat at home are dreadful—92° and 97°. An inferno.

We are cool and at ease in this wonderful air, the river gently lapping our garden walls and inviting the boats and larger ships on their way with freight.

This month of lazy delight is appreciated, I assure you. Our routine here is quiet—few guests, and only for tea and an afternoon visit. A stroll around the charming garden or a short drive and we settle to the shady delight of the veranda. Perhaps I shall muster enough energy to continue the revision of my address book. So many R.I.P. crosses against so many names. One is very conscious of the flight of time, and one's inevitable departure to other realms of many friends.

I had all the German accounts and photos of the K.P's rites. Burial was in the Hohenzollern castle grounds. The daughter is still with her mother abroad. Louis Ferdinand is now the titular head of the family. The marriages of all the children appear to be happy. Prince Louis's wife is the Grand Duchess Kira, of the old Russian noblesse. As a very young man he was a popular worker in the Ford plant at Dearborn. He has visited me in Ridgefield.

Now to lunch and contemplation of this lovely scene—I am

always clear in mind when I can come to Nature and learn from her unhurried, if inexorable, progress.

All good greetings, GF

August 3, 1951

Dear Miss Stotler:

Downpour and most gratifying cool, after the home heat. We sit by a fire in wool frocks and rejoice in the billows that dash against the garden barricades. At present books and catnaps are my happy routine.

As to galleries and pictures, I feel a bit like King Ludwig; if I might enjoy them alone, taking my time, and musing at the lovely splendors. I hate to march through galleries, herded with the mobs, with tired feet and eyes.

A friend praised the permanent collection of photos in the Museum of Modern Art, where Steichen[164] sits three days a week; she was certain I would be happy to go and admire, likewise renew a fleeting acquaintance, since many years ago he did photograph me.

I would prefer a stroll, alone, through his fairyland garden of delphiniums, rather . . . but their beautiful coloring is nicely portrayed in the garden books, to be enjoyed without chat or social business.

The most successful photos I ever had are those from the early Berlin days by a great artist soul, Georg Gerlach. He seized the moment I felt spontaneous, and made that *Manon* head that is my preferred. The eighteenth century has always been of nostalgic interest, though I cannot say why, unless some obscure atavism urges the response . . .

One is made from so many strands . . . how can one know which is only a thread in the pattern, and which the principal motif?

I hear guests, so for today, good wishes. GF

[164] Born in Luxembourg and trained in Paris in new technical methods, Edward Steichen elevated black and white photography to a high art. In the United States he was involved in photography for the armed services in both world wars. He became famous for his photographs of well-known people published in *Vanity Fair* and *Vogue*. They were distinguished by his subtle use of light and shadow and his ability to capture the personality of his subjects. In 1947 he became director of the Photography Department of the Museum of Modern Art.

August 8, 1951

Dear Miss Stotler:

Pouring cold rain, the river tranquil and like a ribbon at our garden's edge. None the less, we are off to Watertown on business for the day.

We spent a few hours in Ottawa recently, a handsome city, a three-and-a-half hour's ride through rich farmlands with the river winding in and out of pretty villages. I hadn't been there since my *Carmen* tour in 1926 . . . a long time ago!

The days pass quickly. Friends come in and we have no formal program. I do none of the sports, so am not disturbed in my inclination to remain on the porch.

The current *Saturday Evening Post* has a vivid article on Acapulco that would give you an idea of this lovely spot, though it seems that it may soon become like the overcrowded resorts here, abroad, and in South America. Soon there won't be an island where one can be sure of seclusion.

This North country has its own charm—frontier history and colorful legend.

Friends who lunched recently with our great General report him an amazing man! Alert, keen, in wonderful physical condition; with positive ideas on those subjects he knows first hand from a lifetime of experience.

I read that English royalty must by-pass New York, but will visit Blair House.[165] Poor things; they have a rugged Canadian schedule, and quite properly, owe that country their first attention. Blair House, is, of course, a tacit official gesture.

A letter from Lilli Lehmann's niece (83) bemoans what she fears is the "Entschadung" [vandalization] of Frau Lilli's resting place. Can I do anything? I shall try to find out if this is really true. The last time a friend had been to the grave where there was a splendid urn, nothing in the area had been disturbed. I see no reason for any unhappy deterioration, the urn being of permanent substance.

London praises a superb Flagstad concert (to my mind she is only half herself in this avenue) and the same press notes that she will forego the heavier Wagner roles (alas!) and choose lighter ones. A confession of waning powers she is not wise to admit.

[165] Located in Washington, D.C., Blair House serves as the U.S. President's guest house for distinguished visitors.

This month of complete relaxation is appreciated for I anticipate a busy Winter with local matters. I do sleep well here—the air is something special, rare and pure.

It seems our puppies are smart as can be!

Kind greetings, GF

August 10, 1951

Dear Miss Stotler:

I do not recall, as you do, that I told you at our first meeting, "I am interested in transcendentalism." I cannot claim to have any deep knowledge of it; only a dim feeling of motivations beyond my controlled thought or reason, like small points of light, at times, that one might call intuitive . . . I rather think this definition from *Funk and Wagnalls* best expresses this feeling. *Transcendentalism has been applied in the language of the Emersonian school, to the soul's intuitive knowledge of things divine and human . . . so far as they are capable of being known to man.*

How can one put his finger on the gossamer of such delicate experience? I cannot even describe the sensation of being beyond material reasoning or compulsion. I am very practical in matters of daily living per se. How define my soul—unless this nebulous form of the dictionary gives a hint?

Referring to another letter—I do not doubt that you saw the flying saucers. I am sure they do exist, and all this nonsense of denial is silly. They no doubt have something to do with research work, and as such, will in good time present their purpose. Several of my magazines carried well documented accounts as well as sketches of their various designs. Our officials do not reckon with the keen nose for news of the press, so all the mystery is furnished by the former, it would seem. I was much interested.

In re Chaliapin[166]—I knew him first in Monte Carlo, where the presence of his Italian wife and a troop of progeny and nursemaids apparently detracted in no way from his reputation as a lady-killer. A great blond giant of a man with a marvelous voice and great acting ability. He was always a good comrade, although his habit of dropping into Russian in recitatives where cues were none too easy in any

166 Feodor Ivanovich Chaliapin (1873–1938), though Russian-born, lived outside the USSR after 1921. Possessed of a powerful bass voice, he was also a fine actor.

language, could be provoking. I recall especially Caruso's difficulty with this in *Don Giovanni.*

Now to the village and many chores.

Best greetings to you, GF

August 15, 1951

Dear Miss Stotler:

I know of no memoirs written by the Crown Prince save those from the First World War. The general press has not been too friendly in the obituary notices—perhaps to be expected . . . Well, it is now a matter of the past and can harm my friend no longer.

Our weather continues superbly cool, while humidity reigns at home, to the discomfort of all.

I believe Frau Lilli's urn, in Grunewald [Berlin], is in the American occupied sector. The niece is a recluse, and I fear, a bit "touched" in the head. She occupies the lovely villa outside Salzburg that I knew so well, but can use only one room; alone and deserted, it seems. I sent a friend to see her last year; reports were far from cheerful. Death is the most charitable solution in such cases.

Moods? Everyone is liable to them, dependent on many causes. No doubt you are fatigued unduly, and the body cries out for relief from physical and emotional strain. I take full advantage of this peaceful routine.

Each puppy has gained four pounds since I left!

All good wishes, GF

August 20, 1951

Dear Miss Stotler:

Fog and warmer weather. The cargo boats go full blast by our garden emitting their long hoarse calls to advise of their position. The river joins Lake Ontario just below us and the local pilots take over to navigate the tricky channels through the islands to the ocean. But a fog horn is a desolate cry, all the same, and of almost a human note of distress.

Some military men were here and I was much interested in their observations. One was, to let Ike get the GOP nomination, and send Mac to Europe as a soldier and administrator. Also make the DPs [persons displaced by World War II] paid mercenaries with the reluctant Europeans, all under USA command, but so placed as to cause no friction between hereditary enemies, and not drain the U.S. of manpower. Anyway it's a thought, and the DPs might thus justify our interest in them.

They are of the opinion that Taft could not win the presidency when Ike has the "build-up." I would prefer to vote for Taft.

May your weekend be happy, and with a breeze. GF

August 21, 1951

Dear Miss Stotler:

A ripsnorting downpour, blotting out the river, even the huge trees in our garden. The rattle on the roof gives a very pleasant feeling. One is so relaxed and protected in this gay cottage that the mood is wholly agreeable.

I have been re-reading here *Days of My Years* by Pierre van Paassen, a report of his experiences since the First World War. Much of it rings with dreadful veracity today. It is a sad book.

He is evidently anti-capitalist, but as an humble reader I would not know where to place the blame for the defects he deplores, save on the varied patterns of human behavior, not necessarily on a system. The book leaves one with confusion and many matters unresolved, but the brilliant worldly figures who course through his pages all have their weaknesses.

I have been approached to write another book. The idea falls *not* on fertile soil. There is too much pulp poured into the refuse tubs as it is. Too many, too futile! The last volume of [the philosopher George] Santayana is deadly boresome—an old hermit in his Roman cell with no message to send out. To be genuine, any writer must present his era in its harsh light—and as I see it, to what end?

The Autumn flower catalogues are entrancing . . . at least *they* carry no taint of human frailty.

Now to lunch and general chat of the fishermen who are not dismayed by inclement weather. They *fish* no matter what.

Best greetings, GF

Home
October 3, 1951

Dear Miss Stotler:

Well, here we are, home again and on the threshold of Winter. Falling leaves like golden coins, drifting this way and that—a Danae shower.

I am minded of your query concerning a future life. One must hold to something, faith or belief; I have my own thoughts about this business. One sees the seasons change, all nature burgeons, sleeps and reappears, following the age-old pattern. For me the application is just as good for a human. Progression continues, perhaps with a fusion of the individual rather than a separate identity; what does it matter? I cannot embrace the rituals but they have their place for those who can.

The Babylonian evening was a dinner and quasi-business affair, most enjoyable. I had not seen some of the friends for ten years, since the Mexican trip. Several live there and were in the city for only a short visit.

Mexico has its own brand of politics . . . one understands there that mordida (polite graft) is a definite part of any transaction; thus there is no public hysteria about sudden disclosures of fiscal scandals, but a steady percentage of expected gratuities when service is rendered . . . the old pattern of Europe.

I do not know the young Roberta Peters, but she is the pupil of a friend of mine, who speaks very highly of her ability, good voice and ambition. I regret that *Life* portrayed her in such vulgar style, but that is no doubt the agent's idea of original publicity. Today there is no limit to the brashness employed to get before the public, and often real talent is obscured by these shoddy and unnecessary means. I do not know her background at all. She sprang into a MET performance [as Zerlina in *Don Giovanni*] at last minute notice, with excellent press, and had genuine success in the British Festival under Beecham. We can do with some new talent if it is really promising.

Hearing Mario Lanza last evening, I could only regret that this fine youthful organ was wasted in yelling over a radio program. He should be studying serious music to become a real singer in opera. A very pleasant chap on the screen, and certainly with vocal potentiality, but the voice will not last long if he continues in the present ear-splitting expenditure of natural clarion-like scale.

I am sure you had real delight in the current Loan Exhibit. How well I agree with the lovely French portraits.

In all Berlin collections my choice would have been the small gallery at Sans Souci in Potsdam, which was a marvel of dainty *Watteau, Lancret, Greuze,* etc. All small canvasses, but of such enchanting delicacy, the proper setting for a young lady in her furbelows of another era. Where are they now, I wonder? *Boucher* and *Fragonard* . . . they had such a palette for illusion and color charm. I shall love to have the promised catalogue. Thanks.

I shall also be appreciative of your offer of the coming Taft book. This man has been my choice right along. He is honest and fearless, and no one has a better brain. The smear campaign will continue on all sides, but he will not lose in stature no matter what the outcome.

Flagstad will not come before the New Year to the MET. Her Carnegie Hall concert is scheduled the first week in February. The novelty of *Alceste*[167] in English will not tempt me to go, despite Mr. Bing's essay at something out of the ordinary.

I hope the hunters leave you in peace—as well as the hunted!

Our greetings, GF

October 6, 1951

Dear Miss Stotler:

The true autumnal days are here. At the moment, a dull sky and hint of showers, the gardens somehow pitiful in their obedience to the chill nights and brisk winds. I have the last of the vivid zinnias and marigolds at hand, and their pretty splashes of color, in various vases, lend a sunny gaiety to my study.

We are off to clean the halls for the clinical preparation of the Blood Bank, a voluntary job for us Red Cross workers; but we are given rent free the rooms, and cannot, nor do we, complain. I have a fine canteen chairman, who is most competent in the kitchen, happily.

Before Korea, you perhaps recall we had a regional blood program. Most of the states signed for it, and the voluntary donors gave through the Red Cross. But once this ghastly Korean war presented urgencies, we had to speed up the business—hence the

[167] Opera by Christoph Willibald von Gluck, first performed in Vienna in December 1767.

Blood Bank drives and our hectic efforts. At the moment the urge is for fresh blood, not plasma. This fluid is flown to Korea immediately.

We have been plagued by the gossip that the Red Cross sells blood—a shameful lie. The organization is not too popular and I surmise because the local committees are less than tactful and polite at their desks. New York showed me this snobbish attitude clearly—a great pity.

To put your mind at rest, we do not anticipate actual bombing here, save perhaps an incendiary stray. A very expensive explosive is more likely to be used in crowded sectors or factory sites, for damage to material and esprit—too costly to waste on a few humans and field areas. I am only repeating what our military opine.

The Garden woman is publicity mad, so perhaps this affords her some sort of pleasure.[168]

Now to a meeting, and the bracing autumn day.

Our best greetings, GF

October 28, 1951

Dear Miss Stotler:

Yes, I am assailed (as are most people of some public news), with subtly worded invitations to subscribe to this and that; one's family tree, for example. I wrote that the young man designated as

---

168 Miss Farrar enclosed this clipping with the letter.

Mary Garden Sails in With Cargo of Gems

With $500,000 worth of jewelry on her neck, her ears, around her wrists and on her fingers, Mary Garden, onetime operatic soprano, arrived yesterday aboard the United States Line's *America* for a last visit to the States.

The flash items:

A six-strand pearl necklace, pearl bracelet and an emerald bracelet, several sapphire, ruby and diamond rings, and, to brighten her up a little, an emerald diamond pin.

The Scot spinster, now in her 70s, explained that she is booked for a nation-wide lecture tour. She started herself off on the right note:

"American men are most charming and companionable—not like the Latins. And I don't like dumb men . . ."

Five-feet-four and still at her old-time singing weight of 110 pounds, Miss Garden said she'd be here until December, then Winter in Scotland and Summer next year in Corsica—"The one place you can live with nature."

"You can bathe any way you want," she amplified archly, "and no one pays any attention."

This reminded the older ship news reporters that years ago she had reportedly swum in the nude off Corsica, which she confirmed. "I love it," she said.

agent would not be welcome. I have all the family history at my finger tips, and am indifferent to any further inclusion in vellum at high costs.

Recently an imposing committee invited one to subscribe to a proposed American Shakespeare Theater to be built in my neighborhood; much stress laid on combatting the woeful state of the theater, present entertainment, etc. The sum of $552,000 is the starting point, with special grants later for an Academy whereby aspirants will be instructed by the "great" how to carry on in the old tradition. My letter was one of regret, and quite formal. But the thought did persist, with the formidable wealthy patrons heading the gesture, that it would be more simple to have *them* fund the enterprise and see what happens!

I recall well the splurge of the Century Theater in New York by some of the MET directors, with high purpose to promote operas and plays. I sang at the opening with [Julia] Marlowe and [Edward] Sothern appearing in *Cleopatra.*

The theater cost a fortune, was most unfortunate in acoustics, looked like a Roman bath—marble, plush, etc.—not feasible for opera or plays. It was given over to *The Miracle*[169] a pageant by Max Reinhardt, and later to the ballet. In the end it was torn down, a complete fiasco. I hope the Festival House mentioned will not suffer the same fate.

I am glad that Taft has declared himself, and do not think he has made a mistake. It now remains for the layman to use some kind of sensible reasoning and vote in an able, honest man.

Some Mexican friends are due any moment and should bring a happy change of thought.

A pleasant weekend to you, GF

October 1951

Dear Miss Stotler:

I was interested to hear last night, Henry J. Taylor, who has been the length and breadth of Scandinavia, include in his talk, Finland, whose people elicit his warm admiration. With their four million people, and Russia at their door, they succeed in paying their honorable debts, keep themselves fit and tough, and make the daily

[169] In which the English beauty, Lady Diana Manners, starred as the nun.

routine of the Russians stationed there so miserable they know not where to turn—all with no shouting or chest thumping.

We, with our great abundance, and sixty million still move in fear and trembling, waiting on those rascals and doing everything a self-respecting individual condemns . . . heigh-ho!

One ponders, in a different field, on that wonderful old elm (1729) in Wilton, that has succumbed to the Dutch elm disease and has to be removed. If it could become vocal for a time . . . what could it not reveal?

One feels so sorry for the suffering English King[170] and his family: decent people. Sad that they should have this ordeal. I imagine the malady is a fatal one, for so serious a surgery case.

Now to dress for dinner.

Our greetings, GF

November 9, 1951

Dear Miss Stotler:

Here is a blast from a Boston paper sent to me by an enraged patriot. *Era of Tolerated Corruption Will Shock Historians. Boston Sunday Herald*, Oct. 14, 1951. Most of our citizens are as apathetic about the Blood Bank. I think we do not deserve our great good luck so far.

I fear the sparkling Evita Peron[171] is a very ill woman with the dread malady. Too bad. She has at least the brains and the courage for the glamorous role she plays. Up from the gutter, if you will, she rises, while many born with more advantages sink to a low level, indeed. One hears that she is a sufferer from uterine cancer—surely a dreadful ordeal for a young, handsome woman. One hopes she confounds her medical advisors.

The birthday party in New York was a happy and intimate one. Mrs. G. was touched by the little surprises we had prepared for her. Lilies-of-the-valley were flown in from California for table decorations with silver and crystal. The living room was a mass of smilax

[170] The operation for lung resection took place September 23, 1951. On February 6, 1952, King George VI died in his sleep at Sandringham. He was buried at Windsor on February 16, 1951.

[171] A motion picture actress, Maria Eva Duarte (1919–1952) married Juan Peron, who four months later became President of Argentina. She was immensely popular because of her extensive welfare programs and was deeply mourned at her death in 1952.

and gardenias. All of us were of the same vintage and it was an evening of dear memories.

I note with real pleasure that in a recent *Life* three gracious ladies of the theater carry the title cover page—[Lynn] Fontanne, [Katharine] Cornell and [Helen] Hayes. This is a source of delight to those of us who associate them with the best traditions, certainly a welcome change from the previous dubious females in strange postures . . . like the demoiselles in the bordellos. However one must go far to find a Bernhardt, a Duse, or an Agnes Sorma . . .

I must tell you that I have a most beautiful TV, the anticipated birthday gift of Mrs. Gilmour as she believed the opera opening would be broadcast. I would never have thought to have purchased it for myself, but it is a magnificent gift and will provide diversion for family and friends, especially when Winter snows keep us indoors.

I can appreciate your disinclination, perhaps heartache, to place the Dogwood home for eventual sale. But one must think of the uncertain future, one's waning energy, and the responsibilities that abound with large acreage. How well I understand the desire for one's own roof; rentals are never to my liking.

I nearly forgot to tell you that Mrs. G. met a relative of yours, Mrs. Kuhn, while lunching last week with [former Met contralto] Mme. Marion Telva (Mrs. Elmer Jones), where it was discovered that you and the lady are related. They were in New York.

The Korean situation will not better. Conflicting stories come out. Now, per General [Hoyt S.] Vandenberg [Air Force Chief of Staff], the possibility of need for attack in Manchuria. Well, we would have been farther along had the powers that be in Washington given MacArthur a free hand. As it is the toll in American lives stands at over 100,000. Not pretty reading.

Our puppies are all over the house, to the despair of Margaret. They are so lively and want to be with us all the time. When the "Wasserleitung" [water control] gets to be a more reliable affair this will not be difficult, and they may come where they will.

Even at this early age they show such dissimilar dispositions. Luka is alert, active, curious, and takes every initiative. He is into every corner, whips up and down stairs like a whirlwind, and has no fear of anything. Little Bubi loves to lie on the knee, cradled in the arms; cries at being left behind by his wild brother, but is much slower to adopt the tactics. Very gentle, very loving.

As they grow into their harness we can take them outside, but now they would be impossible to handle, especially as the big garage dog, a nice blundering collie-shepherd beast is as frolicsome as they, and would be off to the woods with them in no time.

All good greetings, GF

November 26, 1951

Dear Miss Stotler:

Thanksgiving Day was crisp and sunny. I spent it with a charming group of old friends. As I have remarked, the circle narrows, but memory holds the departed ones in close touch.

The NBC concert was supremely beautiful—I hope you heard it. The *Meistersinger* soliloquy, Hans Sachs's gentle resignation to matters in his world, was like a caress from the strings—truly heartwarming. There was no lessening of the vigor of the Maestro's beat; nothing escaped the perfectionist and the orchestra responded nobly.

I think the so-called spark of energy lies mainly in the mental processes. When one has vitality there, it shows, whether or not expressed in physical gesture—but the combination is highly gratifying.

Personally I think it is not good for orchestras to have to accommodate themselves to a constant stream of guest conductors, each man having his own beat, conception, and method of inducing the musicians to obey. How can it be otherwise? It is like so many opera performances. If the cast is always changeable, no one knows the intention of the other; thus the smoothness and detailed ornaments are lost, and each newcomer ill at ease; though it is true that many operatic roles require all too little interpretation so long as the voice responds.

You asked what role I considered the most difficult. Each one had its pages and demands. No role ever gave the easy feeling that one could sail through it. The combination of vocal and emotional appeal, once on the stage, proved a quite different thing than when the score was rehearsed, calmly and with mental attention, at home. There is some devil in the theater itself, with the added stimulus of the audience, that transports one into another realm. One is aquiver with nerves. I read once that Man of War ran a perfect and controlled practice hour, but once the bugle sounded he knew the same expectancy and had nervous chills until the race started and he was on the course. So much for the purely magnetic communication of the moment.

My TV gave a very comprehensive account of Taft in his several tours and the speeches he made. I am all out for him. This dry, matter of fact, pleasant manner suits my humor. I want someone with his feet on the ground—and for *Home Policy First*!

All good greetings to you, GF

November 30, 1951

Dear Miss Stotler:

Weather at the moment, crisp and sunny. May it so continue. Each such day one less of dreary Winter.

The *Call Me Madam* is rough and vulgar, but hilarious in its blunt political matter. I laugh even now, recalling the brass-lunged [Ethel] Merman, on whose shoulders rests the whole show, and her easy mugging of all the points that are scored. Our matinee was a party of ladies and we all enjoyed loud laughs with the packed theater. The material is fit best for New York where there is no brake on the provocation for lusty haw-haws.

Yes, I know what "chitterlings" are; certain Southern dishes do not find favor with me. Pork and fowl seem to be the preferred diet—so many of my friends do not care for red beef, veal, or lamb.

Too bad you had a bout with the liver; it can be a most cantankerous member of our combination. I had reason to give mine a drastic reproof last week and it has been sweet and docile since. I think I had a bit too much gaiety, with hours not quite so tranquil as usual—the cause of the malaise.

Our best greetings, GF

1952

(Envelope marked in Ilka's hand, "Heartening letter.")
February 16, 1952

Dear Miss Stotler:

Your letter of Thursday as well as that of Tuesday, here at the same hour, breathes much of misery and pain. I am relieved for you that you have already bespoken the hospital room, and *please, this time*, do go through with the matter and be once more your gay *well* self. I feel certain that once the ordeal is accomplished you will wonder why you tortured yourself in raising such barriers.

Every day of delay has only lessened your strength. I do not mean to be intrusive, but such constant pain only prolongs this matter to no purpose . . . be a good girl and get it over with!

I thanked yesterday for the exquisite bouquet in honor of the good St. Valentine . . . I could see myself wending my way to a luncheon at Delmonico's, in a smart victoria behind high-stepping horses and equipage to match those lovely days. All was gay, one was young and full of illusions and life was at the peak of happy adventure. I was privileged to so enjoy it at the time despite hard and unremitting routine.

All this circa 1906—1907. What days!

We have brought some lovely branches of forsythia into the house which thanks to the water are blooming; delicate yellow sprays that betoken Spring, indeed.

A few uncomfortable hours, less than at present, and you will be fit as a fiddle again . . . go through with the plan for surgery![172]

GF

February 16, 1952

My dear Aida:

To thank you again for so kindly advising me of the final decision of Ilka . . . now she will surmount the convalescence, and never have to bother with such anguish more!

I shall send the wire today, hoping it will be less disturbing and she may gain some measure of our hearty good wishes. Now if she can be patient and allow complete healing in the hospital, she'll gain all the more quickly.

---

[172] The surgery proved successful and the patient made a good recovery. The following letter from Miss Farrar to Aida Truxall reflects the former's concern.

She has had such a dreadful struggle with her apprehensions! Not the happiest way to spend her birthday, but the results will be the blessing.

It is good to know you gain strength and have such gay plans ahead. Thank you again for so kindly phoning, and with every good wish to you and your husband.

Cordially, Geraldine Farrar

1953

November 25, 1953

Dear Miss Stotler:

A perfect SPRING day, blue skies and sunshine; what a cock-eyed world indeed!

I must confess that radio and press with the various slants on the espionage doings upset me no end. I cannot understand why decent people keep harping on the "invasion of privacy," etc. Does not the man in the street *want* the apprehension of malefactors? Why hinder the few committees that are trying to get nefarious elements out of our important posts? The only means to do so is exposure.

Well, it all makes for a strange situation, especially incongruous at this time when we celebrate the one truly *American* day of gratitude for our country's survival and the promise of its greatness. Perhaps those dour Puritans did not have the most ingratiating manners but they were people of principle and fought to attain and keep it. Well, life has lost all semblance of simplicity unless we insist upon it for ourselves, which I try to do.

No, I have not read Edith Wharton in some time; do not know *The Reef.* So many of her books are dated without the enduring human characterization that makes great works live on. 1912—what ages ago that seems!

The Toscanini concert [with the NBC Orchestra] went off well, though I must confess the choice of offerings, *The Tragic Overture* and *Don Quixote*, are not my special favorites. The Maestro seems to have recovered his immense vitality, at least in the concerts.

A happy holiday to you, and good health. GF

My good Margaret has had her 70th birthday and is inclined to resent it.

Thanksgiving Day, 1953

Dear Miss Stotler:

Such unbelievable weather, real Summer. One almost pants with any exertion. The maintenance men are still raking leaves that fall just enough to make it a permanent and expensive job.

The bill for the January tree damage by the hurricane has been sent me. One wonders if this item, of considerable importance, is likely to be a yearly matter. However this is part of the home responsibility, and as such I accept it, rather than fly to a rabbit warren, as do many of my friends, and pretend they are comfortable. That is not living, to my mind.

The Opera opened with scant observation, in the papers, of the singers, but much nonsense about the designs, set in 19th century Paris, and *not* in 16th century German environs, as the great Goethe wrote in his *Faust.* Judging from the sketches and report it could have been *Bohème.*

Goethe was not mentioned in the program . . . of course this will not trouble that august spirit. In Germany this opera was always billed as *Margarethe*, since it represents but an incident in the hero's life. As you know, there are two other operas on the same theme, in which I have sung—[Berlioz's] *La Damnation de Faust* and [Boito's] *Mefistofele*, both very expressive of the musical settings, French and Italian, with Faust the hero in one, the Devil as such, in the other. As our traditional better known and loved favorite is the Gounod version, I see no reason for transposing the century from the more picturesque setting of the poets. What will these moderns do next?

Unlike you, I have no hunting problems, but the deer are becoming a menace in their mad escapades. Two people near here have had their cars damaged by deer smashing blindly into them. The animals break their necks—no pretty sight, and the car driver is shocked into hysterics . . . I fear the animals from the nearby preserve are lacking in food and drink.

Time now for the holiday jaunt into the country for the Thanksgiving bird. I shall be home in good time; no more driving at night. The fogs are deceptive and dangerous.

All good wishes, GF

December 8, 1953

Dear Miss Stotler:

First of all, thanks for the Dimling's candy, a treat at all times. The carrier brought it on his rounds this lovely morning.

The weather is truly beautiful; crisp air, sunny skies, and more greensward than ever I obtain in Springtime. Birds caroling from every branch.

Yes, I think the MET is wholly unsatisfactory to be touted as *the* opera house of the world. Between the performances and the nitwits in the entr'actes I fled for air and other thoughts. After the "Jewel Song" [in *Faust*], a nice ride in these hills was refreshing.

[Ferruccio] Tagliavini seems not to be in the company. [Jussi] Björling, I am told, is too fond of his bottle to be a reliable member, though he is announced now and then. [Salvatore] Baccaloni must wait, without doubt, for those operas, *Barber*, *Elisir D' Amore*, etc., where the buffo role is dominant.

Miss Munsel,[173] after her *Melba* film (which I did not see, so cannot render a verdict save the observations of English friends who were pretty severe), now seems to be devoting most of her time to her offspring. A recent photograph with it, and recommending some kind of diaper (adv.) is the latest addition to the publicity man's column.

Miss Peters is, by far, the more talented. She is kept busy, and studies hard. I do not know her, only see and hear her on TV. She is pretty and poised. The voice shows signs of serious attention, always good and apt to be unusual in these times.

Yes, I heard the agreeable reference to myself at the [Boston] Philharmonic entr'acte. How many memories! That old concert hall should be kept always as a revered shrine, so many of the truly *great* have stepped onto its podium. As a young girl I heard Joseph Hofmann in his American debut, Lilli Lehmann, Nordica, Melba, Sembrich, Carreño, not to forget Kreisler and Rachmaninoff. The wonderful Boston symphony under Karl Muck, as soloist often, with this finest band in the world at that time, and *not* union wrecked!

All good greetings, and try to keep cheerful. It will do no good to go on the rampage. We are helpless in this complex pattern of modern life. I am trying to get out from under as much as I can, a "sauve-qui-peut" [save yourself whoever can] scrutiny. If I take care of *my* problems, there will be one less on the Federal payroll.

GF

The new *Faust* setting seems to amuse the young opera goers. I listen to their comments and say nothing. What is the use to argue against ignorance and lack of taste?

[173] Born in Spokane, Washington, in 1925, Patrice Munsel joined the Metropolitan Opera Company as its youngest member in 1943. She was vocally unprepared for the difficult coloratura roles she was required to sing, with the result that her delicate voice was damaged. However, she continued to charm audiences for many years in less demanding performances than grand opera calls for.

December 18, 1953

Dear Miss Stotler:

Weather bitter cold but dry and sunny. The premises sparkle, a million diamonds of cheer. I like it thus; one feels alert and ready for action.

Our simple home decors are done and the pines give out a wonderful aroma. Christmas seems so real in the country . . . the city is gaudy, and somehow artificial. We are well, and this is the greatest blessing of all.

I shall listen a few moments to the *Bohème* tomorrow, as the Musetta [Jean Fenn] is the pupil of a friend of mine and has earned a genuine success. It is good to see her serious efforts rewarded. I was invited to attend, but that is another story. I shall hear, at ease, and in quiet.

I shall welcome the lovely blue candle of which you speak, and it will join its twin on the upper hall bookcase where it can be seen. I do not light these candles as their beauty without matches is quite sufficient, and besides we are chary of fire hazards.

Clocks? I have small table ones all over the house, but no so-called grandfather's clock; that left the family long ago, but I do like their friendly tic-toc . . .

You were writing of the handsome Ludwig of Bavaria.[174] In my youth there I do recall so many tales from peasants who could remember him in his fantastic escapades. Always a poet, seeking beauty and illusion. Easy enough to allow such fancies to play on one's imagination, so beautiful is Bayern and its many legends.

How thrilling for your mother and her school friends, the

[174] Ludwig II of Bavaria spent a happy childhood in the ancient Castle of Hohenschwangau, which his father, Maximilian II, had restored. Here the boy's romantic imagination was stimulated by the fine alpine setting of the castle and by its interior decorations, including paintings and frescoes of medieval heroes, among them the Swan Knight, Lohengrin. On the death of his father, Ludwig, aged nineteen, became king of Bavaria. He was greatly loved by his people, less so by his military-minded cabinet. Becoming more and more reclusive, he found his chief joy in the music of Wagner, whose career he subsidized, and in employing his flair for architecture in the building of fabulous and expensive castles. In June 1886 Ludwig was declared insane and within days his body and that of his doctor, whom he was presumed to have murdered, were discovered floating on the edge of the Starnberger See. He was deeply mourned by his cousin, the Empress Elizabeth of Austria, who had always sympathized with him. Today Ludwig is best remembered for his support of Richard Wagner and for his wonderful castles, Neuschwanstein, Linderhof, and Herrenchiemsee.

meetings in the park at Nymphenburg with Ludwig exercising his greyhounds.

Our village looks very pretty and inviting, the greens gradually taking their part in the holiday trimmings.

Best greetings and cheerio, GF

December 19, 1953

Dear Miss Stotler:

Many thanks for the always kind thought and the heavenly roses—great luscious blooms that are so perfume dispensing! Sturdy of stem also, which means that with my daily care they will smile at me for a long time.

Snow is in the air and I am off to lunch with friends before we have too obvious a reminder.

We keep well, and of course busy with many little chores about the house, always so cozy and inviting at this season. I trust your holidays are gay without undue fatigue—too often the price paid by the generous hostess.

Our best greetings and thanks again. GF

December 24, 1953

Dear Miss Stotler:

It now looks as though the weekend would be very cold, clear, and with no snow in these parts. No Babylon for any of us which suits us well. Christmas should be in the free and open spaces when possible, to my mind.

I am sorry that your poor little Toto has a recurrence of that spinal ailment. I recall so well when our Hansi was thus afflicted; all we could do was of no avail, so we had to put him to sleep and out of his misery. Poor little mites, they should not have to suffer.

I doubt if the world settles to peace and good will in the coming 1954—but at least the individual can do his or her best to bring some measure of it to the immediate circle. I am too much of a realist to *expect a volte face* [turnabout], but I can *hope* some integrity and decency may come of the veiled future.

Yes, it might be interesting to follow the path of my portrait. The one mentioned in the Seattle collection was presented by a donor whom I did not know. I hated to sit for my picture; even a quick photo was a chore. As I recall with von Kaulbach, we enlivened the sitting hours with matters of the moment, musical and artistic. Munich was ever a fascinating city and the environs gave one much stimulation.

These sittings lasted from an hour to three or four, according to the light and the discretion of the artist. I was then of such lively temperament that an induced position after a time would get artificial to my mind and I would beg for a little diversion and walk about the studio. These hours also had to be according to the *Kur* I was then taking at the sanatorium of my devoted Hofrat [court councilor] in the city, likewise a good friend of the artist; hence the permission to pose at this time.

The pose which you and Miss Aida saw in Mrs. Gilmour's New York apartment was as Traviata, the role in which the artist heard me for the first time. It was the first he did of me. Through my dear vom Raths this portrait business was concluded. This family had been patrons of both von Lenbach and von Kaulbach. Several of their best examples hung in the Berlin home.

I am very thankful, this holiday season, having been really a child of good omen. I try to deserve my blessings. If I fail it will be because of faulty perception, not inconsiderate heart.

The warmest of greetings to you from our household. GF

December 31, 1953

Dear Miss Stotler:

The sun and blue sky are most welcome, with now and then an errant flake just to remind us that it *is* Winter.

I expect to be tired as usual, after the midnight gaiety at Mrs. G.'s New Year's party tonight; then I shall have no more to consider until the February birthdays come along.

Well, I am personally grateful for many blessings. I owe none of them, at least visibly, to the GOP, but to a traditional American background, decent family relations, a code that suited the region from which I sprang, and the results of independent and enthusiastic initiative . . . alas that it has become such a castoff in favor of paternalism in our political plans. All the social crutches in the world of schemes will not compare with the sturdy individual effort at progress.

It may be interesting to sum up at the beginning of a new

year—but I rather think a *daily* scrutiny of our motives would be a wiser thing.

May you speedily seek and find another baby puppy. One accepts a newcomer in infancy with interest and affection. In no way need it be a usurper.

Our best wishes, and *Good Health*—with it you can do so much.

HAPPY NEW YEAR! GF

1954

January 11, 1954

Dear Miss Stotler:

Bitter cold, but a bright and cheerful day; Winter at last, at its best. The snow is light and feathery, the roads well sanded, and as my travel on them is only to the village, I am not incommoded.

I did listen to the [President Eisenhower's] *State of the Union* message; and was much interested in the overwhelming spontaneous applause that greeted that part where punishment should be meted to the subversives. It did not go far enough in my opinion, for there should have been deportation added to the loss of citizenship. Will you tell me how reasonable men of integrity can afford to discuss any sort of pact with these murderous foes? The UN is more and more culpable to my mind, in permitting the constant denial of our fundamental principles . . . Well, I fulminate and can do nothing, like many of my opinion. Alas that it should be so.

The book on the Arctic regions reminds me of the cruise I once took to the great Northland. We came within 500 miles of the Pole, and I stood on deck at 3:00 A.M. to watch with other shivering mortals a most fantastic iceberg—happily far enough away to be without danger to us.

The play of light and shade in the sky and on the water was breathtaking . . . but it was an awful amount of water! I was happy to get to my stateroom and shut out the gale and the bleak, if thrilling expanse.

We had, at another point, an excursion on a glacier, where the Catholics held a Mass. This time the sun was dazzling, the snow very inviting, the air like wine.

Way up beyond Spitzbergen we were told that our ship, the old luxury liner *France*, would be the last to undertake so far North, this somewhat precarious travel. We had three remarkable Norwegian pilots, fine, wonderful men, quite the Viking types. I felt great confidence in their knowledge of home waters.

I hope the *Tannhäuser* will be good; it is a favorite of mine, and I have cherished memories in the role of the gentle Elisabeth.

Best greetings, GF

January 18, 1954

Dear Miss Stotler:

Another heavy snowfall, so pretty, in great squashy flakes that drift around aimlessly. The postman is having his troubles in this deep ermine.

You should be careful about trudging up that hill, as well as physical labor too demanding . . . the thought makes *me* shudder. As to being "winded" as you say, you should not expect superhuman efforts to go without some natural remonstrance.

And why do you *not* stop at the sign, rather than invite a police ticket? Surely it would be more simple . . . no? What an obstinate little woman you are, to be sure, for one so intelligent in many ways!

I note you are still hunting Pekes; may your search be successful. My two rascals are gay and lively, love to play in the snow, and of course get submerged, but they manage to work their way out of the drifts. The exercise is good for them.

I shall sit with fancy work at hand during the opera and listen to the good old-fashioned *Trovatore*. There are ructions it seems, at the august institution, and one conductor, [George] Szell, has terminated his visiting contract according to the press. I fancy conditions are not harmonious, and the atmosphere generates unstable moods.

No, do not return *Human Events*. I like this paper very much, together with the *U.S. News and World Report*, whose editor David Lawrence has a daily column in the *Herald*. Good frank reading.

I have no end of things to occupy me and feel very cozy and snug in my rooms.

All good wishes to you, and do take better care of yourself. GF

January 21, 1954

Dear Miss Stotler:

Fog—fog . . . one sees nothing and the ceaseless drip of the thaw makes one hope to have the snow disappear. I would welcome this for the release of so much white burden on my roofs.

On Sunday night I noted with admiration that Toscanini can obtain, with modest talents, immense effects of beautifully balanced singing and orchestra. . . . There is everything to be said for guidance.

I shall listen with enthusiasm for the remainder of the *Masked Ball* next Sunday night. Then the Maestro rests for another month.

Do you have the *Chicago Theater of the Air*? Our time is at 10:00 P.M. This hour gives some lovely performances of opera and operetta, and finds promising young singers who are nicely trained and give good accounts of themselves. The *Chicago Tribune* is the sponsor.

All good wishes. We are in fine spirits with all the Winter changes.

GF

I saw a sweet Peke in the arms of a friend. Blond, with a saucy little black face and lovely fur. Still timid from too many home changes, but he is in good hands now.

My roly-poly Bubi has had to have his last baby tooth out, by Miss Sylvia's careful hand. He was good as gold, but now wants to be babied at every moment. Both are so terribly spoiled.

February 12, 1954

Dear Miss Stotler:

Heavenly advance of Spring! One gasps in a fur garment. We are off to Danbury to shop; the girls want to look over the larger store supplies there, I fancy in view of Easter home offerings across the sea.

Puppies are indeed a responsibility, but so engaging, and they have a *future* . . . I should not worry about the color of the new Peke. If you brush him well his pelt will be silky. The clay color can be very soft, and pretty also, with a slight cast of black.

As for the foolish Irene Castle, she has been one of those animal fanatics whom I do not trust at really *knowing* half of what they so loudly speak. How insane an idea, to offer herself as a rabies guinea pig; quite disgusting and unnecessary. Some intelligent person will, I hope, prevent such a display of publicity.

I too, have a certain reserve about all the "shots" now in vogue for any and all ailments. The tempo of present living is good for no one, but there are commonsense measures on which to rely; nature gives one a hint . . . but pills and piqûres are supposed to work instant wonders.

I feel that these over-medicate often to the point where the patient has little normal resiliency. I have seen sad results from friends who have tried to burn the candle at both ends. They pay a price and learn too late how dear it is, alas.

I did listen to the opera matinee, and got a certain nostalgic mood, but the radio results were not such as awaken wholehearted enthusiasm. I want to be fair, and thus admit that without action, costume and expression, one's hearing is alone in the estimate, thus there is no flattering composite to give the picture its true value. Often the vocal irregularities are not well handled by the studio technicians, who, it seems, are the real arbiters of what the production should be. Too frequently they fail to understand what the singer might desire in the way of nuances, etc. I had this out many years ago with bright young electronic geniuses. One can make no impression on that kind of mind. *Machinery* is the watchword. I am not likely to endorse it wholeheartedly. To me it is the next best thing.

My tulips are still radiant banners of sunshine here in my study. I shall let your order for the Talisman roses stand; they are always beautiful. I would *not* care for a blue rose, perish the thought!

Our best greetings, GF

February 20, 1954

Dear Miss Stotler:

Springlike air and sun make one very drowsy. I find none of us has the usual zip with the too sudden rise in temperature.

The Valentine party was most happy. The young people, sons and daughters of the dear contemporaries, were delightful and intelligent. They are married, with infants already in school, and these young parents have a very interesting outlook. It was agreeable to listen to them, and since the world must be theirs, one is happy to find at least in this circle, such stability of thought. It was hopeful, something I have *not* observed in any press or radio outlook. We are primed, I feel, too much by the personalized view of the prima donna reporter, who has become a glamorized figure with a public avid for *his* slant. I have my favorites too, but give scrutiny, of the aural kind, and use my own inner sentiments as gauge.

I am not so very surprised that your friends bought you the red Peke. Indeed you are not daffy to want a companion for the new Toto. The two of the same sex should be most happy pets. If you keep Mei-Ling as well, you will have to watch most carefully at her time, unless you wish to raise a family. The little female is, I take it, a "pensionnaire"? Even three are not too many for your care and pleasure, so may all go well in your doggy world. How nice of these ladies to have thought of an Easter egg that is sure to please you.

Yes, I do like my distant correspondents, and have no wish to know them personally. People weary me very much; the impact of their energy when one must put up a guard. One cannot speak freely, for fear of discord or fancied hurt. Whereas I find that in knowing only the written words that express the thought, I am free to squander my observations as I will. If it is not a happy reaction, then the writer need not reply; if otherwise, and of stimulating interest, then one enters upon an impartial field of thought exchange. It can last as long as this free expression is spontaneous.

I have ties of this kind in South America, South Africa, Australia and Japan. Most began with inquiry about records or other musical matters. It is fascinating to note the manners and expression of these various sources, and to keep up a steady and very interesting flow of exchange.

I have a party tomorrow, Friday, and then my own birthday on Sunday. We are very gay!

All good greetings, GF

March 3, 1954

Dear Miss Stotler:

I have been so preoccupied since my birthday I doubt *when* I can get to my desk for usual correspondence.

My birthday party was a most beautiful one, and with a special happiness that perhaps was a forerunner of the later news, as you will see in this reading.

The girls, with the help of our laundress, managed splendidly, and at the cost of much fatigue; so that the next day, when Margaret came in, I was not too surprised at her news. She was in tears, the dear, good soul, but she would have to stop working. Her 70 years were too burdensome for continuation.

I understood it perfectly, and Miss Sylvia and I are making plans at once to sell this *ark* and all that I do not carry with me to her little cottage in the Fall. Her tenants will move then.

We must choose wisely, to fit certain furniture to the smaller areas, but it has to be done, and we forge ahead.

Margaret will stay with us until the Fall. We can obtain no help, so this is the result, plus my growing inability to negotiate the stairs. There is much confusion, for I have to see agents and consider many things in the new line—you can guess we are not idle!

The death of my oldest friend in Berlin has saddened me very much. The poor dear was in the Ost [Eastern-Russian] zone where none of us can make contact.

I shall have more leisure later. For the moment we are planning like mad for what is to come. Simplicity in all is greatly to be desired.

All good wishes, GF

March 8, 1954

Dear Miss Stotler:

We have been moving fast!

I have had the builder and the plumber of Miss Sylvia's little house here to construct an additional room there. I shall duplicate my study, my bedroom and my smaller salon as they are here. All very easy, and the zoning permit in order.

I did not hesitate an hour in the decision. None of us can take care of this place any longer, and Margaret's statement only did me a good turn in bringing it clearly before my eyes.

There is *no* help at any price to be obtained. With 22 rooms and 72 windows, you can imagine the task of those devoted girls. I shall hope by careful planning, to make these last months as easy as possible. Sylvia is cursed with an ulcer condition for which relaxation and lack of tension is the prescribed program.

She and I will make out very well, and the one level floor will be a godsend. Miss Sylvia has sold the house where I built the studio, but she has this corner bungalow, new, with a large lot at the back that will insure our complete privacy . . . It is a sweet place.

I suggest you put down Tuesday, April 20th to come here. I fear your visit will not be as tranquil as I would wish, but it is the only time I have free.

My dear Berlin friend was the daughter of that fabulously wealthy family who were so wonderful to me on my coming to Berlin, the vom Raths. Through them I had the audition with the Hofmarschall, later at the Schloss, and so many dear kindnesses that my heart swells in gratitude. All down the years I was in close touch. When the parents died in the First War, the daughter was in command of immense wealth. A fine city house, a country estate. Well, you know the usual landowner's *Gut* [possessions] at that time.

Then came the bloody business. She was living on each pearl from her wonderful necklaces, and such other jewels and art objects as were left after the First War's disruption. The last war found her in the Ost zone and I could do little for her in that part of the city.

It is heartbreaking that decent fine people have to be victims of such times . . . and perhaps she is better off, at rest. She had nothing left.

I do not know the immediate cause of her death, but underneath it all was the food lack and the cold and the tension. I have just here at hand a world of miserable children, their too slender bodies and the pictured haggard faces of the older people—perhaps after all, death is the kindest medium.

We are well and busy. We go forward with new plans in good spirit, knowing it is the wise thing to do, and *at once*.

Best greetings, GF

March 16, 1954

Dear Miss Stotler:

We continue to dismantle things little by little, but it is a task that takes time and energy. I am delighted that so many of my favorite articles can be easily accommodated . . . just needs attention to choose wisely and not be swayed by sentimental feelings to clutter rooms.

I have reserved for you twelve very attractive plum colored plates. I hope you will like them, and they will be ready for you to carry away when you come April 20th.

Happily I shall be able to house my favorite porcelains in their accustomed niches, which under glass assures their safety.

I am glad that I sent most of my music to the New England Conservatory long ago. No, the piano will not go into the new quarters. I never touch it, as you know. What I want in music is available in other mediums. The piano will be sold at auction along with other pieces.

I shall get to the books soon; that is more arduous, and must invite reflection. The attic is an area of such magnitude that I must wait until the weather is milder so we do not freeze. The March winds are vocal near the roof.

I have at present no intention to leave *anything* to any public organization, knowing how embarrassed all such institutions are when there is not a financial grant for care. It is amazing how objective one can become. Symbols of what was a life long ambition and achievement become just happy—or sad—records of that time, and as such are of little consequence in the years that bring other, inner reflections.

I am distressed to learn that Aida is again hospitalized. Poor child, indeed. Happily Miss Sylvia is doing nicely with the affliction that is as temperamental as any spoiled singer. Thank goodness she is well at present. I shall try to keep her so.

I shall be leaving for Cape Vincent at the end of July and hope by that time to have most of the accumulation out of the way.

Our best wishes, and heigh-ho for merry Spring! GF

March 24, 1954

Dear Miss Stotler:

Snow of all things! Bright sunshine however, and the rays will soon disperse the light ermine cover. We want to uncover bulbs, etc., but that must wait.

We are making excellent progress. The attic is fairly neat, since many moons, I may add. I disposed via the flames of all the family portraits, bibles, and the books in which my little Auntie took such pleasure. She had a great leaning to the church ritual, Unitarian, and found much comfort therein. I cannot keep any matter of privacy for alien eyes and fingers. A nice feeling of order and a balanced book.

Easter will be here soon. I hope Aida mends and will have more hope of release from pain.

All good greetings, GF

April 5, 1954

Dear Miss Stotler:

Your Saturday letter at hand seems to breathe great fatigue on your part. Would you not do well to reconsider making your trip on a Sunday? Never too agreeable.

I have no way of knowing what the future plans for the Maestro will be; he has always been an unpredictable man. I do not see how even his valiant spirit can force nature to obey in the arduous task of conducting. I would prefer to have him leave in the super-glory of his last performance. But then I have observed, that few, even among the greatest, ever consider their own retirement. One merciful thing did occur, that Caruso did not overstay his time. Fate stepped in and made the dramatic decision.[175]

I shall go to lunch Saturday with Mrs. G. here in the country, then we shall listen to the radio *Parsifal*. We have for many years made Good Friday of *Parsifal*, a rite that was so enjoyable; however, we can no longer breast the MET mob. The country beauty and quiet will lend themselves happily to the mood.

Easter Sunday she and others come here for lunch; a quiet gathering of old friends.

A happy and *restful* Easter it seems to me should be your portion!

GF

April 8, 1954

Dear Miss Stotler:

I was not present at the last Toscanini concert. I never go to these evening affairs outside Ridgefield. There were no birthday celebrations for him, only the immediate family at hand, with the regard not to impose further fatigue on the Maestro after the magnificent performance.

It did, indeed, carry a finality that was heartbreaking. It is hard not to feel a deep sorrow, that so much glory and beauty, housed in one frail body must pass from our earthly ears. I fear this genius will be an unhappy spirit in the inactivity to come.[176]

My own farewell was of an entirely different nature. I was

[175] Shortly before Christmas 1920, while singing his most taxing role of Nemorino in *L'Elisir d'Amore* at the Brooklyn Academy of Music, Caruso suffered a severe hemorrhage. The performance was stopped and the audience dismissed. On Christmas Eve, despite chest pain, he insisted on making his scheduled appearance at the Metropolitan as Eléazar in *La Juive*. He never sang again. In the spring he and his family returned to Italy, where his health seemed to improve. On August 1, 1921, however, he was stricken by pleurisy and died the following day.

[176] Toscanini's farewell concert with this NBC Symphony was given April 4, 1954, at Carnegie Hall, shortly after his eighty-seventh birthday. His career began in Italy where he became conductor of the La Scala Opera in Milan in 1898. In 1908 he came to New York where he conducted at the Metropolitan until 1915, when he returned to Italy. From 1928 to 1933 he conducted the New York Philharmonic Symphony Orchestra. In 1937 he organized and conducted the orchestra of the National Broadcasting Company. His career spanned seventy years and brought him the reputation of being the world's greatest conductor. To Miss Farrar, his firm friend since her opera days, he was always *The* Maestro.

happy to be released from the crushing exigencies of my profession. I never had the tremendous vitality that others were so fortunate to possess. I needed rest and seclusion, and a professional must offer not only the performance but be, as well, at the social service too often. This I avoided as much as possible. The long banquets, receptions, etc., were anathema, because I did not have the stamina to endure them . . . nor the crowds that meant well, but drew out one's strength like leeches . . . I was drained to the last ounce.

Kreisler wanders about New York, handicapped by failing eyesight—he will *not* wear glasses, and deafness—he will *not* wear a hearing aid; so this dear soul is a difficult vis-à-vis for any conversation. He nears his 80th birthday.

I listened to Ike. It was all such an obvious effort to calm—one would think the public needed constant doses of soothing syrup to meet coming events. There is no hiding—is there not such a phrase in the Bible? And unless humans rectify their self-made evils, they must and will suffer the consequences. The H-Bomb may come or go—the age is indeed monstrous; but in reading a most fascinating novel of Louis XV and his employment of gunpowder against the cross bows of his opponents, well, the picture seems the same as now, uneven balance because someone invented the former to the dire consternation of the ignorant public. The *new* is always epochal.

History, sometimes with this backward glance, induces a philosophy that is constructive. Humans, it appears, have always been fearful of something or other.

All good wishes, GF

April 28, 1954

Dear Miss Stotler:

Gentle, misty rain; the grass is grateful but the blossoms droop. However, it *is* Spring. It is hopeful and lovely.

I think I wrote you in re the visit of the Librarian. *All* my data is desired for the Congressional Library, including the professional and civic activities. I am busy as a bee getting the whole mass of material properly tabulated for eventual easier reference in filing in Washington. It is a chore, indeed, an every day routine. So everything will be consigned to the national organization, which is very pleasing in thought.

Les Miettes is my name for the small cottage; and thus it will be "crumbs" in comparison with this too large house. My study, to be built, and our living quarters are facing the back woodlands, which I intend to plant with every kind of flowering thing . . . Thus I shall not feel crowded, and the eye will be constantly delighted.

Yes, Caruso was an excellent caricaturist; he sketched with great expression and economy of line. He sat forever with pen in hand drawing on any available surface. I believe he was as happy then as when singing. I am glad you like the self drawing. I used to protest his sketches of me—always with enormous mouth and "tombstone" teeth. "But Geraldina," he would counter, "You know I *always* see you with your mouth open."

I treasure a buckle which he designed for me, my monogram surmounted by a robin, and circled with the motto, *Farrar Fara*, Farrar will achieve.

Happily we keep well and have plenty to occupy us, as you may imagine.

All good greetings, GF

May 3, 1954

Dear Miss Stotler:

The country is so pretty now; the rains have loaned a freshness to all and done the parched land much good. I am taking the girls for a drive to have a change from our home labors as we amble through the countryside. It does one's spirit good.

Some friends who have large houses and families, so they need house help, tell odd stories of the difficulty of getting service in the country. One waitress would not dream of going for the Summer where she could not don her swim suit every afternoon. Another must leave Friday to be gone, with pay, until late Sunday, of course not in time for dinner. Cooks apparently are helpless without an extra kitchen maid to peel their vegetables. What next? Wigs and white gloves for the table retainers?

Now for some fresh air and fresh thoughts. Happy weekend!

GF

May 14, 1954

Dear Miss Stotler:

You have just called. I cannot understand why you did not

receive my letter telling of my bout with the flu germ, the reason for silence. Well, thanks for the inquiry, and all is once more serene.

Mr. Hoover, Treasury Secretary Humphrey and Senator Byrd should have a mighty interesting broadcast on *Coast to Coast* May 25th. I think it will be worth while to listen; they should have some highlights of value. Mr. Hoover, especially, is an amazing man, with his feet on the ground and practical suggestions to offer always.

I have been greatly saddened by the death of the Crown Princess,[177] a sweet, gracious lady . . . She will be buried tomorrow in Hechingen, beside her husband and the two sons. I can see her now, arriving as a June bride along the *Unter den Linden*, the avenue flower-bedecked and gay with bunting. She was a shy, charming figure. I have been looking over some of her letters, all so pretty and feminine, pertaining to our several interests, music, dress, etc. It was thrilling to be young and live in a romantic, brilliant era.

I do hope your household cares will be less and that you will get some manner of leisure with your friend. I have cancelled the date of your coming; let us leave it until you have a more relaxed mind and can really enjoy a little trip away. I shall be here until the end of June.

I am glad Miss Aida is improving. The Sulphur Springs should be an agreeable change.

All good greetings, GF

May 24, 1954

Dear Miss Stotler:

I am still a busy bee; the records are taking time for they must be played and judged for the best choice. I am sending those of early dates when the machine was still in its infancy and got such a boost by engaging opera singers to further the interest. 1901 saw my beginning in Berlin. The LP's of recent date can be obtained in other collections. I was only interested in the aforesaid, for my purpose.

We have quite a few people seeing the house; the agent and Miss Sylvia attend to them. One never knows what is merely curiosity and who is a serious visitor.

You are very kind to offer a garden token, but let us wait till I have all my possessions placed, before we come to the outside embellishment. I have a woodland to clear and the dogs' play pen to

[177] Crown Princess Cecilie of Prussia died on May 6, 1954.

set out in the most favorable place. I am taking out all electrical equipment in favor of gas, for I never want to be without facilities when our storms are so heavy and frequent. Both my girls are towers of interest and strength. We shall manage nicely, and when the time comes to depart, in the Fall, our program will have been laid out. I go whether or not the house is sold. That is in the lap of the gods.

All good wishes, GF

June 1, 1954

Dear Miss Stotler:

No, I do not feel the least bit saddened in the contemplation of change. I've had a happy time here and I shall make another happy sojourn in the new little home. I am too interested in planning to let my humor become rancid with rotten and confused political matters. I can do nothing about them and I will not waste energy in a futile gesture. I listen and venture no opinion; no need to get into an argument over the teacups! No, it is not Nirvana, but a resolute determination not to be spendthrift with my emotions. I'm far from stale in the pattern I'm outlining for Les Miettes!

This morning I went over every *pen fancy* and replaced in boxes, labelled, and ready for transportation there. Your pen and skill have more than illustrated so many of my amusing experiences, while the care the attention you gave their creation is fully appreciated. So much has had to go—we cannot bulge out the walls. It is like losing some part of my person, but it must be.

I shall like to think the little silver box will be welcome for your vitrine. The gift of a friend of long ago.

Now to the post and a breath of fresh air.

Greetings, GF

June 14, 1954

Dear Miss Stotler:

No, do not send me the book. I want something in another vein when I have the leisure. There is a certain brutal realism that is not pleasant to me. Hemingway, Steinbeck, Dos Passos. Not from me will these writers receive the commendation that has been accorded them. Their pose in press photos is enough to disgust me.

A tragic story, via a Berlin magazine, of a young man insinuating himself with such evil skill into the entourage of the Crown Princess, that the executors find she had left him State, as well as personal jewels. Probate Court is hot on his heels. Poor, unhappy woman—at 68 to be so misused by a scoundrel of 31! Alas, alas!

The agents show the house, Miss Sylvia present to point out to the ladies certain little commodities that would escape a man's notice. The visitors are very grateful for her courteous guidance.

The heat is really overwhelming. I must dress now for the Garden Club, fortunately in a spacious home where it will be cool.

All good greetings, GF

I hope your doggies will eventually recover from their nursery woes and prove a little less worrisome, in health.

June 28, 1954

Dear Miss Stotler:

The days are flying and we have so much to clear before I leave for the Cape. Then the auctioneer will consult with Miss Sylvia in my absence and list all that goes on sale. Today I have completed the last minute check-up in the attic, and so can depart with a nice feeling of ease.

The Crown Princess was a charming person, not unduly perceptive, due to her background and the protective aura that surrounded all children of that era and family. I fear she was fond of the rascal, and her trust and friendship were unfortunately misplaced. Further news from overseas indicates that the family are most unhappy about it . . . and of course, with the State jewels in question, they might be held responsible in her name.

The enclosed is just the shocking, sad finale. It is good to know the rascal is to be in the *prison* hospital, and thus is brought to legal hands. Such a gay, charming wife and mother should not have had to meet such a condition in her later years.

May you have a pleasant Fourth, distant from noise and nuisance, as we intend.

All good wishes, GF

July 19, 1954

Dear Miss Stotler:

This will be my last letter from home; I am nearly ready to leave for the Cape. The humidity is again in force; we are weary of trying to breathe the heavy air, or lack of it.

I, too, think genealogy is interesting, but I am not impressed by it to the point of snobbishness, which seems the usual American idea. At some time, as I understand my own coat of arms, some Norman squire did his liege lord a favor (so the story goes) hence the emblem. Today we hand over a nice block of preferred stocks or bonds . . . seems a little more practical, since we all have to regard the necessity of living expenses.

The various forms of the name are amusing, Ferriere, Ferrers, Ferrara, etc., according to the pilgrimages of the bearers, and no doubt the influences of the current background.

Thanks for the return of the German item. The scandal still goes on according to the German papers, some of which were sent to me. General criticism from my friends that the family should not engage in aftermath . . . though this seems a bit shortsighted as there are matters entailed that could not fail to be made public when the accounting for State property is in question. I should think, declared "incompetent" would be the best solution.

At any rate it is a very sad remembrance. I read that only Louis Ferdinand was able to reach his mother just before she closed her eyes. Conditions being what they are, there was general relief when one lad married a British bride, and the girl, an American. Life has not been kind to any of the old noblesse . . .

I agree with you that it would be absurd to alter the status of little Pee-Chee. This breed is so dainty, and gives no trouble when in season . . . just keep her aloof. The alteration always leaves an animal too early encumbered with fat, and disinclined to frisk.

We keep well. Our best greetings, GF

September 24, 1954

Dear Miss Stotler:

Confusion reigns; and we hope for fair skies as it is very hard to display things in a downpour. We have a huge tent that takes care of the more solid articles, on my front lawn. A herd of elephants would be at home!

Visitors will soon be coming and the actual sales will be the three weekend days. I hope I live that long without collapse as well as Margaret and Miss Sylvia! Both are busy every minute and the phone is in constant use . . . people do ask such silly questions, but are given a polite answer, of course.

This is my third auction, but in the case of the other two I was away and had nothing to do with the matter save select what was to be sold. *Now* I flee early and remain away until the closing hours. I shall indeed rejoice when the week is over.

In haste, GF

September 28, 1954

Dear Miss Stotler:

The hectic week is over and most successfully, but we are all very tired and need time to settle to normal again.

The weather was perfect, happily, so that the huge tent that made visitors comfortable in chairs, with coffee and sandwiches served, was much appreciated. A country auction is always a pleasant event, given fair skies, and on this occasion there was widespread interest. I was away every day as I do not favor crowds nor the curious, and retired to various friends until evening. Everything was most beautifully handled; the auctioneer, a man of charm and repute. The results were financially most gratifying and not a single item was left over. The New York dealers were out in full force and we did not need to trek anything to Babylon . . . it was all very well ordered.

The house is swept clean, ready for the new owner. All is in order at the cottage save the panelling of the study and the terrace to complete. We have already (hopefully) dated our moving vans for the 16th of October.

Both my girls were valiant, courteous, and at attention; but they are tired and I shall be glad when we have less demand on our time and strength.

Now we concentrate on the new little home and all it will offer.

I keep well, if a bit weary. GF

September 30, 1954

Dear Miss Stotler:

This superb Autumn weather continues. The foliage is dry, and not too colorful, but it is arresting all the same. This permits the outside painters to get Les Miettes in good order.

Never having lived on a street, name or number, I feel no need to designate. Fairhaven had its thick hedge for privacy, but in the little house with an open lawn we will not be so shielded. The mailbox is sufficient to give any clue

Les Miettes
Ridgefield, Connecticut

Just right for friends who are welcome. The whole town knows where I am going and is very interested about the exodus.

Yes, thanks, I have been given several copies of *The Untold Story of General MacArthur* [by Frazier Hunt]. The arrangements of its chapters in the *U.S. News Report* made me burn with anger. What kind of dirty politics went into the humiliation of a great man and soldier!

We shall be glad when all this confusion is over; too hectic for any enjoyment.

All good greetings, GF

October 25, 1954

Dear Miss Stotler:

I will send off a few lines so I may sit down a little and rest my tired feet. This is truly Bedlam, though all is going well, with fine weather and willing workmen hurrying as they can. But paint and wax have to dry, so we cannot hope to get furniture into the studio until the end of the week. . . .

Yes, Cecilie has her infant, and I hope life in Amarillo is pleasant. She will miss the green and the trees—ours gave her a wave of homesickness when she paid me a visit—but she is young and will adapt. She has a nice lad for husband, and he seemed truly devoted.

Wednesday Margaret's effects will be sent to New Jersey. We shall have her here on and off for a visit—this will seem less final than a definite departure. Our threesome was always on a friendly basis; both my devoted members were rarely loyal in this impersonal day of indifferent cooperation.

In haste; we keep well but are really tired. GF

Farrar made her debut as Marguerite in *Faust* at the Royal Opera House in Berlin in 1901.

Farrar as Mimi in *La Bohème*.

Farrar was outstanding as Carmen, first in the opera and later in a film version.

At the triumphant premiere at the Met in 1906, Farrar sang Butterfly in a cast that included Louise Homer, Enrico Caruso, and Antonio Scotti. *(above)*

As Zerlina in *Don Giovanni*, Farrar was a member of a cast directed by Lilli Lehmann at the Salzburg Festival.

Farrar was unstinting in praise of Kirsten Flagstad, referring to the "heart-warming and heart-breaking beauty" of her voice. *(above left)*

Of Antonio Scotti in *Tosca*, Farrar wrote, "Toscas may come and go but there is only one Scarpia." *(above right)*

In Tosca, Farrar was a diva in the grand manner.

Farrar was glamorous in *Turn of the Wheel*, a movie about Monte Carlo made in 1918.

A backstage party at the Met, following Farrar's final matinee, *Zaza*.

Farrar in a film role as Joan of Arc.

On a visit to Mexico in the 1940s.

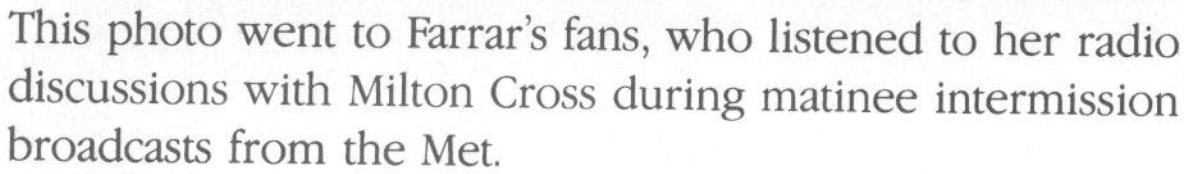

This photo went to Farrar's fans, who listened to her radio discussions with Milton Cross during matinee intermission broadcasts from the Met.

Margaret Gellatly, "the dear good soul."

Fairhaven, Farrar's "Early McKinley" home in Ridgefield, Connecticut.

Les Miettes. "My study overlooks the glory of the woodlands."

Farrar in her Red Cross uniform. *(right)*

On the veranda at Fairhaven with her beloved Mutzi and Hansi.

November 1, 1954

Dear Miss Stotler:

The pouring rain did not make the remainder of the moving very easy, none the less, we *are* out of the big house, and Monday I turn over the keys to the new owner. Glory be . . . what a load off my shoulders!

The girls worked like beavers, the matter of linens, china, etc., being out of my province. For some time we shall have delays, carpets and draperies, so that we cannot place everything until they arrive.

My study overlooks the glory of the woodlands, just now in flaming beauty, and all is quiet as can be. The bulldozer is promised for Monday to open a path between the house and the woods, so that we can enter them at will.

The rain keeps the boys quiet in their garden house. They are so shockingly spoiled, with never any discipline. After I paddle them with a newspaper, Miss Sylvia cajoles with a piece of cake and sweet words, and of course they yell all the more for such ministrations!

Polio has struck the New Milford district, an hour from here. Schools are closed and doctors busy with the gamma globulin. I hope it prevents . . . this is a fearful disease—no one knows the source nor apparently the absolute cure.

Now to the coffee break—most welcome after so much activity.

All good greetings, GF

Election Day[178]
November 2, 1954

Dear Miss Stotler:

Dreary weather for the voters, but the spiritual skies weep more than the natural elements in my opinion. I go to vote with no enthusiasm. How can one endorse the people who should be our superiors, and who offend in so many ways?

Yesterday was glorious, frosty and cold. At 8:00 A.M. Miss Sylvia and I were at the big house ready to turn over the keys and see that all was well. An hour with the lawyers, and now I am a free woman; no property or real estate and no *white elephant* to plague me. What

178 An off-year election in which the Democrats narrowly regained control of Congress.

a joy not to own a large area that I cannot protect or keep free of trespassers. It is very still here; our neighbors might as well be on the moon for all we see or hear.

My first beautiful chairs came from New York yesterday. Carpets due tomorrow for the same part of the house. The general color is a delicate aqua green, save for the pine-panelled living room and new study; these are in natural wood. The carpets are old rose and aqua green. The French and English prints are here from Fairhaven, with a portrait or two as well.

I have no time to see friends, but once we are ready for inspection I can invite a few in at a time. We are small, and can only handle six comfortably for tea. I serve no lunch or dinner—Miss Sylvia must not be put upon; she has enough as it is. I take people to Mr. Tode's Inn where we have the best.

All good wishes—in haste, GF

November 15, 1954

Dear Miss Stotler:

Rain and fog with a mild temperature that is not seasonable; however it is convenient for our plans. It seems that many friends, obeying my injunction *not* to send any housewarming gifts that would only add to the confusion of the moment, have had the very sweet and welcome idea of outdoor bulbs that will bear a gay welcome in the Spring.

As my maintenance man was preparing the soil in general, it was easy to continue and draw out the design for my small area. I accept, as does Miss Sylvia, your very kind offer for our "friendship garden" and we shall employ its generous elasticity in permanent adornment.

I will draw a small sketch of the road. We should have a pleasing allée of flowering shrubs at all times, in rotation.

Where my small area of flowers will be is at the front part of the lot. We shall be protected from the lane (public entry) by spruce, dogwoods and lilacs. Later I shall erect rough country railings. It is such fun to plan, and Spring should show results.

All the carpets are here. Of course everything could not be *too* smooth; and carpenters had to come in a hurry to shave down the doors (eight) that I could open closets, the velvet pile is so thick.

The Christmas cards still stare at me, and I seem not to be able to clear my desk for action of this kind. The time is far too short for all one would accomplish, while the energy flags at the end of a long hard day.

Our best greetings, and again, thanks. GF

December 7, 1954

Dear Miss Stotler:

We are *at last* complete in our furnishings, the *lares and penates* in order, and it all looks mighty pretty. I think with gratitude of the sweet environment here, as compared with the worries and burdens of the all too large house. It does look a bit lonely as we pass by, and the neighbors say they miss the lights.

Officials tell me that my exhibition in D.C. looks very fine, topped by the von Kaulbach portrait loaned for the occasion by Mrs. Gilmour to whom I gave it years ago. Thanks be, I did not need to undergo the well meant but fatiguing excitements my presence would have entailed. I cannot understand why professionals pathetically refuse to relinquish the limelight to a younger—and often more appetizing generation. Well, at any rate, the collection is well placed, and no longer my responsibility.

I am sending one of the printed articles that may interest you.

I am well and active *because* I recognize just how much I dare undertake. I am not really able to go down, despite most cordial invitations to be a part of the opening.

There is little news save the usual pre-holiday excitement. The village tree will soon bloom into myriad lights, carols will fill the air, and the post will be filled with gay reminders of good wishes from far and near.

Dimling's sweetmeats just arrived—second delivery, since we live in the village. The carrier rings the bell, all so convenient, and I need not don Arctic equipment to sally to the post office as in other days. Thank you! Always so welcome.

The news reel yesterday gave such a good interview with Mr. Hoover on his Berlin visit. He and Chancellor [Konrad] Adenauer represent the finest of their kind—*men* not political *Affen* [apes].

May all go well with you . . . Happy Holidays! GF

[Enclosure]

THE LIBRARY OF CONGRESS
WASHINGTON 25, D.C.

Press Release
for IMMEDIATE Publication

No. 55-31
December 2, 1954

GERALDINE FARRAR'S NOTED SINGING CAREER
RECALLED IN LIBRARY OF CONGRESS EXHIBIT

An exhibit of photographs, manuscript letters and mementos from the recently acquired Geraldine Farrar Collection was opened in the Library of Congress today. It reflects the brilliant career of a prima donna of the opera and concert stage whose name became, in this country and abroad, a synonym for great art, dramatic vitality, exquisite singing and striking beauty.

The exhibit represents only a part of the extensive collection that Miss Farrar gave the library last spring, but it fills the entire North Gallery on the Main Building's first floor. It may be seen until February 28.

Miss Farrar was born in Melrose, Mass. and grew up in New England. Her voice and talent developed so precociously that at the age of 19 she made a sensational debut at the Royal Opera House, Berlin, in the role of Marguerite in *Faust*. Five years later, in the fall of 1906, her debut at the Metropolitan Opera House in New York proved equally sensational; from that time until her retirement from opera in 1922, she was a favorite of the New York stage. From 1922 to 1924 she was on concert tours and in December 1927, reappeared on the New York concert stage. She enjoyed also a successful career as a motion-picture actress, beginning with *Maria Rosa* in 1915. Her other films included *Carmen, Joan the Woman, The Woman and the Puppet, Temptation, Shadows, Hellcat, The Woman God Forgot* and *The Devil Stone*.

Among her operatic performances were the roles of Madame Butterfly, Manon, Mignon, Mimi, Elizabeth, Tosca, Zerlina, Gilda and Violetta.

Photographs of Miss Farrar costumed for her many parts are exhibited. The mementos shown include a blade for the act of hara-kiri in her role of Butterfly (a gift from the American traveler and author, E. Burton Holmes, in appreciation of her performance); a piece of the old floor of the Metropolitan Opera House and a framed portion of the Metropolitan's old "Golden Curtain." On the back of the frame of the last mentioned is a note to Miss Farrar from Fred Hosli—"Inclosed find part of the 'Golden Curtain'—have thought of you when we were taking it down—many a bow you have taken before this curtain. Best regards from the Boys back stage."

A large group of autograph letters from celebrated persons are included; among the correspondents are Irvin S. Cobb, Mary Pickford, Rosa Ponselle, Deems Taylor, Lotte Lehmann, John McCormack, Julia Marlowe, Ernestine Schumann-Heink, David Belasco, Richard Strauss, Lilli Lehmann, Sarah Bernhardt and Giacomo Puccini. Two autobiographies are shown—*Geraldine Farrar—The Story of an American Singer* (Houghton Mifflin, 1916) and *Such Sweet Compulsion* (Greystone Press, 1938). Examples of her activity as poet and composer are also included. A portrait of Miss Farrar, painted by Friedrich August von Kaulbach has been lent to the Library for this exhibit by Mrs. Howard G. Gilmour of New York City.

December 23, 1954

Dear Miss Stotler:

I have been greatly moved these last two days, having the privilege to hear General MacArthur in the flesh, also to see him briefly on TV. Our station WOR with some 25 million listeners covered his visit in fine fashion. The papers have their own reasons no doubt, for extracting from context . . . however, he is in my opinion a *great* man, indeed the greatest living American.

Well, I wrote as I felt I must, to add my steadfast admiration, and feel the better for it, as if I had communed in some measure above the trivia of the day. God bless him and his helpmate.

At last I have concluded all the Red Cross post and it is delivered to the Chairman. A task of repetitious boredom really, as one senses it means (despite a fine record which I have faithfully put down on paper) only another appeal to a public already wearied to death of the never-ending arrival of similar stuff. Of course without the horrors of war, few people realize the excellent work that is really done, for the very veterans who now suffer from that sad period.

Indeed I do wish you lots of luck in getting ahead with the sale proposition [of Ilka's house]; one cannot presume on one's strength forever. Alas, it soon wears down.

Best greetings meanwhile, GF

December 29, 1954

Dear Miss Stotler:

The weather is too mild. Many are afflicted with flu that seems to haunt the holidays till colder days arrive.

I shall close festal joys with the New Year's party . . . then one can revert to routine till February brings along the many birthdays. I believe there is to be a public manifestation on the 2nd for Kreisler, on his 80th anniversary. He will like this for he is a genial soul, echter Wiener [genuine Viennese] . . . and you know how gregarious these delightful people can be.

I have brought all the white porch furniture from Fairhaven for our terrace later. The several figurines are just enough to be pretty and not intrusive. I have plans for more greens, laurel and such, with a line of hemlocks to screen pleasantly our line at the road corner . . . I fancy some greens also must be placed in the woodland, as it now seems all the trees there are deciduous . . . all a pleasant reflection for later plans.

I wrote to Aida and told her if possible to come along with you and see this sweet place. I do hope she is better.

All good wishes, and HAPPY NEW YEAR! GF

1955

January 5, 1955

Dear Miss Stotler:

The fine weather continues, praise be, and one can get so much underway. Miss Sylvia and I went to shop in Danbury; some things still needed for the house. Also I stopped by the Ford dealer and ordered a new car, a very handsome two-toned aqua tint that is pretty without being too spectacular. He tells me that the ladies have set the fashion for the pastel hues in cars. I have the same exhilaration that used to accompany a new hat!

I very much fear you will never be able to curb the big dog's infatuation for moving cars. I tried for fifteen years to induce my police dog to some kind of precautionary conduct, to no avail. He was always arriving after some episode in which he had been worsted, and would *never* learn.

I know so little of the stock market, that is in the hands of my counsel. They know I do not hanker for a change, but want the measure of conservative security. I should think, however, if your General Motors dividends were satisfactory, you would not be wise to change. Isn't the industrial field our best bet? General Motors, oil, electronics, etc., would seem to be the best buy, but of course all will bear watching.

May your Sundays be happy. On three succeeding ones the WOR radio will give one act of *Tristan* with Flagstad and the lamented Furtwängler.[179] I own these recordings and they are superb. Today's *Marriage of Figaro* was no special treat. I detest anglicized Mozart.

February 5, 1955

Dear Miss Stotler:

The snow is here, a light covering in the sunshine, and weather is consistently cheery. My new car is promised today and I am in a high state of excitement. The model is *Fairlane*, 4-door sedan—very pretty.

MacArthur's appearance on TV shocked me and gave me a heartache. I think he is speaking as a prophet and a truthful one too. I had a feeling that he was far beyond the contemporary scene, but already visualizing it from the edge of another realm. Perhaps the soldier-statesman has become completely the philosopher and hints

[179] Wilhelm Furtwängler, renowned German conductor who had died in 1954.

at the incalculable destruction we invite. Or is it that we are fated to encompass our death and, en masse, begin the weary toil to reassemble civilized standards? One knows so little, and few inspire faith or trust.

I am looking over flower catalogues, all with such charming brilliantly colored pages. But I must go carefully, and not clutter up our small land plot.

All good wishes, GF

March 19, 1955

Dear Miss Stotler:

A beautiful day of sun and promise of Spring. Will the elusive maid be with us on the official opening this Monday? I shall hold on to the wools and furs for a time.

Tristan is having hard going, the lovers very sour over the radio, without the flattery of lights, costume and action. Nor do I find the entr'acte chat of Flagstad of sufficient value to be attached to her superb vocal accomplishments. Oh, these texts compiled in the recesses of the pen-pushers! What commonplaces indeed.

A newcomer to the MET is very fine—I've known her records for some time, Renata Tebaldi.[180] A pleasure to read that not all critics are immune to fine vocalization allied to dramatic fire.

Miss Sylvia and I keep busy, a joy in this band-box. My study provides a sweet retreat, facing the woods and companioned by them.

All good wishes and a speedy return of your car, restored. I know what a nuisance it is to be without one.

GF

March 24, 1955

Dear Miss Stotler:

Well of all the debuts into Spring! Rain, then sleet, then snow. One is glad to stay indoors, busy with happy, if trivial tasks.

Yesterday's "Omnibus" program [on television] had the last of

180 A lyric soprano, Renata Tebaldi was born in Tesaro, Italy, in 1922. After highly successful seasons in Parma and Milan, she came to the Metropolitan Opera. There her beautiful, typically Italian voice was to delight audiences for years to come.

the story of the Boston Adams family. It was most ably presented and one had, from direct quotations or authentic material, a very correct idea of matters of the moment, at various periods, and how they were handled by a remarkable family.

The prognostications of the last Henry Adams are being fulfilled at this writing. One wonders what induced him to foretell, with such acumen, the many forces that would shape our land. Greed, the lust for power, immigration which imposes alien precepts. . . Very well presented in simple narrative, and so pictorially that a child could grasp the salient changes. It engendered a chain of thought—not too happy.

It will be a joy to view the arrival of undiscouraged Mother Nature in her Spring attire, and I for one will not let the nation's boiling pot disturb my thrills at something *God* made.

All good wishes, GF

Good Friday, 1955

Dear Miss Stotler:

I'm on my way to Kensico, and post my thanks for the pot of fragrant hyacinths here in my study. After they bloom, the bulbs go into the garden where they'll continue for some time. Such lovely augury of Spring. It's sunny but a crisp morning; however there is cheer in the air.

I awoke early and heard all *Parsifal* on the radio, a Bayreuth offering of a few years ago. The music is very impressive, and with the sun in a sky of dawn, quite a spectacle apart from the scenic picture of the opera itself. How many beautiful things we can enjoy in our own hearts—and music certainly conveys its healing for any bruise or disillusion.

I hope your Easter may be a happy one, such as you would wish. My house is redolent with lilies, tulips and such—a garden in itself.

All good greetings, GF

April 13, 1955

Dear Miss Stotler:

May the weather be fair and your trip most pleasant. I think you will find Spring a bit less verdant in our area. I'll meet you and your friend as arranged, Friday, 22nd at 12:30 at the *Tode Inn*. We are sorry that Miss Aida does not feel able to make the trip; she always enjoys a few days in New York.

I hope to have quite a bit of planting to show you when you come. Your kind thought and check have been invested in most beautiful roses; they are destined, in part, for the upper terrace here at the study door. In two years they should be well established. I got them from the rose growers, Jackson and Perkins, whose catalogues are entrancing.

I am not sure you will have real pleasure wielding your gavel. It is hard to bring harmony and cooperation in a committee, and then, so often, the head has to pitch in and do chores that should have been shared. I can recall the spurious interruptions at times with us, "point of order"—you would think we were the Congress sitting, and sometimes we are just as dumb.

I am glad that my civic duties are behind me. I realize that my years dictate retirement; it is better to look back on their activities than to have them on my agenda at present.

A Blood Bank is scheduled for the 15th. I am glad I no longer have the chore of persuasion for this. The Chairman is a wonderfully energetic person and succeeds because of this as a business man. One wonders when the ulcers may kick up—they seem to be the usual aftermath of pressured organizations.

You spoke of Miss Peters—I think her the most talented and hard-working singer at the MET. She appears to have gifts in all directions. She has made great strides since her debut, and continues to work without stint.

Well, this is a lovely Spring day—the moment when, if ever, we should be grateful for the burgeoning earth and all it means to us. Alas, we all too often fail to see and bless.

All good wishes, GF

April 28, 1955

Dear Miss Stotler:

Your Monday letter announces your safe arrival home. We have the rain also, like November; my planting is at a standstill. Miss Sylvia has opined the new moon was a watery one!

Yes, it is unfortunate that the Salk vaccine [against polio] has been co-incident with the death of several children. The press has sounded an alarm, which may even become hysteria. A pity, for parents are going to suffer confusion.

The *Homestead Steak House* is unknown to me, but the locale brings back earlier memories when fine restaurants were all along 23rd Street, with lovely residences as well. Changes—changes.

Now to shop in the chill drizzle.

Best greetings, GF

May 18, 1955

Dear Miss Stotler:

Another lovely day after a nightfall of needed and refreshing showers. As we have planted quite a bit this was most welcome; the newcomers are very happy and nodding upright in their new home. Our small garden area is very gay and inviting.

Tomorrow I go with my gardener to hunt azaleas now in bloom, to be sure of the proper colors. I am not partial to the magenta harsh tints—too many now on view. My laurel is planted at last, and in two years I hope to have a leafy framework to enclose my border lines.

My rooms have their tiny vases of lilacs, pansies, and lilies-of-the-valley. Truly this is a magic time . . . the old earth renewal plays its role and all humans react pleasurably to sun, cheer and warmth. The pagan legends have much to elaborate this picture.

This heavenly weather has made me forgetful that I have to be careful when driving, of draughts. I was *not* careful and had a most unpleasant neuralgia in head and neck for three days. I ought to learn, but the fragrance of the drives in the back roads drove all thought of such prudence away, so I pay with a stiff neck and bleary eye—but it will pass.

I can never sit outdoors, alas, for everything that has wings makes at once a feast of my person. I keep inside and *look* . . . but Miss Sylvia is happy there with her sewing or a sunbath as she wishes.

Your Friday letter speaks of the possibility of constructing a new home. I would say, make your own plans, and abide by what you feel is for your wish and comfort. A glass roofed-in garden would be delightful.

I shall never forget the exotic and charming one at Mrs. Jack Gardner's in Boston. One came from a windy, dull day into a fragrant, blooming area, a delight to all the senses. At the time of its erection she was very much criticized for almost everything her fertile mind evolved. She was a lady of firm principles, and once she took on a purpose she did not swerve. Her immense fortune allowed great expenditures, and most of the time, I am told, in the purchase of art treasures, she harkened to excellent advise.[181] I knew her slightly.

I, too, am disturbed by all the pro and con in the press. I have little confidence in the declarations of the pundits. An honest difference of opinion is one thing—the slanted imposition of one is something else.

The programs at Yalta, Casablanca and Potsdam have been suspicious for a long time, and the public is not duped by the censored "mis-Geburts" [abominations] that now become officially public.

The GOP will have waited, no doubt, to make political capital, but I fear this will fail in view of their many flops.

The photos of FDR, as you say, show the complete breakdown. His doctors and advisors should have heavy punishment for their denial of his condition. It is said that the wife insisted on the last term. The Washington miasma breeds something more nefarious than just malaria!

I like it not that the Russian General Georgi Konstantinovich Zhukov "might renew pleasant ties" with *Ike* and *Churchill.* A fine victory they brought us. See the tragic result!

Well, this is enough harangue for a lovely Spring day.

All good wishes, GF

June 15, 1955

Dear Miss Stotler:

The skies have cleared and the day is superlative. The men are cutting grass and the bloom is abundant over the areas . . . very pretty to see.

I have a friend in the airlines who did me a service by going to see and describe the first flight of the Lufthansa to our shores. I was invited to go to the airport, but the early hour and the long drive

181 The vivacious Isabella Stewart Gardner (1840–1924) had befriended Bernard Berenson during his student days at Harvard. The eminent art critic later assisted her in assembling a fine art collection for Fenway Court, her home in Boston. She willed both her home and the collection to the city for a museum.

made the idea out of the question. At any rate I was there in imagination. They use our Constellations but have added fuel in their wing-tips, and thus have no need to stop and refuel between here and their home ports. They arrive here at 10:00 A.M. and depart that afternoon for home. Amazing!

My first ride was the *Viktoria Luise*, the finest Zeppelin of that moment. Then many plane rides in Germany [on] Lufthansa. We shall see much competition now, for they are making great plans to enter the air-ways and have all the talents for so doing.

Every day living in this simple and charming villino is only a pleasure. I wish all my contemporaries could experience the peace and ease that comes with a decision to simplify. Miss Sylvia and I sleep like infants—all so quiet, no nocturnal disturbances.

All good wishes to you. GF

June 23, 1955

Dear Miss Stotler:

The days are hot, but we are cool and comfortable in our green shelter. The poison ivy nuisance is abating and Miss Sylvia is well of her attack. She is very susceptible to it.

I have had tea groups in several times weekly; only four or six at a time.

This makes for pleasant chat and no strain upon the household.

The top level conferences have had their counterparts since Woodrow Wilson got his messianic ideas. They will come to the same conclusion, if I read history correctly, and the character of the Russ. One has only to see *him* in action at the UN to realize, even without an interpreter, that this is a very clever and unscrupulous adversary. That he will never yield, we have heard too often. How anyone can sit down to his vituperations, knowing full well that this is the evil that keeps the world in a straitjacket, is beyond me.

I speak, of course, of [Vyacheslav] Molotov.

Meanwhile, why do we act like children, and force, even for a semblance of goodwill, a ten-gallon hat on this Muscovite? Only one person looked more miserable under its brim and that was the late Calvin Coolidge.

Adenauer is a fine gentleman. It is remarkable that he can at his age, undertake the travel entailed. But of one thing I am sure, the Russ will put nothing over on him at Geneva.

May your weekend be happy. We are having here odd exhibitions of hail and electric skies.

Best greetings, GF

July, 1955

Dear Miss Stotler:

The heat is still upon us. I can only manage to do something worthwhile in the morning. After lunch, till sunset, it is very humid and one's energy is gone.

I have just seen the sport car, Ford *Thunderbird*, the smartest thing on the road. If I had garage space I would buy one just for the pleasure to drive such a slick affair. Long, low lines, jet black relieved by ivory leather upholstery. Of course the winds would play on my sinus and there would be trouble—but *oh* what a beauty it is!

Poor, gifted Isadora Duncan; I knew her quite well, especially in those days when she had the dance school at Grunewald [Berlin].

Her sister [Elizabeth] was the real head and co-ordinator, a fine, talented woman only lately deceased in Germany. Isadora provided the monies and réclame with her dancing. It is a pity she got involved with the Russian angle, but then her powers were on the wane, and she was sentimentally attached to her Russ poet,[182] a boor and beast, if ever there was one.

She had a bad time in her youth. I remember the family from early days in New York. The quiet sister; the excellent Augustin, who became a fine actor; the odd Raymond, who "went native" even in those days; Isadora, with her advanced ideas.

No money till she came to Paris and Germany. In the latter country she had her most legitimate success. I thought her compositions lovely, though she was much ahead of her time, the old-fashioned ballet type being the usual attraction for dancing.[183]

She was not especially cultured, but was not noisy or objectionable until later when she was not really in mental order. In those early dance classes in her studio, the small children, who later

182 Her much younger husband, the Russian poet Serge Essenin.

183 The popularity of Isadora's naturalistic dance style, and her outspoken criticism of classical ballet, stirred much controversy. On one occasion a duel was fought by an ardent young balletomane for the honor of the classical ballet.

became the most potent argument for her dance ideas, were like angels. They made a picture like a Donatello frieze.

Well, sic transit, etc.

All good greetings, GF

Pennywise
Cape Vincent, New York
August 12, 1955

Dear Miss Stotler:

A breeze today, probably due to the hesitant "Connie" on the Virginia coast or her sister hurricane "Diane" enroute from Puerto Rico. At any rate we are breathing normally. I shall be glad when Autumn strikes a note of chill—nor complain of snow . . .

You may correct your friend as to any TV appearance of me! Someone is in error, but *not GF.* This folly I would not commit, I do assure you! Have I a twin somewhere? If so, she is unknown to me.

Yes, I think Schumann-Heink and Lilli Lehmann were ironclads. Both had superb physical equipment; both knew early struggles so that their achievements were a proud acknowledgment of their gifts and grit. Remarkable people. I can better evaluate their concentration from my present years. But even as a young student with Lilli, I sensed the difference between her Teutonic application, and my own needs for certain compromises rather than the hammer process by which she so superbly bent all efforts to her own purpose. The two were great musical figures. What they obtained from *life*, I would not be able to say.

Both insisted as do so many, on public acclaim long after the bloom was gone, and only a forceful projection, style and tradition permitted a shadow of what their prime greatness must have been. The human voice, like one's face, cannot withstand the years without surrender in so many subtle ways. That impresses me always. I do not see why anyone should fear the years to which we all must bow, if we are alive to have them imposed upon us! There are compensations. If one does not find them or admit them, and refuses adjustment, one may be uncompleted in the life cycle. Many unhappy souls are. But—it is everyone's problem, to be handled individually.

The qualities of notable personalities are so very different.

[Teresa] Carreño[184] and Calvé had the seduction and fascination of beautiful women. Marlowe was lovely in a more restrained way, the English reserve perhaps, and a haunting voice. I knew her quite well. [Her husband, Edward Hugh] Sothern never appealed to me—probably a hard working actor, but withal a stilted one. I sensed no spontaneity . . . Perhaps the opera is the fullest expression of such; when soaring in song, so exultant and free!

This humidity is promised for another month. Alas, one can only gasp and think of snowflakes tumbling down!

Best of good wishes, GF

August 21, 1955

Dear Miss Stotler:

I must thank you for another copy of the beautiful magazine, *Connoisseur* at hand. What a pleasure to touch and peruse its lovely pages! I cherish the more gracious aspects of earlier masterpieces. The "modern" look in furniture, paintings, sculpture, ceramics, etc., does not appeal to me. I see no reason to revert to the primitives of Dordogne![185]

I liked Anne Morrow Lindbergh's reflections re the lesson of the shells [in *Gift from the Sea*, 1955]. Though I do not react so favorably to the seashore, I can enter into her musing and her calm; for instance, in the contemplation of green—be it in trees or mountains. I sensed in her observations much depth of feeling, and the need of freedom for herself, if only for a little while. Her cares have been many and her sorrows known to all.[186]

Her mother also showed singular gifts. Some of my friends are graduates of Smith and recall Mrs. Morrow's unusual endowments.

I clipped, some time ago from *Saturday Review* a splendid article, a speech before a certain body honoring Charles Lindbergh upon his acceptance of the Guggenheim Medal. It says so well and so simply what I have felt all along as to *character* of the individual and its influence in our day of so many evils. The progress of man's mind

[184] A Venezuelan, Carreño was considered one of the foremost women pianists since Clara Schumann.

[185] A reference to the paleolithic cave paintings to be found in the Dordogne region of France.

[186] The firstborn of the celebrated aviator and his wife Anne was kidnapped and murdered in 1932.

and its application is of little value if he forgets or ignores the more lasting values of human betterment.

Now to the usual village shopping. Greetings, GF

October 6, 1955

Dear Miss Stotler:

Gentle but persistent rain, with falling leaves like burnished coins—bright flashes of color in the air.

So your milestone was re-dedicated and you have concluded the occasion. I so often wonder if future generations will be interested in several corner stones in European houses where early records have been encased in sealed crypts.[187] My records, circa 1901, went in among others of my era. They will sound odd no doubt, after a hundred years, in view of rapid electronic development!

Lilli Lehmann was responsible for the cornerstone of Salzburg's Mozarteum and made its dedicatory address (1903). Now no one seems to realize her tremendous effort in making Salzburg a true Mozart place of reverence. It seems all dates from Max Reinhardt. Without wishing to detract from his career of eminence, none the less, Salzburg *did* come to life and early glory by reason of Lilli and the Emperor Franz Joseph's cousin, the Archduke [Eugen] who was our patron. He assumed expenses!

I am more incensed on *her* account than otherwise, for she worked only for artistic achievement, obtained it, and should be forever its shining goddess of the Muses![188]

Now to town for shopping, darting in among the rain drops. All's well!

Greetings, GF

October 21, 1955

Dear Miss Stotler:

As you perhaps read or heard, we have been flooded again, and worse this time, in the same areas as after the hurricane.

---

[187] In 1907 recordings of performances by Caruso, Kubelik, Farrar, and Kreisler were placed in the vaults of the Paris Opera to be opened in 100 years.

[188] Miss Farrar said that for gala seasons at Salzburg, artists came and gave their services gratis "for love of Lilli, and of Mozart."

Ridgefield, with other areas, was cut off, and only now are phones and foodstuffs once more accessible. The army engineers moved in and are repairing roads and bridges with commendable skill and speed. Food also arrives. But there has been tragedy—loss of life, and great property damage. And exhausting efforts on the part of all relief agencies.

I never saw such rain. The TV pictures of surrounding districts are terrifying. We had three helicopters at rescue work in outlying neighborhoods.

I hope you are well removed from any Pennsylvania district that suffered? Our news is only of local value, involving the plight of neighbors. We are physically well and grateful for our many blessings. This house is a jewel, so tight and snug, a real haven!

Best greetings, GF

Saturday evening, December 11, 1955

Dear Miss Stotler:

The mighty strains of *Meistersinger* ring out as I sit in my cozy study. The music speeds my pen, and it is easy, in its eloquent flow, to shut out the harshness of this modern world; though I dare say that era, too, had its trials and tribulations.

Our village is gay; green ribbons and lights lend a festive charm. There'll be carols at Memorial Park where a pretty créche has been set up, but I'll be prudent and remain at home. The wind is bitter, though the stars sparkle and the sky is serene.

I go again tomorrow to see my ill California friend. She and her husband leave Wednesday for their Arizona ranch—I tremble for them both. So ill, and they can't stand our cold. Poor dears; close friends these fifty years.

Mr. Kreisler will have his 80th birthday the 2nd February . . . almost blind and hearing nothing. Many organizations will honor him. I don't know if he can publicly divide himself in so many pieces! A lovable man and a great artist.

I am so discouraged at our policies; one cannot make a dent in what I believe is a firm determination of the "one-worlders" to change our great land to the *welfare* state. Rotten equivalent! Alas, I see its nefarious shadow!

All good wishes, never the less! GF

December 23, 1955

Dear Miss Stotler:

We have snow falling in pin-point sheets that are very pretty to see. Trees and houses are lightly veiled, and the birds flashing through the woods at the feeding stations make a gay and appropriate Christmas picture.

I do love this kind of Winter in the country, and the comfort we have after the "baronial halls" of Fairhaven. I used to wonder at times if the house would not take fire from the strain we put on the oil burner. The third floor was an Arctic horror.

The little dogs are such pets, and do not care to roam now. The vet said we could expect no interest in a female, hence our hope of getting a puppy from our sweet little Luka came to naught.

Why did you not give a whiff of chloroform to the little street waif that you found? I have done this frequently. Just tie a little muslin around the muzzle and gently place the saturated cloth over the nose. One or two inhalations suffice for deep and painless sleep. For a larger dog the vet usually gives a piqûre . . . all very humane and sans peine.

I am not sure I agree as to the horse and buggy days. Do not forget that we had all too many examples of cruelty to animals and the SPCA had to step in. I suppose all depends on the character of the human involved. Some would be kind under all circumstances—others would not. As against the evildoers in autos, there are still hundreds who pursue a decent code in driving.

Of Lena Geyer seemed to me to be a composite of prima donna habits and actions. The authoress [Marcia Davenport], came to me and obtained all the Lilli Lehmann details. She wished to be exact in the delineation of that great artiste's background and training. The reference to the royal family was gathered, no doubt, from the usual gossip sheets. [Since Davenport is] the daughter of Alma Gluck,[189] a lovely singer and a pupil of Marcella Sembrich,[190] there was much that was authentic in the background of the musical world.

[189] Alma Gluck (1884–1938) was born in Bucharest but came to America as a child. In 1909 she made her debut as Sophie in Massenet's *Werther*, and until 1918 continued to delight audiences with the clarity and beauty of her lyric soprano voice and the charm of her personality.

[190] Marcella Sembrich (1858–1935) was a Polish-born coloratura, celebrated for the "velvety" brilliance of her voice which maintained its tone quality evenly from the lowest to the highest note of her wide register.

I had a letter from Welitsch only the other day, describing the fabulous opening of the Wiener Oper[191] of which she is a member. I regret that we do not have her at the MET. She used her voice without stint and I fancy was in retirement for a time to recover. This happens to us all and is no cause for alarm. A delightful person, handsome, skin like a peach, big blue eyes, laughing mouth. She has a keen flair for dissection of her roles. I liked the way she told me she went about her interpretations, intelligent and colorful.

Mr. Bing has engaged a very fine singer in Tebaldi. I have heard and admired her records only, but the reviews have been excellent and she seems to be in demand. Another is coming to join next year, Maria Callas,[192] a fabulous singer but without the sweet caliber of voice. A fiery person who seems to exult in startling effects. So much the better. These two should stir up some superior interest in music.

As for all the young people who are "heroine" worshippers, one is happy that they obtain such an outlet for adolescent emotions, but one has to be careful to keep them at a distance, for the impulses sometimes are annoying and lead to unpleasant incidents. Miss Garden had a most disagreeable experience of such an "exaltée" who brought a pistol with her to the hotel and came very near to using it. Press reports exaggerate and one has a most unfortunate incident to combat.

All good wishes from house to house. GF

December 24, 1955

Dear Miss Stotler:

The lovely shining snow and blue sky have dulled; we are now having miserable icy rain and I fear there will be many road accidents. Such seems to be the unfortunate case on holidays. The floods

---

191 The opening on November 5, 1955, of the rebuilt Vienna State Opera house was a doubly joyous occasion since it celebrated the recently completed withdrawal of the post-World War II occupation forces from Austria. The opera selected for this event was Beethoven's *Fidelio*, symbolizing the triumph of freedom.

192 Maria Callas (1922–1977), born in New York of Greek parents, began her career with the Royal Opera of Athens. In 1956 she joined the Metropolitan Opera, where her magnificent coloratura voice and her dramatic interpretations made her one of the great stars of her era. She is credited with the revival at the Metropolitan of such bel canto works as the operas of Bellini, Donizetti, and Rossini, which had been largely neglected since the so-called "Golden Age."

and devastation in the Northwest stir us here with a sympathetic shiver; we know what those rushing waters mean!

It seems to me there has never been a more handsome assortment of Christmas cards. Very appealing, from the tiniest greeting to lovely ornaments for the mantelpiece. I have put out as many cards as I can in windows and mirrors, also in broad trays, very colorful, and carrying a thought from each donor.

This will be Christmas Eve. We shall enjoy music and television and not breast the ugly weather.

I should not repine about any holiday withholding, as your letter says. You have always been so generously disposed—surely to such an extent as to last a lifetime.

You remember how hard put we were for the Red Cross pageant curtain? And lo, out of your store of good things came the glowing red and blue yards that were our pride at the festal moment? And the posters—no sooner was our need expressed than they appeared. . .

I do hope that you will get in order with your apartment affairs; and may your worries in the fluctuating financial world lessen, indeed.

It is nice to know that Aida is improving. A note from her expressed pleasure in their travels.

The cheeses have just come, and again I thank you for such delicious consideration. They are a most delectable addition to my supper trays.

I wish everyone could be as content!

The best of good wishes, and a betterment of your resources in the coming 1956.

The doggies join in too! GF

1956

January 3, 1956

Dear Miss Stotler:

I have been at my desk these last few days; such a pleasant feeling to clear things out and start the New Year afresh. Cards continue to arrive, which prolong the agreeable surprise to hear from distant friends.

The weather after having been superb, cold and sunny, has given way to grey, dreary skies and icy rain.

I had friends in for tea on the 28th, all the festal activity I enjoyed. Many here are ill with colds or exhaustion, and friends in the city were having too much of a good time to suit me.

I am sorry that you have to worry about the condition of your factotum; but you will need to prepare for her finale; one should not be always alone, especially as you are isolated. Will you not try to find someone to make certain accommodations?

May 1956 bring you a happy change in your concerns and offer you only the best in energy and spirits.

Our good wishes, GF

January 15, 1956

Dear Miss Stotler:

All is in good order here, and by some instinctive feeling, one senses Spring. Even with the wind blowing a gale, and a thin layer of ice holding firm the garden spaces . . . perhaps, after all, only wishful thinking?

I am having great delight in playing my various symphony records. The *Reformation* of Mendelssohn is of peculiar beauty and uplift; and Strauss has woven such magic with his tone poems. I think my favorite is *Death and Transfiguration*, perhaps because of its imagery.

I have a fine recording of Toscanini's Traubel Wagner which makes me wonder and deeply regret that this warm, magnificent voice is no longer heard at the opera. How can she be content with the spurious Broadway farce? What a pity.

The television is improving, really, quite a few good films. The vivid Disney productions, the *Zoo Parade* from Chicago on Sunday afternoons, quite delightful. *Peter Pan* has delighted millions in its second showing; I do not care for Barrie whimsy, so saw it only once. Helen Hayes had a commemorative *Dear Brutus.* Lily Pons repeated part of her gala program, looking very chic and singing well.

Maurice Evans has directed some fine plays. The NBC Opera group have done more than well. I believe next Sunday will bring from them *Cosi fan tutte* to participate in the Mozart festivals.

Why do you not think of acquiring a good machine and thus provide some variation of home routine? I had mine as a birthday gift and it made its debut so charmingly with the young Queen's coronation.

We are grateful to keep well and busy. No need to seek superficial activity, voyaging hither and yon. So many travellers on return can tell you nothing of beauty or history—only the shops and the dreary cocktail round.

Keep well! Best greetings, GF

January 17, 1956

Dear Miss Stotler:

We have at long last, the promised blizzard. The white curtain descending in a steady stream, which will mean a cozy day indoors.

I think you are missing quite a vicarious pleasure not to enjoy the garden brochures. They color a dull day like this, induce dreams, and cost one nothing in physical activity. The reproductions are so vivid they almost emanate a perfume!

The weekend had many interesting TV offerings. The *Magic Flute* was charming, well sung and projected like the gay and fantastic fairy tale it is. The camera again permitted leeway in lighting and pictorial effects that were well conceived. One must lay aside all thought of tradition and what was formerly understood to be an opera composition; this medium is a timed affair, to the last second. All must be fused to the director; voices are gentle without dynamic force—no need of this, since the mike picks up everything to the volume required by the sensitive engineering. Facial expression is limited (I daresay camera distortion would otherwise result) and the synthetic ensemble is smooth and not disturbed by individual outbursts.

One can understand, in this avenue, how little a performer must demand of himself. If he is an obedient servant to the overall director, the mediocre will have good results. Well, just a personal reaction, all this, to a most pleasant hour's entertainment.

We have still two months to go before Spring is within our circle. I *try* not to wish time away!

Yes, I have seen Ike on television, and find him a very ill looking man.[193] I still wish he would decide, for better or for worse, and keep politics out of the picture.

All good thought, GF

January 19, 1956

Dear Miss Stotler:

I realize when I welcome each passing day as one nearer the desired Springtime that it is an incursion on my life span; yet the nostalgia to welcome growing things is strong, and the impulse very natural. I think of that gruesome tale, *The Ass's Skin* [Honoré de Balzac], where each wish fulfilled brought the author nearer his own demise.

I am sorry you find so little comfort in the approaching finale. I admit one has to marshal forces of will and efforts at understanding. I believe that every human being has within himself the eventual submission toward future growth, though I am not wise enough to define it. For me, I believe the *credo* suffices.

Miss Pons on TV was a handsome vision and sang well. It is a delicate but sweet instrument, and would seem to be, in its high octave, very easy in production. Below this scale, there is very little tone, hence the reliance on a restricted repertoire employing the acute roulades. The coloratura is an exacting métier, not quite normal, and with insistent professional use may deteriorate early, even in the most gifted.

We keep well, praise be. Now to the village where I shall consign this to the post.

GF

February 3, 1956

Dear Miss Stotler:

The bright, cold days continue, therefore I have been able to

193 On September 4, 1955, President Eisenhower had been stricken with a heart attack, diagnosed as a mild coronary thrombosis. He was deciding whether to run for reelection.

enjoy a daily drive over clear roads, the hills rosy in a Winter's sunset. One feels a surge of Spring. It is good to be alive.

I think you would have enjoyed the ballet *Sleeping Beauty* very much on TV. The camera allowed a charming venture into fantasy land, while the dancers were disposed in the most graceful of postures.

I do enjoy the ice skating also in this medium.

One had several pleasant surprises. *Tales of Hoffmann* under Beecham employed the same technique as the NBC used here for *Magic Flute*. Usually I am seated on my study couch and often have my coffee or supper tray at hand depending on the hour of the offering. I am idle; save for the enjoyment of the senses. Knitting does not appeal to me, nor crochet, so my hands having been busy at other matters, do not disdain an hour of leisure.

This is the grim period of tax computation, and all that is connected with the dubious business. As for the concise and workable report of the Hoover committee, none of these D.C. politicians have any idea to follow through. My fear is that Socialism will go merrily on till the Red destroyers take over—with no war, only the insidious whittling down of our standards and principles. We have become a weak, sluggish, sentimental people, whom it is all too easy to rob via alleged charity and patriotism. It appears easier to let the government take over rather than maintain our tradition of initiative.

Well, enough of this gloomy outlook. I make my own plans for self-preservation—or what I hope will be!

Our days are quiet but full of pleasant home tasks.

Best of greetings, GF

February 16, 1956

Dear Miss Stotler:

The *Lincoln* book came, as I think I wrote you. I did not see the TV story that was taken from it, but all Sunday I was treated to so many Lincoln dramas that it was amazing. There were more actors with enlarged noses, dank, unkempt hair, and prominent warts, uttering fancied colloquial speech, following each other in sad, unhappy fashion! On one program André Kostelanetz,[194] the hus-

[194] André Kostelanetz, conductor of popular orchestral music, changed the character of this musical form in 1934 by adding a large string section. He was also noted for his sweeping arrangements of popular music. When the brilliant Metropolitan coloratura Lily Pons appeared with his orchestra, they drew record crowds.

band of Lily Pons, and no mean conductor, labored at fifes and drums, more or less muted, to permit Carl Sandburg to drawl out some kind of verbosity, doubtless his own—he read from a book. It is utterly useless to pretend that these offerings do a thing for inspiration or stimulation.

Would it not be far better to allow the noble utterances without this theater clap-trap to hinder and repel? The magnificent statue in Washington would suffice to frame the actual sentiments that have come down to us as the expressions of a fine spirit.

So now we await the decision of the White House incumbent. What a deluge of speculation there has been! Now the report of the doctors would seem to give the President the "go" signal. Well, I wish him the best of luck. We hear that the San Francisco stock market had a decided upward curve at the report, and it was thus released over wires before the market opened in New York. The opposition are probably gnawing their nails, with who knows what black thoughts in their political hearts?

The headlines are apt to keep one disturbed most of the time. And now the horrid truth of the two highly placed British spies, with all it connotes.[195] No wonder our General could not proceed when the leakages were so direct from the State Department.

The current *Life* presents a stinging rebuke from MacArthur to the memoirs of one Truman, which have apparently gotten out of hand re accuracy. . .

They say it takes all kinds to make a world; we well know it takes all kinds to mess it up.

Now to go out in the sun and breath the clear air—refreshing to the spirit.

GF

March 1, 1956

Dear Miss Stotler:

I have been hard put to get to my desk, what with the recent activities relating to my natal day. Came Mrs. Martin with a superb box; she was distressed that there were no hyacinths, so had done

[195] In September 1955, the British Foreign Office had confirmed that two diplomats, Guy Burgess and Donald Maclean, had spied for the USSR before disappearing behind the Iron Curtain in 1951. In February 1956, they reappeared at a press conference in Moscow.

her best, which is always a fine alternative, and I had a most beautiful and unusual combination of blue daisies and freesia. It was heavenly. I placed it in a lovely vase from Munich with the blue city crest. Thanks again for the blooms and your thought.

If weather permits, I shall go to the city to celebrate with Mrs. G. and a few close friends.

The phone rang all day long; it was hard for me to get a bath or comb my hair. Miss Sylvia had to substitute for me on several occasions. I am sorry for you that a birthday does not thrill you as mine does me. Perhaps you linger too much on the accumulation of years, rather than the riches they bring?

I viewed the President last eve in his press interview and then on his Address to the Nation. He looks so thin—the sunken shoulders and the contour of the face indicative of those who must diet and keep *underweight*. How then, does one regain strength and have resistance? His MD had it in print that he gave him anti-appetite pills . . . that is all I want to know about *his* medical advisor!

I do wish him well, but the *Dems* will show him no mercy and he will have to meet their jungle tactics. I *dread* the coming Summer campaign.

All good wishes, GF

March 14, 1956

Dear Miss Stotler:

More snow and sleet, very dreary for one who must go abroad. The little birds have departed to some evergreen shelter, I hope. They emerge for food in the morning hours, and of that we give them and the squirrels plenty.

Our diavolos are brought up from their nest in the warm, dry cellar, and moved into their nice house in the yard, to bury themselves in cedar shavings till supper time. A neighbor recently moved in, a vet, with a handsome but lonesome female boxer. We shall not invite her over. Yes, jealousy is a curious factor. Luka is gentle and forgiving, but Bubi is a meany when a bone is in question; yet in a moment he's all sweetness and loves his brother devotedly. They are really good little boys, but the saying is true in their case, "Dachsies can learn anything but will do nothing"—save what agrees with their own wishes.

No return, please, of the Wiener Burgtheater brochure. I thought it would interest you. What a wonderful restoration for an art loving people! I shall never know what goes on in our erstwhile Berlin Königlich Oper [Royal Opera], but no doubt there are good offerings in that restored house on Unter den Linden, which I, for one, shall never call *Stalin Allee*!

A superb *Richard III* was a three-hour offering on TV last Sunday. Magnificent in all ways under the direction of Laurence Olivier also in the stellar role. In color it must be marvelous; even in black and white it was beyond cavil.

All well here, despite foul weather, GF

March 17, 1956

Dear Miss Stotler:

After a real blizzard we are once more shining white, in a foot of snow under blue skies. A glorious Winter day! The followers of St. Patrick will have no easy march along the avenues of Manhattan, and those in the review stand will freeze in the icy blasts.

In Minnesota, Adlai [Stevenson] and Estes [Kefauver] will slug it out in the [Democratic presidential] primaries. It *will* be cold! The New Hampshire write-in for Nixon pleases me. I haven't given much attention to this energetic hard-working man, but *anyone* who defies the *Palace Guard* and the *Reds* will have much to recommend him.

The current *Life* begins a most interesting "History of the English Speaking People" by the versatile Winnie, in fragmentary condensation with handsome illustrations. A weekly attraction, well worth while. The cover shows Churchill as a doughty gentleman, all bespangled with orders, as becomes his long and brilliant career. He works for *his* empire. How I wish we had some counterpart of the same obstinacy and insularity whose motto was "*America First*"!

Well, I suppose there is a difference between a loose hinged democracy and a tightly knit empire—even if in name only at present—the latter has had a long inception.

All good wishes and fair weather, GF

March 26, 1956

Dear Miss Stotler:

Miserable Easter outlook—one can only hope that fair weather will confound the forecasters and allow a general "bien-être" [well-being] over all. I shall soon don raincoat and scarf for a chat with my handy man. Once the underbrush is removed I can think of an evergreen accent here and there against the Winter bareness. I like the idea, in the country, that there is always something to do, improve or clear. The Winter damage has been severe. We shall replace feathery andromeda, as a hedge, with stiffer material, arbor vitae. It is more resilient and we can prune it to the desired width.

Bubi is not so well as I would like, with arched spine and lameness. I shall see how matters go on for a time, since he does not appear to suffer, but I fear the eventuality. Now to the village.

All good greetings, GF

April 8, 1956

Dear Miss Stotler:

How welcome is the sun! Everyone is impatient for the gentle season, to uncover the garden beds.

You will have had my previous letter, that I did get to Babylon on a singularly fine day, and had such a pleasant visit with my friend. She is very frail, and we cannot make plans too far ahead. She is, however, still planning her usual sojourn at Cape Vincent.

The current *U.S. News and World Report* has a fine outline of the Russian strategy by General MacArthur, which no doubt he foresaw in his earlier days as supreme commander. The map clearly illustrates his résumé. I fear that great trouble looms ahead in that part of the world, since those *against* would not listen to the man who best understood the situation. But *they* have the upper hand, and *our* money.

As for allies, they will serve their own immediate needs and interests—vide France with her Algerian problem and Britain with her Cyprus hornet's nest.

Right you are, it is a fantastic world. Thank heaven I still have my dear little tranquil corner; only the d—d tax intrusions betimes!

You asked about my Easter outfit—very simple. A forget-me-not trimmed hat, navy crêpe frock and a sable coat to withstand the chill that was very sharp.

Save for my little sick pet, all is well here.

Our best greetings, GF

April 23, 1956

Dear Miss Stotler:

Snowflakes are drifting down—big as silver dollars; all the garden efforts at naught for the moment. Easter was premature. Could we not have one date as for other church festivals, and let it go at that?

The WOR station has given us a most thrilling *Walküre*—half a week ago and the rest yesterday. I had from 1:30 until 4:00 a most enjoyable excursion into memory land. I always try to keep Sundays for myself and such programs as have been a feature of the Winter season. A relaxation of mind and body—it makes the whole week pleasant.

My little Bubi is doing nicely, alert and on his feet. We shall keep up his medicine and the eye of the vet upon him for a time.

Indeed, the Monte Carlo wedding[196] had all the makings of an operetta, with overtones not so tuneful. It is to be hoped the young couple may be allowed to complete their travels far from the eyes of the ubiquitous and unmannerly press.

Our best greetings, GF

May 10, 1956

Dear Miss Stotler:

While my precious Sylvia refreshes the linen on the bed I shall try sending a few lines to you, with thanks for your several messages.

My back is improving slowly, still very painful. The MD wants me to make an effort of ten minutes or so at intervals to keep some kind of lubrication going. I try to walk, sit and lie without involving too much the wretched sacroiliac . . . a nasty part of the body when ill—it should be called demoniliac!

The one great consolation is that I hear no fretful inquiry from Gatti-Casazza asking *When I Can Resume Opera Duties*? This used to drive me frantic. It will take some time for me to get real comfort, but I have a wonderful masseuse, and when she is gone, my one companion is the hot water bottle wrapped in flannel. I do *not* cotton to the electric pad—no need to be cremated as yet.

196 The marriage of Prince Rainier of Monaco to Grace Kelly took place in Monaco on April 19, 1956. Public interest in the wedding was intense. More than a thousand journalists covered the event.

Walter Gieseking is indeed a great artist [pianist]. How true the observation of Mr. Lissfeld, these "thumbs down" reviews are purely manufactured . . . I have known some out of pure spite and jealousy.

I hope you acquire a good, solid car, so that you may be spared the sad surprises of your present one. I had the same disinclination re the automatic drive, but came the day in my last purchase, and what a joy of ease and confidence! I no longer fear, really, hills or rough going.

All good wishes, GF

May 18, 1956

Dear Miss Stotler:

A lovely day and cheery. I have a nice rattan seat for the car, which gives excellent support, and have just had a ride of half an hour, driving myself.

I am not going to the Cape, as I may have written you, which relieves me for myself, but I have great concern over my friend. I hope she may soon realize the difficulties connected with this charming but too distant spot. It may be a heartache to dispose of the property but better than having her there, ill, and so far away.

Aida will have a fine trip, as you describe her plans. Not having known the older more glamorous days she will have her own enjoyment of the moment.

All good wishes to you—perhaps you will invest in a new car?

GF

June 7, 1956

Dear Miss Stotler:

What a perfect June day! Night rains keep the greens happy. Roses and honeysuckle make my small terrace a place of grace and charm, and delphiniums decorate the larger space in the other lawn where my little sundial boy keeps watch.

Thank you for the nostalgic interest in the Cecil Beaton book.[197] It brings to mind many scenes and personalities of its

[197] *I Take Great Pleasure*, one of a series of Cecil Beaton diaries. Beaton was a popular English artist, actor, and writer, perhaps best remembered as a designer of costumes and settings for a number of theatrical pieces, including *My Fair Lady*.

era . . . an excellent reference for the modes and extravagances of that time.

In the case of the UN flag—the content of my letter to the press at the time of MacArthur's return—and believe me, I was astonished that it was proposed to greet this great American not with the *Stars and Stripes* but with the UN flag that designated no true banner of our country—or of any country for that matter!

I have a high regard, love and pride in our standard, as all nations have a right to love and pride in theirs. This *one world* bunting is a farce. My flag shall fly to the exclusion of any other foisted upon a stupid people.

I progress slowly and have to rest much. The current *Life* has a very interesting article on the subject of aching backs, even to the elongated X-ray of a dachsie, and why their particular build invites trouble for them—poor little tykes.

I hope the new car will be a happy change. I gather you will try the automatic drive.

The weather promises fair skies; I hope your area will enjoy them.

Our greetings, GF

Independence Day

Dear Miss Stotler:

We are quiet here; too many maniacs infest the roads—we feel safe at home.

Many people have commented on the same vocal quality shared by Miss Sylvia and myself, as we both have a light flow. So many shout or murmur, when clearly spoken words without strain are the best.

I don't wonder the spectacle of the poor, mangled Bozo gave your factotum a severe shock. One wonders what the victim must have suffered before the end came . . . poor beast! Also, to lose a pet—no easy matter. One is haunted by the intelligent eyes, so devoted, so affectionate.

The repercussions of the steel strike are many. One thing does impress itself on my mind. When Labor becomes so big and arbitrary, where is Government? Do not return the enclosed, but I must applaud every word of [Senator Harry] Byrd, a consistent patriot and an honest gentleman. Too few of his kind.

I am glad not to have the long drive to the Cape. The place is beautiful, but sad too, so many friends are gone. Mrs. Gilmour is swayed by memories, but I am not one to essay a return to the unreturnable. The memories *have* to suffice.

Best wishes and good results with your suffering Peke. GF

July 30, 1956

Dear Miss Stotler:

We are, as is the world, horrified at the terrible accident of the Italian liner, *Andrea Doria*, and the Swedish one that rammed her in the fog.[198] The former now lies at the ocean bottom, such a magnificent vessel, so new, and the pride of the Italian fleet.

The scene on TV of the arriving refugees was heartbreaking; some hundreds picked up by the *Isle de France*, that had barely left the Manhattan dock. What dreadful hours those poor, trapped souls had to face till rescue came; then the harrowing account of the manner of their salvage to other boats!

All the welfare agencies are at hand and must remain until the slower moving vessels discharge their portion of crazed humans. Everyone was saved from the two vessels but several have died from shock and injury . . . some hundreds are in hospital. Water is to me, the most treacherous of all the elements . . . I so fear its motion and power.

In re the Kronprinz, he was a wholesome gentleman, an excellent sportsman, and most democratic and affable. He had a discerning mind and alert intelligence, and would have made a just and understanding ruler. The picture you saw was from a snapshot taken at a luncheon when I was last in Berlin. A friend had it enlarged and sent it to me.

Now to some radio music to the soft patter of rain; rather pretty undercurrent to the melodies.

All good wishes and greetings, GF

198 The collision occurred on July 27, 1956, off Nantucket Island. The *Andrea Doria* suffered the loss of fifty lives. Five died on the *Stockholm*.

August 13, 1956

Dear Miss Stotler:

Wednesday, September 12th is reserved for you and Miss Aida; if this date does not work out to your convenience we can arrange another. There is now in process of being built a motel, near Pinchbeck the florist, that looks very attractive, also one on the Danbury road. I could drive you to both places if you wish as a personal view would be best.

I am busy with record researches. I had not thought of this time as a half century since I made my Berlin debut (1901) and subsequent home appearance (1906), but many people have written in kindly fashion, and to the present manager of the MET [Rudolf Bing], as well, wishing to know if some sort of memorial were not in order, to which they could contribute.

This gentleman, who really had nothing to do with my career, nevertheless has hoped I would permit a dinner in honor of the hour. I have, I hope, chosen the proper words of regret, that such a gesture, while greatly appreciated, was not in my present picture, and I trusted to his understanding of my retirement from all public functions, and disinclination to be other than a very private person.

Meanwhile the recordings are to be re-issued it seems, and as many of the master plates have been lost, when Victor Company sold outright to the RCA, I am lending some of my choice selections for this purpose. Thus I have been listening and cataloging, really an arduous chore, with also a bit of wonderment at the passing of time and the disappearance of a lifetime of endeavor in a pouf of smoke! The whole enigma of life and its purpose comes before one and is not resolved.

I was amused at the notice in the German paper you sent me. An oft told tale, happily with romantic and not ugly elaboration. But odd things happen, even here, for instance.

Last week I attended our Garden Club meeting. At the tea-table the very polite maid, in passing the tea and cake, was so eager for me to taste the latter that I took a piece; a delicious bit it was. She waited till some of the ladies were elsewhere to tell me her origin. Her father had been chef at the [Hotel] Adlon—had served me often there, while her mother had been infected also with "Farraritis." She could not wait till I had expressed my pleasure in the cake. Who would have thought a whiff of old Berlin could be found in Ridgefield?

Sunday I go to view the Danish Ballet, and expect to have a most enjoyable time.

No, I had not heard of Christine Miller Clemson's[199] death. I am sorry. A very pretty woman and an excellent singer.

Our best greetings, GF

August 15, 1956

Dear Miss Stotler:

I am nightly viewing the Democratic Convention. The excitement is in the hotel and bars, I fancy, for the proceedings so far are a bit dull, save for the fiery address of the Tennessee Governor [Frank G.] Clement, a sincere enthusiast, who put some critical nails in the Republican plank, all too well. My opinion, of course, since I am disappointed in the present GOP. They have a chance to spike the observations next week.

Eisenhower looks ill and should be kept away from the cruel cameras if the public is to be coerced into belief that he is a well man; and the GOP has no alternative.[200]

I do hope you are able to arrive at some agreeable sale of that part of your property you wish. We are having trouble here; the sale of too small acreage for subsequent developments being the question. The large, beautiful estates are no longer possible to keep up and tax rates are driving the owners to any kind of sale that will bring relief.

We have newcomers who bring in several small children; they rent, and pay no taxes save what may be included in their rentals, while we others have to provide the schools. We have just built one for $900,000, an elementary one, and there is talk of two more. Mushroom developments make extended sewage necessary—all a vicious circle.

This credit idea is not sane. How dare people spend what they have not or what they will not earn? No one wants to face the fact that

[199] Pittsburgh mezzo contralto, Christine Miller, won national acclaim for her performances in oratorios and concerts. She toured with Walter Damrosch and during World War I devoted much time to singing in army camps. She was married to Daniel Clemson, president of Carnegie Steel.

[200] In November President Eisenhower was elected to a second term, with the Democrats retaining control of the Senate.

government is our taxes. It is a general idea that there are untapped coffers to be disbursed for the asking.

Labor is the ruling force—but try to get someone to do a job!

Well, I am not gloomy, despite the aforesaid.

The heat is most uncomfortable and sudden. I have all the fans going and the shades are drawn. The best thing one could do would be to let the hose play on one's body. As I see the children frolic, I envy them their unconscious freedom—one brief garment suffices!

All good wishes, GF

August 25, 1956

Dear Miss Stotler:

I am distressed to hear of your latest mishap. Tumbling over a leash can produce woeful consequences. Two friends of mine have suffered broken wrists from just such an incident. I do hope the pain is lessened and you will have no after effects that worry.

We have again coolness with sunshine for which all are glad. Though it means the approach of Fall, I welcome it. I like the changing seasons and believe the accommodation to them an excellent health sign. I nearly went mad at the eternal sunshine of lower California; then to be engulfed in the equally eternal—or so it seemed—tropical rains.

And this thought brings to mind the cool winds of San Francisco that must have been a god-send to the GOP Convention. Mr. Hoover was given a hearty welcome, truly a patriarchal figure, with sage advice and here and there a touch of salty humor. Dewey was excellent, pointing out the weak points of the opposition but with no smear tactics.

The President looked fine as he came down from the plane. He, and all others should forego the cosmetics no matter what the counsel of Hollywood, and be themselves. And coach [actor George] Montgomery should stay in the dug-out (to use a baseball expression) and not curb Ike in his better gesture of spontaneity. TV is gruelling. It takes great stamina to withstand the lights and heat.

I am having fun getting my Winter frocks at hand: matching skirts and sweaters in cheerful pastel colors that flatter; just what I want for country comfort.

All good greetings, GF

As you have expressed an interest in my estimates of the records I will add a few comments.

I believe I made 160 recordings in all. In an article written for a musical magazine some years ago I listed several examples illustrating different qualities of singing, to wit,

Youthful Exuberance—"Sempre libera" from *Traviata* (T. & T.) and Valse from *Romeo and Juliet* (G. & T.) both made in Berlin at the time of my first recording session in 1904.

Emotion—"Un bel di vedremo" from *Madame Butterfly* (Victor); "L'altre notte in fondo mare" from *Mefistofele* (Victor); and "Lieber Spielmann" from *Königskinder* (Victor and I.R.C.C.)

Vocal Line—"Wonnervoller Mai, O Komm' herbei," Gluck (Victor and I.R.C.C.); "Tutto per te" from *Le Donne Curiose* (Victor and I.R.C.C.); "Via, cosi non mi lasciate" from *Il Segreto di Susanna* (Victor).

Style—"Caro mio ben," Giordano (G. & T.) and "Dove sono," Mozart. The first of these was made in 1906, the Mozart in 1927, an electric recording, one of the few I made.

Color—The "Gavotte" from *Manon* (Victor); "Seguidilla" from *Carmen* (Victor); "Mama usciva" from *Zaza* (Victor). In these three records the color of the voice along with expression and accent portrayed three very different characters. Color also emphasizes the changing moods.

October 25, 1956

Dear Miss Stotler:

After gentle rains, again a mild sun appears, and we shall be able to get on with our planting. The leaves are a golden carpet. It seems a shame to gather them into the compost heap. It has been a beautiful Fall; our vivid hills will be a happy memory.

Re your feeling of intense concentration resulting in a stalemate, I fancy it can apply to all creative effort. I know so often, in composing a role or interpreting a song, there would be the liability of routine without the vital spark. One needs mental refreshment and stimulation.

The apprehension of performances never left me. I *had* to live with this condition, and during youth resiliency comes to the rescue—but the years take a toll . . . *enough is enough*!

I had the anniversary luncheon at the *Inn*. The excellent service and cuisine still prevail. I am making ready the Christmas post and parcels, these dullish days are good for such activity.

All good wishes, GF

November 1, 1956

Dear Miss Stotler:

Thanks for your Saturday message. I can well imagine that you are annoyed by the hunters. My father's 30 acres were constantly invaded, and he told the marauders that the only thing he would *not* shoot would be their dogs. He was partial to animals. . . .

I am reading Churchill's history with pleasure. But it is frightful to think of the sacrifices of subjugated peoples of our own day. All power to Hungary as the first to set a definite pattern of revolt. Yet we sit in conference with the Russ knowing full well that we can do nothing about free peoples until *their* brutality is curbed. Still, an interesting thought, when one contemplates mass immigration, one wonders if it is not a defense against extermination. I recall an erudite Italian once remarked to me, "Italy grew to a nation *because* she has been invaded for centuries." Well, our little moment is but a molecule in the breeze of time. We shall never know where it will be propelled.

Mrs. G. and I had planned to go to the Saturday matinee to hear the new star, Callas, but she was unable to make the effort. Callas has box office attraction and must be an arresting figure on stage. I have only several records to form a conclusion, not quite so proper as did I hear the living artiste. The voice is brilliant, but there is little beauty in it. The other prima donna, Tebaldi, has a lovely quality. Well, it all makes for interest.

I shall be glad when the election excitement is over. The last weeks have seen such a disgusting exhibition of name calling and mud smears. It seems incredible that humans would allow themselves such gutter sniping.

We shall see what the future holds.

Greetings, GF

November 29, 1956

Dear Miss Stotler:

The grey days and cold are here, threats of snow, but not yet arrived. The holiday spirit begins to make itself felt and the village will soon be stringing its colored lights on the main highway, placing the crèche for carols, and decorating all shop windows with fantasies of the hour.

I always have live trees at my studio doors, that look very gay in their tinsel dressing; also this year, we plan to heap the urns at the entrance with colored disks, and green swatches will hang from two new lanterns that now illumine the garage entrance. Thus we shall present a welcome glow from all sides of our little house.

The 26th here was made gay and happy by numerous floral tributes and greetings. I had almost forgotten that it marked the 50th anniversary of my debut at the MET. How far away it seems, as of another century, but a splendid and gracious time, before the wars and strife so soon to follow.

The film *Anastasia* will be a supposedly imaginative story. I knew something of the actual woman who came here.[201] Rachmaninoff played a large financial part in her rehabilitation, as did some Americans. When I was last in Europe I spoke with some who were of the old school. Her sad history had been examined, but there were too many discrepancies to make one certain of her claims. Whether or no, this poor soul had suffered some dreadful fate—another example of the cruel aftermath. I have little doubt but Bergman will be a tender and sympathetic proto-type in this mystery. In the play here, Leontovich was a superb figure as the aged Empress.

I do not expect to go to New York until Christmas Day.

Greetings, GF

December 20, 1956

Dear Miss Stotler:

All is clear and sunny here, real Winter weather. This morning came your package, and I had to anticipate Santa, lest my "thank-you-ma'ams" be delayed unduly. This charming lounging jacket is the very article so needed—doubly welcome at this moment. I shall don it tonight as prelude to my happy Christmas. Many thanks for your

[201] For many years a woman called Anna Anderson, living in Germany, claimed that she was the Grand Duchess Anastasia, daughter of Czar Nicholas II of Russia, although the Grand Duchess had reportedly perished when her family was executed by the Bolsheviks in 1918. Anderson's claim was never established, but a film with Ingrid Bergman taking the part of the would-be Anastasia was highly successful.

thought and your trouble in the midst of so much that is worrying you.

I shall open other packages as the days fly by. The carrier is often burdened when he gets to our door, so is glad of the hot coffee to cheer him on his way.

There have been sad occasions among several friends, death and accidents. One tries to send a word of cheer, but so much depends on the individual understanding and acceptance as life flows on and brings to us all lessons not always clear and often of sad import.

This present day miracle (?) working to keep humans breathing into a helpless and expensive old age, I feel is all wrong. Let Nature single out *her* choice for the longevity, *not* have the person kept over the allotted time for this or that scientific observation.

Well, I did not intend to read a lesson. May you keep well and not overtire in this holiday rush. Again, most hearty thanks for a gift so pretty and so needed.

Our greetings, GF

1957

January 9, 1957

Dear Miss Stotler:

The snow is falling in knife-like slashes, with chill winds and dour skies.

Speaking of my book [*Such Sweet Compulsion*] which you have resumed reading, it is odd to say, but true, that all the chapters purporting to be my mother's reflections were *never* revised, and flowed very naturally, as if I had very close alliance with her thoughts and plans—as was indeed the case. My mother was what the psychic people designate as a "sensitive." She accomplished so much with her intuition and her own energy. I am more realistic, and soon realized that too many charlatans latched on to people of prominence, and not always to the latter's benefit.

There were many who visited Evangeline Adams, who was at that time a popular astrologist. How she deduced figures and events is her own story. She, however, had an excellent reputation, and her analytical charts were delivered at a nominal fee. A friend gave her my birthdate—her analysis would have fitted anyone!

Back to the book . . . My own reflections, necessarily in the first person, gave me more trouble—the difficulty of relating facts without the too great ego-prominence of such narratives; but at the close of my professional activity it was far easier to evaluate events and be objective. Now, as I look back, I am so utterly divorced from that time of fierce activity, with the tension required to achieve a goal. It is fantastic to feel so completely another person. I count this a blessing, for with the years one *must* face changes and admit their compensations, or become a ridiculous figure, still insisting on the homage that has no rightful place in the picture.

At that time I had the impulse to write, and did so, perhaps just a pleasant urge to express that took that medium. I agree that my story was more like a fairytale—youth colored it so, and then the era was one of glamor to intoxicate!

My mother fulfilled her own pattern, and whatever the realm of progress (for want of a better word), she will have moved up to a finer expression of herself. She gave me such a spirit of independence that I am not likely to rely on spurious and faked impressions. I do not explore such fanciful spheres.

There *is* a force that permeates and animates; great souls have moved in its current, also lesser ones. So many ways to express, words of Holy Writ, prayers for enlightenment, each according to his own need and tradition. So far I do not accord with any pattern of ritual, although in it I remark beauty and poetry; but life has to be borne by one's self, using one's individual perceptions.

This is very sketchy in outline but at least an attempt to reply to your questions regarding the book.

All good greetings, GF

January 17, 1957

Dear Miss Stotler:

You will have heard by now that our great Maestro [Toscanini] passed away very quietly in his sleep yesterday. A stroke on New Year's Day gave him no pain, only drowsiness that eventuated in his passing. What a mercy this is, for he dreaded his 90th birthday. The failing eyesight was the only annoyance. He had extraordinary vitality to the last.

So—he goes to Valhalla, and will find his peers whom he so loyally served in the music realm.

No, I have not heard of *Magic Fire*[202] though I guess from your mention it has something to do with "der heilige Richard." Decidedly, the formidable Cosima was the counterpart of her father [Franz Liszt]. She was a stately and aggressive woman who *commanded* at every entrée. I know, for I have been present. A haughty manner, as might have been expected of one in her unusual circumstances. Her's was certainly an era of independent action!

I will not dwell on the complicated program that has been sent to Congress. So far as the budget is concerned, I begin to think that the GOP is fortunate to have a powerful Democratic majority to curb the very fanciful (alas, I fear they will become tangible) dreams of our Chief Executive. That I should live to make this remark! But I am *fed up* with this wide world effort for salvation at our expense.

Our best greetings, GF

January 28, 1956

Dear Miss Stotler:

The ice has frozen us all within our confines. The roads are a dangerous sheet of glass. No one who can stop at home ventures out.

---

[202] *Magic Fire, Scenes Around Richard Wagner*, by Bertita Harding.

The weather man is completely confounded; nothing comes out as he prophesies . . .

I should imagine the Arabian potentate [King Saud of Saudi Arabia] arriving at this glacial moment, might regret leaving his desert climate. Mayor [Jimmie] Walker, with voting public in mind, forbade any demonstration for his arrival when the ship docked, saying openly that the visitor was anti-Semitic, anti-Catholic, and a slave holder. Perhaps true, but after all he was the invited guest of our government. How boorish can you be?

Sir Thomas Beecham (to pass over into the musical realm) suffers greatly from arthritis as does his invalid wife. He is a good workman, but to my mind, when Bruno Walter,[203] now approaching 80, passes from the scene, we will have lost the only conductor comparable to the great Maestro. The others just do not have it.

I listened with considerable pleasure to the radio opera *Rheingold*. Not for the somewhat tepid performance per se, but because the orchestra cannot fail to enthuse one. Failing a Flagstad my attention will be focused on the pit rather than the stage.

All good greetings, GF

January 30, 1957

Dear Miss Stotler:

We have clear skies and crisp air at last, after dreadful fog and high humidity. No one could draw a normal breath.

The Maestro, though not given to public religious worship, was, nonetheless, the traditional Catholic, and all will be done accordingly. Cremation is not to be thought of. The body must take another journey, and once in Italy receive the public accolade accorded here. The whole family will journey there.[204] Another strain on depleted strength, but of course due respect from the living is de rigueur.

The wonderful Academy of Music [Philadelphia] will have a ball to pay for its repairs, which gladdens one's heart. Too often do we demolish the relics that speak so eloquently of our history. I was

203 Bruno Walter (1876–1962) was born in Berlin and made a brilliant reputation abroad as conductor of symphonic and operatic music. He was active in promoting the works of Mahler and Bruckner. In America he conducted the New York Symphony and the Metropolitan Opera.

204 Arturo Toscanini was survived by two sons and a daughter, Wanda, who was married to pianist Vladimir Horowitz.

asked to be an honor guest, but of course had to regret. I cannot take journeys and trip the light fantastic, though many of my contemporaries are able, and accept to do so.

Here in New York the Carnegie Hall I fear, is doomed, for want of funds and unhappy situation, in a spot little likely to produce any harmony or joy in performances. The MET will no doubt be moving uptown; there are plans to include it with other appendages in a colossal center for all kinds of entertainment.

Keep well, and do not overtire—soon Spring will be here and our self-imposed hibernation will cease!

Our greetings, GF

February 18, 1957

Dear Miss Stotler:

Saint Valentine's Day proved a gala one for me. Some friends who are on their flight to Hawaii came in to bring greetings of the moment, as well as their offerings for the 28th. I enjoyed a very happy surprise, since they urged me to open the gay packages at once. I was nothing loath, and the results were merry and touching. About this time charming tributes have a fashion of arriving, which gives me a long birthday, replete with sweet reminders.

I do not know how the sale of the Anniversary records is going. I have no financial interest in it as I gave the permission outright to the young man [William H. Seltsam] who is the founder of the IRCC [International Record Collectors' Club]. He is a fanatic about such rare recordings. You will receive one as your birthday reminder.

There will be a June issue from the Victor of *Carmen*. I have approved the reference plates, and considering the primitive method of the time they have been transferred to LP with pleasant results, I think.

An investment report, *Baxter*, has a very interesting article dealing with the prospect of nuclear substitution for the oil that is becoming too costly to handle. The vacuum abhorred by nature cannot fail to work in all avenues; if resources fail, some bright brain will come up with the substitute.

The report went on to describe in fascinating detail the changes in boat building with new metals and their application to ship construction, and the prospect of great mileage on a few nuclear units.

If we would *trade* and leave ideologies to the individual countries, cease preaching a crusade, and let other nations bleed themselves in their age-old differences, if such is their desire, I, for one would be happier—self-preservation being my first law!

I have no wish for the birthday, though you are kind to ask. It is perhaps a little superior to say I have no wishes, but this is truly the fact. Since we came here life has been so simple and kindly. We have just what gives us pleasure, with the least care. So, content me with a pretty card.

Yes, Mr. Kreisler has the two sad handicaps, but such an affable nature that he lives in his own world and is fairly happy. At 82 one can expect anything in the way of dissolution of one's physical energy.

We are well and have come through the Winter, to this date at least, in good health and spirits . . .

All good wishes, GF

1958

January 29, 1958

Dear Miss Stotler:

Such perfidious weather! I have not put my nose outside the door, but none the less I managed somehow to get a chill. The effects were quite as if I had elected to promenade over the hills in my bare feet!

I have been in bed, and only now, crawl to the desk for some business and a few lines here and there to assure friends I am in the living land.

I have just concluded (good reading for self-imposed bed rest) Will Durant's fascinating *Reformation.* As always when the events of history come to one's attention and one reflects, there appears only the same pattern, the same motivations that have comparable source, even if changing in performance, with our own times. I do not know why we should gratify the Russ by panicking, but apparently a large majority pay them this ridiculous compliment, so off we go on the infallible curative gesture, *spend and spend* . . .

You may indeed wonder why I find it so pleasant to be a lone wolf these Winter days. I find people tire me—perhaps expect me to entertain—thus there is too little exchange of interests, only a monologue. I have regretted many pleasantly worded requests for rapprochement. I will not become a legend—while I live, at any rate. My few and tried friends here also are chary of their strength; when we meet over a teacup, it is a real hour of enjoyment for us all, not a social duty.

Now to the village for shopping. The roads are running with water, but better than ice with walls of snow.

Our best greetings, GF

April 5, 1958

Dear Miss Stotler:

The hyacinths, waxen white, in a gay, flowered pot, are very lovely as to view and fragrance. Many thanks for your Easter thought and card of good will. We have a mild day, sunny with fair skies, a real hint of Spring.

I shall journey to the city to have mid-day dinner with my suffering friend. I watch her failing with a heavy heart and a sense of cruel frustration for all who have to bear up under painful invalidism. This delectable season of renaissance *should* revive every living being and allow refreshment of the body as well as of the spirit. The old "God loves and punishes" idea does not sit well with me. Somewhere along the lifeline, a link has slipped away from the normal pattern with resultant havoc. Such a pity! One grieves to be so powerless to aid.

May your weekend be happy, and Spring come smiling at the earliest moment!

Our good wishes, GF

May 2, 1958

Dear Miss Stotler:

We have had two days of downpour that encouraged the green even more than sunshine, and now the landscape is filled with delightful bloom, my woodlands a sea of dancing daffodils that are always later than in the fields of my neighbors in Wilton and thereabouts . . . they are really enticing. I plan to add to them and am even now busy with selections to be ordered from Holland for the Fall.

The condition of my dear friend is if anything a little more vigorous as to heart and pulse. How this comes about is one of Nature's mysteries. We thought her in extremis, and now she may linger, no one knows how long. I think I may have told you, I made my farewells last Easter. It was then I parted from her. I go about my usual routine as one must with sense and understanding. I have never had morbid thoughts regarding death.

As my own circle narrows, I do not take up with any substitute. When friends have been a part of one's life for so long I feel no need to do so, although one can be agreeable to new faces. There is no counterpart that could enter into the many experiences that cement friendships over the years.

Our village is very excited over the program, to continue all Summer, of the 250th anniversary of its settlement. There is a great searching in various attics for dresses, bonnets, glass, furniture, china—any item of the era. The Garden Club will open and hold sessions at the old school house with the original desks and blackboards; you will recall it at the conjunction of West Lane and the main road near my former corner—the Peter Parley School. The typical red little building.

I have nothing to do; I have expressed my regrets for all public gatherings; but I can help, mainly by interest in clerical needs and phone calls.

All is well. We keep busy and rejoice in the lovely Spring, here at last.

All good wishes, GF

May 19, 1958

Dear Miss Stotler:

Imagine my amazement to have the nurse of Mrs. G. phone to me last week that she wanted to talk with me . . . Which she did, entirely lucid and gay; would I come in to visit her? I would be allowed ten minutes.

Of course I flew in Saturday afternoon at the designated hour, and was overjoyed to see my friend, smiling and rosy, as if having wakened from a deep and refreshing slumber, like Snow White! She mentioned in passing that she had been very ill—nothing further about the lapse of five weeks. The doctor is baffled, sufficient to say. She is like a little rosebud, cheery, with her old sense of humor, and disposed to say only the pleasant generalities about news of the day, and our mutual friends. She is free from pain, and that is a blessing indeed. I shall go in again when the MD allows it; the nurse will let me know.

A gay greeting from Aida sent from Rothenburg. What a dear, quaint reminder! She had found my name in the Hotel Eisenhut register, heaven knows how many years ago.

We keep well and busy; always some chore to have our domain cozy and trim.

Our best greetings, GF

October 6, 1958

Dear Miss Stotler:

This 40° drop to crisp, fresh air is most gratifying to me, and I don woolens with great pleasure. We have still a gay garden, and my multi-colored mums provide delight outside and fill the vases in my rooms. A very cheerful picture.

I am better after a long tension, and am gradually regaining my interrupted slumber. My sweet friend[205] had been in her country house since June, and though she was so desperately ill, with rare occasions to get out of doors in her little wheel chair, I like to think she had a happier surrounding than in the city. The sun was warm, the birds sang lustily, and her rooms were bright with bloom.

There is much food for reflection on my part about prolonging life when it becomes suspended animation only. But I say little about such matters, the mores being what they are.

My friend was carried to the little country church down the road from her house, and as she had presented it to the community, it was fitting to hold the simple service of farewell there. A professional friend of ours was at the organ, and we devised a soft undercurrent of those selections she had loved—The Prize Song (Meistersinger); the 3rd act Götterdämerung; Death and Transfiguration (Strauss); Good Friday Spell (Parsifal). Episcopalian service, brief, and some noble Psalms read in a quiet voice—all was appropriate. The abundant floral tributes were arranged outside the church entrance; we walked through such an aisle of delicate bloom and fragrance. . .

I keep busy and am happy to have energy and will to do so.

Keep well. All good wishes, GF

November 19, 1958

Dear Miss Stotler:

This weather is April-capricious—grey weeping skies and muggy air. If it keeps up we shall have our bulbs mistakenly trying to bloom out of season.

How did I spend Armistice Day—now re-christened Veterans' Day? As usual, quietly at home. It is a sad farce in my opinion. No matter the agony of those who have lost more than the chirp of a bugle can assuage, we keep on with the same hates and confusions that lead to other massacres. I made the gesture when in service, but no more.

You inquire about my portrait, the von Kaulbach, which you and Aida saw in Mrs. Gilmour's New York apartment. It is now being exhibited at a showing for the benefit of the District Nursing Association in New York. Then it goes to complete my collection at the Library of Congress where it will have a fine home and permanent

---

205 Mrs. Gilmour died in Stamford, Connecticut, on September 26.

residence, unless we are all blown to bits . . . when nothing will matter.

The affair of the village clock dangles in midair so far as the factory delivery is concerned. They can give me no definite date so here we sit. I have informed all members of an indefinite delay. Our cement base is in readiness. I had such a time to get the man to do it as he wanted to rake leaves. No use to get ones self into a temper; the price is too high.

Enough of these trivial concerns. All are well.

Greetings, GF

December 9, 1958

Dear Miss Stotler:

The last file of the clock affair is placed in my cellar cabinet. You will have received press notices. This is my last civic gesture of responsibility. I am glad our group brought it to a successful conclusion. The clock is ticking away in perfect fashion and looks as though it had been there for years.

I have a new recording of Flagstad that is a marvel of masterful singing. Also superb are the Lieder records of Elizabeth Schumann.[206] It is a joy to hear this exquisite artiste. She was a charming colleague of another era who passed away some time ago.

I had ten guests for Thanksgiving dinner at the Inn—the circle who used to meet at Mrs. G's—in memory.

Good wishes to you from all here. GF

December 19, 1958

Dear Miss Stotler:

Clear and cold, a bright sun shining on our be-decked Christmas trees, a pretty sight. The generous Dimling sweets are here—truly a year round remembrance these many years. Highly appreciated. Our roads are clear and shopping in the village is no problem. Otherwise I do not roam the countryside, finding my interest in cozy quarters inside. Many interesting books but I'm frank to confess, of timely topics rather than my earlier preferences though I do miss my

206 Elizabeth Schumann sang at the Metropolitan Opera in 1914–15 when she made her debut as Sophie in *Rosenkavalier*. Her high soprano was much praised.

erstwhile pleasure in French and German originals rather than English translations.

Miss Sylvia and I are ready for the Winter. My two diavolos are content to snooze at length in their little house but have a brisk walk daily before their supper hour. They are little, middle aged gentlemen, a bit ponderous and white about the muzzles, but happy and in good condition.

Well, the world moves on, and humans are drunk with dreams of outer space conquests . . . I can do nothing about that!

Best of greetings and all good wishes. GF

December 22, 1958

Dear Miss Stotler:

You will have had my acknowledgment for the Dimlings and now this missive is to thank you for the beautiful red roses, arrived yesterday, and richly glowing on my study commode. Particularly effective against the snowfall of last evening, which means a white Christmas.

The birds cluster about our feeding stations; some frisky squirrels come and go, charming in their impertinence, for they dispute the birds and are voracious.

My fir trees glitter with dancing baubles outside; in the large living-room, in the crèche, prisms of light play on the crystal surface. Very sweet and intimate—and so quiet; that is my wish.

I shall have no guests nor have I issued any invitations to the excellent fare at Mr. Tode's Inn. Most of my friends here have met with problems which mean strict calorie count; under these conditions who can face a table laden with tempting provender? I enjoy my many greetings, and the cards, pretty now, and less inclined to that hideous "modern" touch that has nothing to do with the spirit of the day.

I shall open packages on Christmas Eve, all in a glittering array in the living-room. Miss Sylvia and I like to linger over the gay ribbons and pretty papers—not to forget the messages.

As my diavolos are not resigned to ribbons on their collars, I shall put the trimmings over their doorway, out of reach of inquisitive noses and paws, so they, too, are part of the festive scene.

Again, my thanks, and may whatever you plan be happy in result!

With best of good wishes for health and high spirits. GF

Index